ITALIAN BED AND BREAKFASTS

A
CAFFÈLLETTO
GUIDE

MARGHERITA PICCOLOMINI

MICHELE BALLARATI and ANN MARSHALL

RIZZOLI
NEW YORK

First published in the United States of America in 2004 by
Rizzoli International Publications, Inc.
300 Park Avenue South
New York, NY 10010
www.rizzoliusa.com

Second edition © 2006 Bed and Breakfast Bon Voyage S.r.l.

2006 2007 2008 2009 2010 / 10 9 8 7 6 5 4 3 2 1

Printed in China

ISBN-10: 0-8478-2817-4
ISBN-13: 978-0-8478-2817-3

Library of Congress Catalog Control Number: 2005933280

The Traditional Balsamic Vinegar of Reggio Emilia
protected designation of origin P.D.O.

*Traditional Balsamic Vinegar is made by fermenting and acetifying cooked grape must which is then aged for **not less than 12 years**. **Extra Vecchio** can be used to describe vinegar that has been aged **not less than 25 years**.*

For further information contact:
Consorzio fra Produttori di Aceto Balsamico Tradizionale di Reggio Emilia
Phone 0039 / 0522 / 508908 - Phone and Fax 0039 / 0522 / 508910
www.acetobalsamicotradizionale.it - e-mail: abtre@re.camcom.it

Welcome to Italy.

Barilla

Italy's No.1 Pasta

CONTENTS

✳

A New Way To Travel in Italy

Bed-and-breakfasts have long existed throughout Europe, particularly in Britain, but also in Germany and Austria, where "Zimmer frei" signs are ubiquitous. But in Italy, they are a relatively new, though fast-growing, phenomenon. Bed-and-breakfasts have quickly become the ideal accommodation for discerning tourists who want to see beyond ruins and fixed price menus to the heart of the country—to have a glimpse at the way the people live.

The highly successful Caffèlletto books were the first guides to high-end bed-and-breakfasts in Italy, where the current trend in tourism is away from impersonal (and increasingly expensive) hotel accommodation toward this new, and infinitely more rewarding, way of visiting the country. Bed-and-breakfasts bring guests into closer contact with their hosts and the Italian way of life in private homes, some of which are also historic buildings. The owners of such establishments are hosts in the true sense of the word and many are even personal friends or relatives of the Caffèlletto staff. Everyone participating in the project was chosen for their ability to communicate in English, extend a warm welcome, and enhance their guests' stay in every way possible.

By staying in bed-and-breakfasts, visitors can discover parts of Italy they might otherwise never have known—little-known but no less beautiful monasteries, markets, museums, natural wonders, and more, away from the well-trod tourist routes. Moreover, Caffèlletto is an innovative approach to travel in that it inverts the conventional concept: instead of "we want to see Rome, let's start looking for a hotel," the approach is more akin to "we would like to stay under an ancestral roof covered with wisteria and have homemade jam for breakfast," until the grandeur of Rome is almost a secondary consideration. That said, many of the houses and villas in the guide are within easy reach of Italy's most important landmarks and picturesque cities, offering guests the best of both worlds: proximity to the sights, and a quiet, elegant haven to return to after a long day.

Caffèlletto requires all its members to meet and maintain certain criteria of hospitality. The hosts should be people whom it would be interesting to meet under any circumstances, who enjoy receiving guests, and who take pride in their home and the corner of Italy in which they live (and often have lived for generations). Their homes should also have historical associations, beautiful gardens and views, and be furnished with taste, while offering every comfort to their guests—starting with breakfast, for which a very high standard is set. Caffèlletto is your guarantee of high-class hospitality.

If you do not find the accommodation you are looking for in our guide, please don't hesitate to contact us directly as we constantly have new houses to propose. In addition, Caffèlletto is always looking for new members and would be delighted to hear about any similar establishments that you may know of. Likewise, we are always interested in the opinions and suggestions of our guests.

Here is how you can contact us:

RESERVATION OFFICE
Via Procaccini 7
20154 Milan, Italy

Tel.: 011 39 023311814 or 1820
Fax: 011 39 023313009

CAFFÈLLETTO GUIDEBOOK
Via di Marciola 23
50020 San Vincenzo a Torri
Florence, Italy

Tel.: 011 39 0557309145
Fax: 011 39 055768121
E-mail: info@caffelletto.it
Internet: http://www.caffelletto.it

CATEGORIES

✻✻✻   Three stars indicate that your room has a private bathroom.

✻✻✻✻   Four stars indicate that, in addition to the above, the room is part of a prestigious property.

We have added the special **Caffèlletto** category with its own logo for the particularly discerning traveler eager to find luxurious accommodation in exceptional mansions of historical significance or situated in beautiful locations.

RATES

Rates are for the year 2004 and are on a per person, per night basis, including taxes.

◯   I. 28.50 to 45 Euros

◯◯   II. 45.01 to 60 Euros

◯◯◯   III. 60.01 to 80 Euros

◯◯◯◯   IV. 80.01 to 100 Euros

There is an extra charge for single occupancy in a double room.
Any optional services you may require can be arranged directly with your host.

ARRIVALS AND DEPARTURES

Please inform Caffèlletto or your hosts of your estimated time of arrival, which will otherwise be anticipated between 5:00 and 8:00 PM.
Rooms should be vacated by 11:00 AM on the day of your departure.

CAFFÈLLETTO PROPOSALS

Caffèlletto is offering "package tours" of some of our most historic, stately, or interesting houses to coincide with seasonal events, festivals, or gastronomic, cultural, and artistic highlights of the year. Groups of four to eight people can attend the Palio in Siena, follow the musical calendar of the Maggio Musicale Fiorentino, or take part in a guided itinerary of Italy's antique fairs, to name a few options. In the fall, Caffèlletto can arrange active participation in the wine-growing regions of Italy. In November, guests can be taken on guided tours of the olive harvest and oil presses where sometimes, late at night, it is possible to taste the first olive oil of the season. In the Alba region of Piedmont guests can enjoy a variety of truffle-based menus. For those interested in local crafts, Caffèlletto can organize, among others, tours of the crystal works of Colle Val d'Elsa, the violin makers of Cremona, the glass factories of Empoli, the papier-mâché artisans of Lecce, or the silk works of San Leucio near Naples that date back to the reign of the Bourbons. Selected houses, palazzi, and castles can also arrange cooking classes, courses in furniture or painting restoration, painting on china, and much more. And, finally, guests who are well known to the Caffèlletto staff can also request private tours of art collections or gardens of villas not usually open to the public.

HOW TO BOOK

Having made your choice, if there is a fax or telephone number listed for the property you wish to visit, you can either contact the owners directly or, if you wish, Caffèlletto can make a booking for you (there is no extra charge for this service). Our booking service includes the confirmation of your reservation, a map and instructions for reaching the property, and our help with any queries you may have.

You may contact us by phone, Monday through Friday or at any time (even in the middle of the night!) by fax or e-mail. Once we have received your message, Caffèlletto will proceed with the booking and confirm it within forty-eight hours. At that time, you will also receive all the necessary information on how to get to the house you have chosen and how to pay for the accommodation.

PIEDMONT

Piemonte (Piedmont) comes from the Italian "ai piedi dei monti," which literally means "at the foot of the mountains." Located in the northwest corner of Italy, Piedmont borders on both France and Switzerland. The snowcapped peaks of the Italian Alps are constant beacons on Piedmont's horizon. The popular ski resort, Via Lattea, is near the village of Sestriere. On the whole, Piedmont is a picturesque province of rolling hills, particularly in the Langhe and Monferrato regions. Piedmont has a well-deserved reputation as one of Italy's most outstanding wine regions, especially for

8

reds—Barbaresco and Barolo, Dolcetto and Barbera—and arguably for Italy's best white wine, Gavi; there is always the tantalizing certainty of a fine dinner at the end of the day. Asti, world-renowned as the home of Spumante, present at every Italian toast, has since waned in popularity.

One of Piedmont's most famous dishes is the Swiss-inspired fonduta (fondue), most sublime when dusted with white truffles from the Alba region, a purely Piedmontese invention. Dogs are trained to sniff out the rootlike truffles embedded under tree trunks. A medium-sized truffle today costs the equivalent of an average month's salary.

Piedmont is generally better known for its food and wine than for its hilltop castles, abbeys, or cultural landmarks. Turin, the capital city of Piedmont, is also less recognized as a city of magnificent baroque architecture than as the home of the Fiat. For centuries it was under the dominion of the House of Savoy, which commissioned most of the splendid buildings in the city. In the nineteenth century, during the unification of Italy, Turin was the country's first capital city, followed by Florence and then Rome, and the House of Savoy became its first royal family. Today, Turin is becoming something of a melting pot as many workers, lured by factories, are emigrating from the south.

THE LOCAL RECIPE

The cuisine of Piedmont is extremely refined and reminiscent of the French. The wonderful tartufi bianchi (white truffles) from Alba are part of its tradition. The use of butter and sauces is also more characteristically French than Italian. However, there are several typically Italian specialties, such as agnolotti (ravioli filled with meat, spinach, or ricotta cheese); rich brasato al Barolo (beef marinated in Barolo wine and stewed over a low flame); and bagna cauda, a warm garlic and anchovy sauce that accompanies a variety of crudités, such as the delicate local cream-colored cardi (edible thistles). Excellent cheeses, similar to their French cousins, abound: fresh or well-seasoned toma (goat cheese), the tasty and quite rare Castelmagno, and Boscaiola, which is similar to Brie.

Monferrato Onion Dip
Ingredients (serves 4)

1/2 pound cream cheese or ricotta cheese	2 tbsp. olive oil
1 small red bell pepper, peeled	1 tbsp. paprika
1 scallion	salt to taste
1/2 lemon	

In a blender, puree the scallion and red bell pepper with the olive oil, paprika, and lemon juice, and a pinch of salt. Stir into the cheese until a creamy and even mixture is obtained. Serve with toasted country-bread slices.

ORNAVASSO (VB)

INFO: CAFFÈLLETTO, ITALY

TEL. +39 023311814 OR 1820 · FAX +39 023313009 · E-MAIL: info@caffelletto.it

The little town of Ornavasso in the Val d'Ossola is just under an hour from the Swiss border and four miles from Lake Maggiore. It is the ideal starting point for visiting the Lake Region and the Italian Alps. From the peaks of the Ornavasso Mountains there is a view of over seven different lakes. Activities include walking, riding, mountain biking, canoeing in the alpine valleys, and excursions to peaks such as Monte Rosa.

The house, dating back to the late 1800s, is in the center of town with a view toward the mountains over sprawling lawns and centuries-old trees. There is an adjoining farm with horses and other animals. Your hostess is the headmistress and

possesses encyclopedic knowledge of the culture and history of the area. Her son, Fulvio, is a sportsman and can give guests guidance on all the main sporting activities in the area. Nearby are the thermal baths of Bognanco, where guests may take to the waters and follow a number of health and beauty cures available.

ROOMS: On the first floor there is a double room with a private bath; in the attic there are two large double rooms, both with bathrooms. Furnishings are simple and cozy.

AMENITIES:
English and French are spoken
Private parking
Children under the age of two stay free of charge

WHERE: The nearest railway station is Ornavasso, .5 miles away, while Milan's Malpensa airport is 25 miles away.

CATEGORY: ✳✳✳ · **RATE:** ○ · *Member since 2001*

ARONA (NO)

IL GIARDINO DI ALICE ◆ **VIA MOTTO MIRABELLO 51** ◆ **28041 ARONA, NOVARA**
TEL. +39 032257212 ◆ **FAX +39 032257145** ◆ **CELL +39 3358066483** ◆
E-MAIL: info@ilgiardinodialice.com

Il Giardino di Alice (Alice's Garden) is found in Arona just above Lake Maggiore, surrounded by a magical forest of chestnut trees. The house itself is a wooden chalet with a terrace overlooking the lake. The interior is welcoming and in excellent taste; here everything is chosen, to encourage relaxation and the shedding of city stress. Your hosts are both involved in psychology and, for anyone interested, they offer specially monitored weeks to help you escape from what they call "modern madness." Alternatively, guests may choose to go mountain biking or for walks in the woods to pick mushrooms, or chestnuts to roast on embers in the fireplace. The lake itself offers a host of attractions.

ROOMS: One double room, the Girasoli Room (Sunflower Room) with a bathroom (with shower); a single room, the Rose Room. On the floor below there is a suite with two double rooms, the Viola and the Mimosa Rooms, which share a bathroom, and a room with three beds and a private bathroom. Minimum stay two nights.

AMENITIES:
English and French are spoken
Parking on the premises
Children under the age of two stay free of charge
Taxi service between Milan's Malpensa airport and Arona is available on request

WHERE: The nearest train station is Arona, 2.5 miles away, while Milan's Malpensa airport is 17 miles away. By car take highway A26 toward Gravellona–Toci and exit at Meina. Drive to Montrigiasco; in the main square turn left at the Buoni Amici bar and follow directions for Il Giardino di Alice.

CATEGORY: ✳✳✳✳ ◆ **RATE:** ○ ◆ *Member since 2001*

SCIOLZE (TO)

**IL QUADRIFOGLIO B&B · MONTARIOLO 24 · 10090 SCIOLZE, TORINO
TEL. +39 0119814044 · FAX +39 0118178721 · CELL +39 3355426712
E-MAIL: rccilquadrifoglio@libero.it**

Il Quadrifoglio may mean four-leaf clover, but this bed-and-breakfast is a veritable paradise for lovers of four-legged creatures, particularly horses. Adults can visit Turin just fourteen miles away or venture into the countryside to sample the famous wines, cuisine, and truffles of the area, while children can enjoy the ponies and swimming pool. Furnished with a spare charm reminiscent of a clubhouse, with posters and

prints of horses on the walls, this is a horse lover's idyll. Surrounded by a park extending over 148 acres, Il Quadrifoglio is ideal for hiking and is fully equipped for equestrian events.

ROOMS: One apartment with a small sitting room, well-equipped kitchenette, a sofa bed for two, a bathroom (with shower), and a double bed in a loft accessed by a wooden stairway. Two twin rooms both with bathrooms (with showers).

AMENITIES:
English, French, Spanish, and some German are spoken
Private parking
Soccer field
Swimming pool
Horseback riding lessons; guests may board their own horses
Use of kitchen and clubhouse
Television set in every room
Children under the age of two stay free of charge
Pets are welcome

WHERE: The nearest train stations are in Chivasso, 9 miles away, and in Turin, 12 miles away. The airport, also in Turin, is roughly 15 miles away. By car from Turin take SS 590 Val Cerrina, which borders the right bank of the Po River, until you reach Gassino Torinese (roughly 10 miles). Once here, turn right at the crossroads toward Cinzano. Take SP 97 which goes up through the hills; turn right at the crossroads until you reach the Regione Montariolo. The entrance to Il Quadrifoglio is on the left.

CATEGORY: ✳✳✳✳ · RATE: ◯ · *Member since 2003*

PINO TORINESE (TO)

INFO: CAFFÈLLETTO, ITALY

TEL. +39 023311814 OR 1820 · FAX +39 023313009 · E-MAIL: info@caffelletto.it

This bed-and-breakfast is only seven miles from the center of Turin, in the midst of countryside full of vineyards and scattered with old farmhouses and flocks of sheep that yield an excellent local cheese. On the border of the regional park of Superga, the house is situated in a natural preserve where no new houses have been built as long as anyone can remember. The windows of the house overlook the Chieri plain and the Alps in the distance. At 1,815 feet above sea level, climatic conditions are considered perfect. In the past, children of delicate health were sent to mountain retreats at similar altitudes, not too high with regards to oxygen but high enough to escape the effects of pollution; plants and trees thrive as well at this height.

This small hamlet made up of twenty families is composed in part of local people who work the land and others who have come from the city to restore some of the old houses. This house in particular dates back to the late nineteenth century. Your hosts have refurbished their home with respect for the region's history and traditions (only local stone has been used in the process). The finer details of restoration have

been paid close attention to; for example, the household linens are hand-woven and, traditionally, of pure cotton. Breakfast and dinner rely heavily on produce from the vegetable garden and the orchard. Whether using jams, fruit juices, or various preserves, your hostess is adept at menus featuring authentic local specialties and vegetarian cuisine. In the warmer months both breakfast and dinner are often served in the garden. At an ideal distance from Turin, to visit the capital of Piedmont, the house is also near enough to Superga Park for outdoor enthusiasts who enjoy walking, hiking, and admiring nature.

ROOMS: A double room with a bathroom and two other rooms—one double, one single—with shared bath. All rooms have private entrances.

AMENITIES:
English, French, and German are spoken
Laundry service is available
Parking on the premises
Dinner can be served on request
Swimming pool and tennis courts not far from
  the house
Enological and gastronomic tours, cooking classes,
  and individual Italian instruction can be arranged
Pets are welcome

WHERE: Turin's train station is 7 miles away and the nearest airport, also in Turin, is 11 miles away.

CATEGORY: ✳✳✳✳ · **RATE:** ○ · *Member since 1999*

RIVA PRESSO CHIERI (TO)

INFO: CAFFÈLLETTO, ITALY

TEL. +39 023311814 OR 1820 ◆ FAX +39 023313009 ◆ E-MAIL: info@caffelletto.it

Twelve miles from Turin, the Mulino della Torre (Tower Mill) ceased to function as a mill at the beginning of the eighteenth century. The tower is an important landmark that dates back to medieval times, and was once used to spy on enemy troops. A handsome nineteenth-century complex surrounds the historic buildings, once the residence of Countess Paolina Serra, a leading figure of local lore whose monogram is entwined in the wrought iron of the parapets. Pale yellow with a rusty tiled roof and surrounded by a garden and tall trees, the Mulino della Torre is typical of houses in Piedmont. It is just outside the country town of Riva presso Chieri and has a lovely

inner courtyard flanked by a low stone wall. It is a place with a fascination all its own. Your hostess and her three daughters will make you feel at home instantly. If requested, they will prepare breakfast for guests, or, for those who prefer to do it themselves, there is a small kitchenette amply stocked with homemade cakes and jams.

ROOMS: A pleasantly furnished apartment with private entrance, large dining room, kitchen corner, small sitting room with a sofa bed, and a double bed located in the overhead loft space. Bathroom with shower. Minimum stay two nights.

AMENITIES:
English, French, Spanish, and Dutch are spoken
Children under the age of two stay free of charge
Small pets are welcome

WHERE: The nearest train station is in Chieri, 2 miles away, while the airport in Turin is 15 miles away.

CATEGORY: ✳✳✳✳ ◆ **RATE:** ○ ◆ *Member since 2002*

PINEROLO (TO)

INFO: CAFFÈLLETTO, ITALY

TEL. +39 023311814 OR 1820 · FAX +39 023313009 · E-MAIL: info@caffelletto.it

The Villa Il Torrione at Pinerolo, a medieval town thirty-five minutes from Turin, is surrounded by a park—and not just any park—landscaped at the beginning of the nineteenth century by Xavier Kurten, the landscape gardener for the kings of Savoy, who planted exotic trees, bushes, box hedges, and plane trees alongside the centuries-old oaks. There are sequoia trees, cedars, and cypresses, including a variety called bald cypress, with huge roots snaking above the ground, as well as magnolias and pygmy horse chestnut trees, a giant ginkgo tree, and a *Liriodendron tulipifera* (tulip tree) 132 feet tall. The villa itself is at the end of an avenue of white hornbeams surrounded by olea fragrans (sweet olive), a bush that, in the fall, emits one of the most haunting perfumes in the world. Ivy, too, scrambles up the imposing facade of the villa, framing the windows from their regal positions above the lawns. At the other end of the park is a lake where ducks and swans nest and herons stand on one leg in the shallows surrounded by swathes of bamboo.

Inside the villa itself, many of the rooms are papered and upholstered in riotous chintz, a fitting backdrop to the eighteenth- and nineteenth-century antique furniture. What were once the maid's quarters have been converted into guest apartments. There is still a domestic staff who serve breakfast (ordered to your bedroom by request) complete with orange juice, delicious jams, and homemade cakes.

Villa Il Torrione is not only ideally situated for day trips to Turin and other historic villas in the vicinity, it is in the heart of gastronomic Piedmont, home of the white truffle and some of the best wines in Italy. Pinerolo itself hosts a number of international equestrian events in the fall. It is also only forty minutes from Sestriere, one of Italy's most famous jet-set ski resorts.

ROOMS: Four very comfortable apartments, the first with a sitting room with overhead loft, dining room, two double rooms, one single room, three bathrooms, and a fully equipped kitchen. The second has a sitting room, a double bedroom, and a kitchen with a staircase leading up to a duplex with two more rooms and three bathrooms. The third apartment has a sitting room, two double rooms, two bathrooms, and a kitchen. Apartment number four has a sitting room, double room, kitchen, and a bathroom. Minimum stay two nights.

AMENITIES:
French and Portuguese are spoken
Parking on the premises
Courses in the cuisine of Piedmont can be organized
Swimming pool and private clay tennis courts
Children under the age of two stay free of charge
Pets are welcome

WHERE: The railway station at Pinerolo is .5 miles away, while the nearest airport is in Turin, 28 miles away.

CATEGORY: **Caffèlletto** + RATE: ○○ + *Member since 2000*

16 COAZZOLO (AT)

PIAZZA VITTORIO 5 · 14050 COAZZOLO, ASTI
TEL. AND FAX +39 0141870108 · E-MAIL: coazzolo@coazzolo.com

Exceedingly handsome, this house resembles a French château. Set on a hilltop near Alba, with breathtaking views of Langhe, Roero, Monferrato, and the snow capped Alps in the distance, the house is surrounded by a magnificent garden with stone steps leading down to landscaped terraces of tall trees and meticulously tended lawns and hedges. The house dominates the tiny village of Coazzolo, where fine wines have been

produced since time immemorial. The area is synonymous with great food and the famous Linet restaurant in the main square is a testament to this fact. The surrounding hills are also a paradise for walkers, and a local manège organizes hiking tours. There is an inviting pool shielded from view by old stone walls where guests may swim after their exertions, prior to sampling a glass of the local wine.

The interiors of the Rose Room, where breakfast is served, the ballroom, and billiard room are all that one might expect of a château, with frescoes and plush antiques reflected in the well-honed sheen of the tiled floors. The buffet breakfast features organic products and homemade jams and pastries. In summer it is served on the panoramic terrace. Your hostess, Maria Pia, personally looks after her guests and is happy to introduce them to the local attractions.

ROOMS: Three double rooms with private baths—one on the ground floor with a fireplace, the other two on the floor above with panoramic views. These latter two rooms can be combined to create a small suite with the two double rooms, a large bathroom (with shower and antique bathtub), and a loft overlooking the stairs.

AMENITIES:
English, French, and German are spoken
Private parking
Swimming pool
Children under the age of two stay free of charge

WHERE: The nearest railway station is in Castagnole delle Lanze, 2.5 miles away; the airport is Torino Caselle, 50 miles away. By car take highway A21 Torino—Piacenza and exit at Alba Est, following directions for Alba. Turn left at the sign for Coazzolo.

CATEGORY: **Caffèlletto** · RATE: ○○○ · *Member since 2002*

ROCCHETTA TANARO (AT)

LA CORTE CHIUSA MARCHESI INCISA DELLA ROCCHETTA ◆ **VIA ROMA 66**

14030 ROCCHETTA TANARO, ASTI

TEL. +39 0141644647 ◆ **FAX +39 0141644942** ◆ **CELL +39 3482261846**

E-MAIL: info@lacortechiusa.it

The Marchesi Incisa della Rocchetta, a Piedmontese family whose origins date as far back as the tenth century, live in Rocchetta Tanaro, tending to their vineyards and producing some of the finest wines of the Monferrato region. At La Corte Chiusa, the beautiful nineteenth-century estate housing the historic family cellars, four charming bedrooms have been elegantly restored to lodge guests. Breakfast is served in a lovely dining room with a view onto the porch skirting the courtyard. The guests, welcomed by the Marchesa Barbara Incisa, will be able to visit the winery, its cellars, and the barriquerie and gain a deeper understanding of the winemaking process. Tasting seminars and cooking classes are held for wine and food lovers in the brick vaulted reception rooms and in the new professional kitchen.

ROOMS: Four double rooms, which can be transformed into twin rooms upon request. In one room a third bed can be added. All with private baths. Minimum stay two nights.

AMENITIES:
Open from March 1 to December 31
English, French, and German are spoken
Parking on the premises
Well-behaved pets are welcome

WHERE: The nearest railway station is 9 miles away in Asti while the airport in Turin is 43 miles away. By car take A21 Torino–Piacenza and exit at Asti Est; follow the directions for Alessandria for about 7.5 miles, then turn toward Nizza Monferrato until you reach Rocchetta.

CATEGORY: ✳✳✳✳ ◆ **RATE:** ◯◯ ◆ *Member since 2001*

18 # CANELLI (AT)

LA CASA IN COLLINA, REGIONE S. ANTONIO 30 • 14053 CANELLI, ASTI
TEL. +39 0141822827 • FAX +39 0141823543 • E-MAIL:
casaincollina@casaincollina.com

La Casa in Collina (The House on the Hill) stands surrounded by vines in the middle of the Asti wine region of Piedmont. Although it's a mecca for wine connoisseurs, anyone who stays in this welcoming bed-and-breakfast even for a short time is likely to leave not only knowing more about wine, but with a finer palate as well. It is here that the prestigious Moscato d'Asti, the Ca' du Giaj (House of Yellow, as in "yellow as the Moscato wine"), is grown. A typical Piedmontese house, the Casa in Collina has been in the family for generations. It is above all a home with a cozy sitting room where guests may read, relax, and enjoy breakfast overlooking the owner's vineyards on rolling hills that gradually merge into mountain peaks. Guests who wish to visit the

cellars will be welcomed not only by Luciano and Giancarlo, but also by Armanda and Adele, the grandmother, who is described as the anima e cuore (heart and soul) of the family vineyards. This is not just a wine region but, gastronomically, perhaps the most sophisticated region of Italy. It is,

after all, where the white Alba truffle grows.

ROOMS: Two rooms on the ground floor and four on the first floor, all with their own bathrooms (with bathtubs). There are double and twin rooms and a third bed may be added on request. Two of the rooms have four-poster beds.

All have views over the vines. Minimum stay two nights.

AMENITIES:
Open from March 1 to December 31
English and French are spoken
Parking on the premises
Children under the age of two stay free of charge

WHERE: The nearest railway station is in Canelli, 3 miles away, while the airport in Turin is 43 miles away.

CATEGORY: ✳✳✳✳ • **RATE:** ○○ • *Member since 2001*

CASTEL SAN PIETRO (AL)

CA' SAN SEBASTIANO · VIA OMBRA 52 · 15020 CAMINO · MONFERRATO, FRAZ. CASTEL SAN PIETRO, ALESSANDRIA
TEL. AND FAX +39 0142945900 · CELL +39 3395030545 · E-MAIL: info@casansebastiano.it

At twelve miles from Casale Monferrato, this seventeenth-century country house is in the heart of Piedmont's wine and truffle country. At your request, the hosts are happy to organize wine tastings, where local cheeses and cold cuts are served around the handsome fireplace in the kitchen/dining room. They also offer to accompany you on a visit to their wine cellars. With its green shutters and paved walkway flanked by flowering plants in large vases, the house has an almost southern air while the welcoming interiors are painted ocher and blue to set off the antique Piedmontese furniture and the original terracotta floors. Breakfast is either brought to your room or served in the dining room, which overlooks a country road.

ROOMS: Four apartments, two with one bedroom and two with two rooms, all with a kitchen and bathroom (with shower). All rooms have satellite television.

AMENITIES:
English, French, Spanish, and some
German are spoken
Private parking
Swimming pool
Children under the age of two stay
free of charge
Pets are welcome

WHERE: The nearest railway station is in Torino Vercellese, 6 miles away, while the airport in Turin is 37 miles away. By car from highway A26, exit at Casale Monferrato Nord. Follow the directions for Turin until you reach Torino Vercellese, then turn left at the traffic light for Camino. Here there are signs for Castel San Pietro and Ca' San Sebastiano.

CATEGORY: ✳✳✳✳ · **RATE:** ◯◯ · *Member since 2003*

BRA (CN)

INFO: CAFFÈLLETTO, ITALY

TEL. +39 023311814 OR 1820 ♦ FAX +39 023313009 ♦ E-MAIL: info@caffelletto.it

Napoléon chose Villa Mamoli in Bra as his temporary residence when he was on his way to consolidate his victory over the Austrians. It is the kind of residence, more French château than Italian villa, where one can easily imagine the emperor standing in front of the ornate mirrors and adjusting his epaulets, making the chandeliers tinkle as he marched through the stately reception rooms in his spurs. Perhaps he planned future campaigns in the garden, a mixture of formal Italian clipped box hedges and the more haphazard English style with huge, randomly planted trees and romantic stone balustrades.

The oldest part of Villa Mamoli dates back to 1780. The house was falling into decay until, in 1979, the present owner undertook the major reconstruction required to restore the Villa to its former splendor. With its frescoed ceilings, inlaid parquet floors, scintillating chandeliers, and majestic damask four-poster beds, Villa Mamoli is again ready to receive an emperor.

Bra was originally Brayda, a stronghold of the powerful Longobards, and has given its name to an excellent local cheese. Villa Mamoli is only a few minutes' walk from the center of town, where guests may visit its sixteenth-century Palazzo Traversa and the numerous baroque and rococo facades. In the summer months guests may use the pool which is also everything one would expect of a château with its elegant pavilion smothered in flowering shrubs. In September the area is crowded with people who come from everywhere for the Cheese Fair in Bra and the Truffle and Italian Wines Fairs in Alba, during the months of October and April.

ROOMS: Three double rooms, all with private baths. Minimum stay three nights.

AMENITIES:
English and French are spoken
The Cherasco Golf Club is two miles away
Parking on the premises
Children under the age of two stay free of charge

WHERE: The airport in Turin is about 37 miles away, while the railway station in Bra is about 1 mile away.

CATEGORY: **Caffèlletto** ♦ RATE: ○○○ ♦ *Member since 1999*

CHERASCO (CN)

AL CARDINAL MAZZARINO ◦ **VIA SAN PIETRO 48** ◦ **12062 CHERASCO, CUNEO**
TEL. AND FAX +39 172488364 ◦ **CELL +39 3332608550** ◦ **E-MAIL: hotel_mazzarino@tin.it**

Cherasco is a small town near Alba in the Piedmont region. Once a Carmelite convent, it is here that the young cardinal Mazarin stayed before he rose to prominence as the Gray Eminence of the King of France, and where he negotiated the Peace of Cherasco with ambassadors from other European states in 1631. He called Cherasco "beautiful, like a glimpse of an amorous assignation." Little has changed in the intervening centuries; the only sounds as the sun sets are the church bells and swallows fluttering across the sky.

The library and breakfast rooms open out onto the cloistered garden, a luxuriant apotheosis of irises, peonies, hydrangeas, roses, and vigorous creepers. Breakfasts feature fresh fruit, local cheeses, and pastries fresh from the renowned Barbero pastry shop, which specializes in tempting chocolate confections. The rooms are elegant with an emphasis on red that befits a cardinal's residence. Your hosts are experts on and enthusiasts of the many attractions in the area, not least as regards wine cellars and restaurants. Cherasco is in the gastronomic heart of the region.

ROOMS: Only two rooms are available so it is advisable to book well in advance. The abbess's room has a double bed and a sitting room with sofa bed and a bathroom (with shower). The Cardinal Mazarin's room has a four-poster bed and a bathroom (with shower). Both rooms overlook the garden. Every night your hostess leaves a different delicious chocolate on your pillow.

AMENITIES:
English and French are spoken
Satellite television and a well-stocked refrigerator in each room
The Cherasco Golf Club
Parking on the grounds
Children under the age of two stay free of charge

WHERE: The nearest railway station is in Cherasco, 24 miles away, while the airport in Turin is 28 miles away. By car take highway Turin–Savona and exit at Marene–Cherasco. Take A21 Turin–Piacenza and exit at Asti Est before continuing on the Alba Cuneo road.

CATEGORY: Caffèlletto ◦ **RATE:** ○○○ ◦ *Member since 2001*

VALLE D'AOSTA

This is the last outpost of the Italian peninsula. With France and Switzerland to the west, the Valle d'Aosta is surrounded on three sides by the highest—and some of the most spectacular—mountains in Europe. To the north is Monte Bianco (Mont Blanc), to the east the chain of the Monte Rosa, and to the northwest the massive crystalline range of the Gran Paradiso. You will spend most of your time going either up- or downhill, as only one-fifth of the Valle d'Aosta is below 4,950 feet.

The mountain slopes are thickly wooded with pine trees, firs, and larches, giving way lower down to chestnut groves, beeches, and oaks, then, at 6,600 feet, a marvelous layer of rhododendron shrubs. To protect the region's fifty-seven alpine floral varieties, the Paradisia Garden was created in the 1960s, next to one of Valle d'Aosta's main attractions, the Parco Nazionale del Gran Paradiso.

The Valle d'Aosta had a powerful nobility whose castles can still be seen perched majestically on the hilltops. The House of Savoy used to come here to hunt and to spend their summers. At the turn of the nineteenth century, the Valle d'Aosta was a mecca for elite tourism and much of its patrician style has lingered. The capital, Aosta, with its splendid city walls and bastions, comprises one-third of the entire population. It is here that much artwork and architecture can be admired—an impressive collection

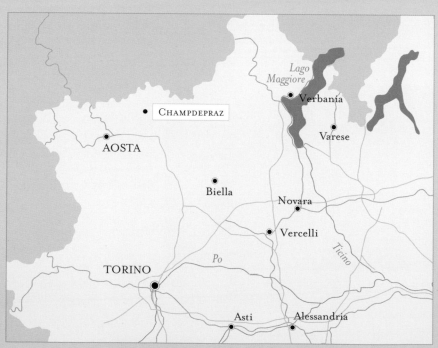

Lago Maggiore

Verbania

CHAMPDEPRAZ

Varese

AOSTA

Biella

Novara

Vercelli

Po

Ticino

TORINO

Asti   Alessandria

of different influences from France, Switzerland, and Piedmont. The Collegiata di Sant'Orso (Collegiate Church of St. Orso), with the sixteenth-century terra-cotta figures embellishing its facade, is of particular interest.

Since the historic breakthrough, literally, of the Monte Bianco tunnel and later the Gran San Bernardo, the region has opened up to tourism on a larger scale, there are several ski resorts and the famous Casinò de la Vallée in San Vincent. This has brought increased prosperity to an area that already had a solid industrial base. Today the inhabitants of the Valle d'Aosta are doubly fortunate, not only do they have one of the highest incomes per capita in Italy, they also enjoy a fair share of the country's natural beauty.

THE LOCAL RECIPE

The Valle d'Aosta is a mountainous region and the local cuisine reflects its geography. Cattle graze freely and supply milk for the many different kinds of excellent local cheeses. Rye bread and cheese comprise the "picnic lunch," which used to sustain shepherds during long days out in the pastures. Polenta (cornmeal) is served with melted cheese or a tasty beef stew cooked in red wine called carbonnade. Due to the abundance of chamois and deer in the mountains, cervo (venison) dishes are common, served with polenta on the side. At the end of a good meal, Valle d'Aosta espresso is served in the typical grolla (a wooden cup with a carved lid).

Valle d'Aosta Espresso
Ingredients (one serving)

1 cup espresso
1 tbsp. red wine, heated
1 tbsp. grappa, heated

sugar
lemon rind

Pour the warm wine and grappa into the coffee. Add sugar and a bit of lemon rind to taste. Pour into the grolla and serve piping hot.

CHAMPDEPRAZ (AO)

INFO: CAFFÈLLETTO, ITALY

TEL. +39 023311814 OR 1820 • **FAX +39 023313009** • **E-MAIL: info@caffelletto.it**

Summer or winter, with its pale blue walls and cascade of white roses tumbling off the balcony, Champdepraz is a welcome refuge from city life. Forty minutes from Turin and only twenty from Aosta, Champdepraz is a village in a green valley, where the famous ski resorts of Cervinia, Gressoney, and Champoluc are at your feet.

The house itself, built at the end of the eighteenth century, is surrounded by a garden with shade trees and lawns. The house is on three floors and is furnished like an elegant Valdostana chalet with com-

fortable sofas in front of a wide fireplace, copper pans hanging from the kitchen walls, and bells for what must be very large cows hanging from vaulted archways. Your hostess renovated the whole house three years ago and lives here herself for many months at a time.

ROOMS: Guests may use a large room 864 square feet in size with an entrance off the garden. The space is cleverly divided into an ample sitting room with a double bed, a kitchen/dining room where guests will find all they need for breakfast, and a bathroom (with shower). Minimum stay two nights; from November 10 to March 1 minimum stay is one week.

AMENITIES:
English and French are spoken

WHERE: The nearest railway station is in Verrès, 3 miles away, while the airport in Turin is 50 miles away.

CATEGORY: ✳✳✳✳ • **RATE**: ◯◯ • *Member since 2002*

LOMBARDY

A northern province bordering Switzerland, Lombardy is the locomotive of Italy, chugging toward Swiss efficiency and affluence. This has led to the formation of some vocal movements to secede from the rest of Italy. (Lombardy is practically self-sufficient industrially and agriculturally and is a national leader in the services and financial sectors.) The landlocked region is blessed with some of Italy's loveliest lakes: Lake Como, Lake Maggiore, and Lake Garda (shared with Piedmont and the Veneto); the Po River courses through the south. In the past, Lombardy was crossed by a series of canals, and sails could be seen bobbing through the fields. In the fifteenth century, Beatrice D'Este, Duchess of Milan, traveled by gilded barge from Ferrara to Pavia to meet her betrothed, Ludovico Sforza. It is to the Sforza family that we owe much of the art and architecture of Renaissance Milan, wrongly considered purely a business center. Milan is the New York of Italy, where achievers in business, fashion, and the arts flock, starting with Leonardo da Vinci. Today, professional shoppers tend to flock in the same direction.

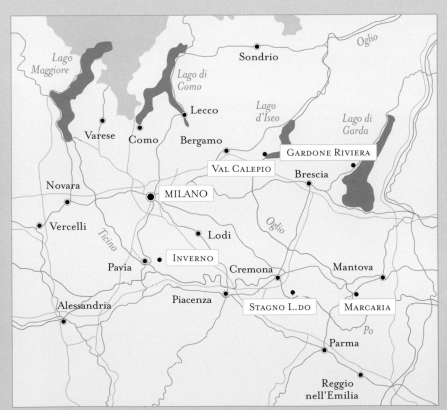

Lombard cities are some of the most beautiful in Italy, such as Mantua, with its Palazzo Ducale, Pavia, with its Certosa (Carthusian monastery), the hill town of Bergamo, Brescia, Monza, and Cremona, where the ancestors of Stradivarius still make violins.

THE LOCAL RECIPE

Risotto is traditionally preferred over pasta in this region. Meat is the main ingredient in many Milanese dishes, such as the splendid bollito misto, a classic dish of boiled meats in a rich meat broth and piquant green sauce; brasato, a braised beef dish; and the original cotoletta alla milanese (breaded veal cutlets). Another favorite is càsoeula, a combination of meat and vegetables both poached and braised. Mantua is renowned for tortelli di zucca (ravioli stuffed with pumpkin and spices), a rich-flavored dish straight from the Renaissance. Cremona offers mostarda di frutta, a perfect sweet and sour accompaniment for the bollito misto.

Panettone Bread Pudding
Ingredients (serves 4)

Panettone is now the national Christmas cake, a sort of dome-shaped, sweet brioche studded with raisins and candied fruit. This recipe uses the panettone left over after the holidays.

3 oz. of diced panettone	1 tbsp. grated orange rind
2 cups milk	6 tbsp. sugar
3 whole eggs	1 drop of vanilla essence
2 tbsp. Grand Marnier	

Coat the bottom and sides of a quart-capacity mold with caramelized sugar (obtained from 3 tablespoons of sugar). Combine the diced panettone in a bowl with the Grand Marnier and the orange rind. Bring the milk to a boil with the vanilla. Let cool. Beat the eggs with the remaining sugar and add to the milk. Mix and pour over the diced panettone. Let stand for a few minutes, then transfer to the mold and bake in a double boiler in a preheated 350° F oven for thirty minutes. Remove from mold and serve cold with custard or whipped cream.

VAL CALEPIO (BG)

INFO: CAFFÈLLETTO, ITALY

TEL. +39 023311814 OR 1820 ◆ **FAX +39 023313009** ◆ **E-MAIL: info@caffelletto.it**

Forty-three miles from Milan is Val Calepio, where this property is tucked away on a hillside among vines, fields, and chestnut groves, a peaceful haven with a benevolent microclimate all its own.

Your hostess has lovingly restored this former farmhouse and it is she who supervises the breakfasts with bread made from her own wood oven and local delicacies, all of which may also be purchased.

Val Calepio is a haven for golfers. There are no fewer than four courses in the neighborhood. It is also only twelve miles from Bergamo, whose magical Città Alta (Upper City) is surrounded by ancient fortifications. Just over forty minutes on the highway are Verona and Lake Garda.

ROOMS: Three double rooms and a single room, all with private baths. Minimum stay two nights.

AMENITIES:

Open from March 15 until the beginning of November, as well as over the Christmas holiday

English, French, and German are spoken

Laundry service is available

Private parking

Private heliport

Dinner may be served on request

Children under the age of two stay free of charge

Pets are welcome

WHERE: The nearest railway station is in Sarnico, 3 miles away, while the Bergamo airport is 19 miles away. Verona Villafranca and Milano Linate airports are also within reasonable distance.

CATEGORY: Caffèlletto ◆ **RATE:** ○○○ ◆ *Member since 2002*

MILAN–PORTA VENEZIA

INFO: CAFFÈLLETTO, ITALY

TEL. +39 023311814 OR 1820 ◆ **FAX +39 023313009** ◆ **E-MAIL: info@caffelletto.it**

Milan is one of those cities with a monopoly on the Art Nouveau period, filled with fine, heavily ornamented buildings. Visitors should remember to look up to admire the cornices, caryatids, intricate wrought iron, and stained glass. This is especially true of the Porta Venezia on the opposite side of a large park away from the commercial and shopping avenues. The Casa Galimberti often has small groups of tourists outside trying to photograph the satyrs cavorting in majolica and wrought iron, the ornate woodwork of the doors, and the porter's lodge. This apartment belongs to a talented young artist and her cat and she will be glad to introduce guests to the intellectual and cultural hub of Milan, as well as the city's insider social haunts. She is also willing to give lessons in watercolor painting.

ROOMS: A large double room with the option of a third bed and a large bathroom with both tub and shower.

AMENITIES:
English and French are spoken
Air-conditioning, television
No smoking
Children over the age of ten
  are welcome

WHERE: Milan's railway station is 2 miles away, while the Malpensa airport is 12 miles away by train.

CATEGORY: ✳✳✳✳ ◆ **RATE:** ◯◯ ◆ *Member since 2003*

GARDONE RIVIERA (BS)

DIMORA BOLSONE, VIA PANORAMICA 23 ⊹ 25083 GARDONE RIVIERA, BRESCIA
TEL. +39 036521022 OR +39 0365638123 ⊹ FAX +39 036563367
E-MAIL: info@bolsonedimora.com

Lake Garda has long been a favorite haunt for tourists because of its perfect setting, fringed by lush vegetation and blessed with the balmiest of climates. This is the only place in northern Italy where cypresses and olive and lemon trees grow. It's no wonder that one of Italy's greatest modern poets, Gabriele D'Annunzio, took up residence here. His villa, "Il Vittoriale," lies just below this fifteenth-century farmhouse. The house commands a magnificent view of Lake Garda and is surrounded by a wondrous garden extending over 865,000 square feet, personally landscaped by your host—a guided tour can take up to three hours! Your host is not only a passionate gardener and yachtsman; he also supervised the restoration work on the Dimora Bolsone, choosing building materials in harmony with the local landscape. His infallible taste is evident in every detail of this enchanting house, from the furnishings to the bed linens.

Breakfasts are homemade, from the bread to the yogurt and the jams, and are served on the terrace, or, in cold weather, in the dining room, whose stone fireplace and vaulted ceiling, decorated with frescoes of lemon trees, lend an atmosphere of pastoral ease. In the Dimora Bolsone's brochure you are promised "serenità estatica"—ecstatic serenity—which says it all.

ROOMS: Three attractive bedrooms with views of the lake. The Tower Room has a double bed, stone fireplace, and a bathroom (with shower); the Lake Room has two

single beds and a bathroom with tub and shower; and the Olive Tree Room has a double bed and a large bathroom (with bathtub). Minimum stay two nights.

AMENITIES:
English and German are spoken
Private parking on the grounds
Children over the age of twelve are welcome

WHERE: The nearest railway station is Desenzano, 12 miles away, while the airport in Verona is 25 miles away. By car, take highway A4 Milano–Venezia and exit at Desenzano. Follow indications for Salò and Gardone sul Garda. In Gardone follow indications for the Vittoriale and then drive up to the house (just over a mile).

CATEGORY: **Caffèlletto** ⊹ RATE: ○○○○ ⊹ *Member since 2001*

BORNO–VALLE CAMONICA (BS)

CASA RIVADOSSI B&B · **VIA TRIESTE 3** · **25042 BORNO, BRESCIA**
TEL. +39 036441520 · **FAX +39 036441033** · **CELL +39 3291049847**
E-MAIL: zanagliodiana@libero.it

This is somewhere worth going not because it is near some other attraction, but merely for the sheer joy of being there. This bed-and-breakfast is in the heart of the medieval hamlet of Borno, an hour by car from Brescia.

At 3,000 feet above sea level, Borno reigns over a majestic landscape in the foothills of the Alps and is surrounded by a splendid pine forest. The old stone house dates back to the Middle Ages, was built over Roman ruins, and is imbued with centuries of history: it walls have witnessed the passage not only of the ancient Roman legions, but as era was succeeded by era, the Celts, the Franks, and the Venetians also passed. There are beamed ceilings in the sitting room and dining room reminiscent of a convent refectory, while the bedrooms all have wooden ceilings and balconies in the style typical of mountain chalets in this part of the world.

Your hosts are two sisters who inherited this charming old house that has been in their family for generations. They have restored it with the same love and taste they put into welcoming guests, serving them breakfasts with custards and biscuits fresh from the wood oven.

A paradise for hikers, the area also offers the possibility of trekking on horseback from valley to valley, and there are ski lifts two miles away, as well as an alpine lake hidden away in the woods.

ROOMS: Four romantic and comfortable double rooms and two twin-bedded rooms all with private bathroom with shower. Three have a loft with the option of a third or fourth bed. Minimum stay two nights.

AMENITIES:
French is spoken
Children under the age of two stay free of charge
Well-behaved pets are welcome

WHERE: The nearest railway station is in Cividate Camuno 8 miles away, while the Bergamo airport is 50 miles away. By car take highway A4 from Milan and exit at Seriate. Take the SS 42 for Lovere and Tonale until you exit at Cividate. Follow the signs for Borno. Casa Rivadossi is in the heart of the historic centre. From the South take highway A4 and exit at Brescia Ovest, follow the directions for Lago d'Iseo and then the 510 for Tonale and exit at Cividate.

CATEGORY: ✳✳✳✳ · **RATE**: ○ · *Member since 2004*

STAGNO LOMBARDO (CR)

INFO: CAFFÈLLETTO, ITALY

TEL. +39 023311814 OR 1820 · FAX +39 023313009 · E-MAIL: info@caffelletto.it

This elongated villa set in the middle of the lush, flat green fields and poplar copses of Lombardy, is near the banks of the Po River. It was once a monastery, founded in the fifteenth century by the Benedictine monks of Nonantola. The villa is called Lo Stagno after the pond on the property surrounded by tall trees mirrored in its waters. The villa is five miles from Cremona, the city of the Stradivarius violin, where violin workshops called "Liutai" have existed since the middle of the sixteenth century.

Since the days of the monks, the complex has become an agricultural concern, owned by various noble families. At the end of the 1990s it was purchased by the grandfather of your hostess who spent all her childhood and adolescence here. She herself is in love with Lo Stagno and eager to share it with guests: "I wanted to give a home to those whose own home is too small to experience the joy of receiving guests," she said. Lo Stagno is within easy reach of all the main cities of Lombardy and Emilia–Romagna: Piacenza, Parma, Mantua, and Brescia.

ROOMS: Three double or twin-bedded rooms all with their own bathroom. If necessary, guests may also use two other rooms: a single and a double (a sitting room with a large terrace). Next to the villa is a house on two levels, completely independent. On the ground floor you will find a fully equipped kitchen, a dining room with fireplace, a bedroom with two sofa beds, and a bathroom. On the floor above is a double room—a large, charming room similar to those in young girls' boarding schools, with four single beds and a bath with a Jacuzzi. Minimum stay two nights.

AMENITIES:

English is spoken
Laundry service is available
Parking on the premises
Dinner may be served on request
Children over the age of seven are welcome

WHERE: The railway station of Cremona is 6 miles away, while the nearest airport is in Milan, 52 miles away.

CATEGORY: **Caffèlletto** · RATE: ⃝⃝ · *Member since 2000*

MARCARIA (MN)

INFO: CAFFÈLLETTO, ITALY
TEL. +39 023311814 OR 1820 + **FAX +39 023313009** + **E-MAIL: info@caffelletto.it**

You haven't seen Italy until you've seen Mantua. Visitors should head directly for the magnificent 500-room Palazzo Ducale that was the court of the Gonzagas for centuries. Mantua is also a city where you would be well advised to dine.

The Palazzo Madella is nine miles from Mantua. Built in 1700, it has remained in the hands of the same family, spaciously disposed around a courtyard and surrounded by lawns, gardens, and orchards. The rooms have beamed ceilings and the original floors and period furniture have been preserved. Breakfasts are served in a dining room dominated by an immense sideboard belonging to the owner's grandmother. Guests are encouraged to taste the local Parmesan cheese and salami with garlic, as well as your hostess's homemade jams, biscuits, and cakes.

ROOMS: Two rooms, one double and one twin, which share a bathroom (with both bathtub and shower).

AMENITIES:
English and French are spoken
Private parking

WHERE: The nearest railway station is in Marcaria, 5 miles away, while the airport in Verona Villafranca is 28 miles away.

CATEGORY: ✳✳✳✳ + **RATE:** ◯◯ + *Member since 2002*

TRENTINO—ALTO ADIGE

The Trentino region—usually grouped with the Alto Adige—is not far from the Austrian border in northern Italy. Both regions used to belong to Austria and became part of Italy in 1918. While there were mixed feelings about this union in the Germanic Alto Adige, the people of Trentino had always spoken Italian and considered themselves Italians, even while under Austrian rule. Austrian influences can be seen particularly in the tradition of hospitality that exists here. Every hotel, guesthouse, or boarding house offers warm rooms with fluffy duvets and good food and wine to greet their guests.

Not surprisingly, some of the food harks back to the days of the Austro-Hungarian monarchy: for example, the local equivalent of Knödel or canederli (dumplings) and a variety of strudel. The specialty of Trento, the capital of Trentino,

34 is called strangolapreti (priest-strangling) pasta—a purely Italian invention. The region also boasts some excellent wines—Traminer, Riesling, and Pinot—while Cabernet and Merlot are popular local reds.

Trentino is a spectacular mountainous region encompassing both the Alps and the Dolomites and equally pleasant in winter and summer. As soon as it starts snowing, skiers descend on the region, especially at resorts such as Madonna di Campiglio, one of the most famous retreats in Italy. The Trentino is also the best freshwater fishing spot in the country with dozens of large and small lakes and countless mountain streams. For this reason, trota alla trentina (trout) is frequently found on menus, as are delicious eel dishes.

THE LOCAL RECIPE

Generally speaking, the cuisine of Trentino—Alto Adige is more Austrian than Italian. Many ingredients, spices, and flavorings are seldom used in the rest of Italy. Pasta is replaced by thick soup and rice is more frequently a side dish. Meat is often smoked and Speck (smoked ham) takes the place of Parma ham. Desserts are often derived from the Austrian tradition as well and are predictably served with a cloud of whipped cream.

Knödel
Ingredients (serves 4)

8 oz. diced stale bread
3 oz. thickly cut bacon, diced
2 whole eggs
2 tbsp. grated Parmesan
1/3 cup warm milk

1 1/2 oz. butter
1/2 onion, chopped
2 tbsp. chopped parsley
nutmeg and salt to taste

Place the bread cubes in a bowl and pour the milk over them. Gently sauté half of the chopped onion and half of the parsley in half of the butter and pour into bread mixture. Add the Parmesan, eggs, and a pinch of nutmeg to the soaked bread. Season with salt and work the mixture until it is well blended. Using your hands form 2-inch diameter Knödel (dumplings) with the bread mixture. Plunge the Knödel into abundant boiling water and cook for ten minutes. Drain and keep warm. In the meantime, sauté the remaining onion, parsley, and the diced bacon with the remaining butter and pour over the dumplings. Serve hot.

MONGUELFO (BZ)

INFO: CAFFÈLLETTO, ITALY

TEL. +39 023311814 OR 1820 ♦ FAX +39 023313009 ♦ E-MAIL: info@caffelletto.it

The Maso Angerer is a beautifully restored peasant house in the heart of the Dolomites, ten minutes from Dobbiaco, fifteen from Brunico, and a half hour from Cortina d'Ampezzo. The ski lifts are twenty minutes away and it is also a perfect place for walking and riding.

The house dates back to the eighteenth century and stands in the middle of a wide meadow surrounded by woods. It is everything one could wish for in a mountain chalet. Old tiled stoves and warm wood-paneled ceilings and floors add to the romantic atmosphere. All you need for breakfast can be found in the delightful mountain kitchen.

ROOMS: Three twin rooms and one double room, each with a private bathroom.

AMENITIES:
English, French, and German are spoken
Private parking
Children over the age of twelve
*   *are welcome*

WHERE: The nearest railway station is in Monguelfo, 2 miles away (a night train from Rome stops here). The airport is Verona Villafranca, 124 miles away.

CATEGORY: Caffèlletto ♦ **RATE:** ○○ ♦ *Member since 2001*

VENETO

The Veneto Region in the northeast of Italy borders on the Venetian Lagoon to the east, Lake Garda to the west, and Austria to the north. Indeed, the Veneto was part of Austria for much of the last century and there are still traces of Austrian culture in the region, including the cuisine. In the mountains, for instance, the casunzei are noodles made with poppy seeds, a typically Austrian dish. The north of Veneto is mountainous and comprises some of the most spectacular peaks of the Dolomites, the Marmolada among them, and there are a number of ski resorts, from the family-oriented to the glamorous, such as Cortina d'Ampezzo. In the south is the fertile Venetian plain and most of the Veneto's lovely cities: Venice, Padua, Verona, Vicenza, and Treviso, as well as Chioggia, a major fishing port on the coast. In the surrounding countryside there are splendid Venetian villas (some of which adhere to the Caffelletto program), many designed by Palladio and containing frescoes by masters

such as Veronese and Tiepolo. Along the Brenta River, between Venice and Padua, are the famous villas of the Riviera del Brenta that can also be visited by boat. The area is also renowned for its wines made of northern grapes, such as Pinot Nero, Pinot Grigio, Soave, and Amarone.

The people of the Veneto, with their lilting dialects, are hardworking but also love to eat and drink—it is not unusual to see people having a shot of grappa with their coffee in the morning—and after they have eaten they love to sing the songs of the alpine regiments who distinguished themselves in both World Wars.

THE LOCAL RECIPE
There are many different kinds of cuisine in the Veneto. In the northern mountain region, the influence of Austrian tradition is apparent; at the same time, fish and shellfish abound near the coast. Risotto is more popular than pasta.

Salt Cod Puree
Ingredients (serves 4)

16 oz. salt cod
2 cloves of garlic
2 cups olive oil
1 cup milk
1 tbsp. chopped parsley
salt and pepper to taste

Place the salt cod in a pan, cover with water, and cook for about twenty minutes. Take the cod out of the pan, discard all the bones and the skin, and flake the flesh with a fork. Boil the garlic cloves in a little water, drain, then mash to a puree. Combine the cod with the garlic puree and work the mixture with a wooden spoon, alternating drizzles of oil and milk, as for a mayonnaise. Sprinkle the mashed salt cod with the chopped parsley and a little salt and pepper and serve cold with toasted slices of country bread.

SAN PIETRO DI FELETTO (TV)

INFO: CAFFÈLLETTO, ITALY

TEL. +39 023311814 OR 1820 ✦ FAX +39 023313009 ✦ E-MAIL: info@caffelletto.it

For Italians, Conegliano—in the Venetian countryside near Treviso—is associated with good food and wine, as well as with long lunches followed by walks in the woods or through the vineyards.

San Pietro di Feletto is just such a place, a large country house built in various periods over several centuries. The atmosphere is convivial: a long dining table under beamed ceilings, a tiled stove, and walls lined with copper pans and wooden boards and baskets made by your hostess. The house has always been in her family and she used to come here for holidays as a little girl. Sabina now lives here year-round with her husband, children, and dogs. She will recommend visits to the cellars in the area which produce the local Conegliano wines as well as the excellent Prosecco (champagne), and suggest restaurants such as Da Lino and Il Castelletto where, depending on the seasons, menus feature mushrooms, asparagus, or the famous radicchio of Treviso. The magical hilltop village of Asolo is only a half hour away by car.

ROOMS: There are two apartments, both on three floors: the first with a large sitting room, dining room, and kitchen downstairs; two double rooms with bathrooms and two double rooms that share a bathroom on the first floor; and a music and reading room with two communicating bedrooms (one double, one single) that share a bathroom on the second floor. The second apartment has a sitting room on the ground floor and two double rooms with shared bathrooms (one with bathtub, the

other with shower) on the first floor; upstairs, a suite with a twin room, sitting room, and bathroom with Jacuzzi. Minimum stay two nights.

AMENITIES:
English and a little French are spoken
Laundry service is available
Parking on the premises
Swimming pool
Pets are welcome

WHERE: The Conegliano railway station is 5 miles away, while the airport in Venice is 20 miles away.

CATEGORY: ✳✳✳✳ ✦ RATE: ○ ✦ *Member since 2000*

COLLALTO DI SUSEGANA (TV)

MASO DI VILLA–RELAIS DI CAMPAGNA ◆ **VIA COL DI GUARDA, 15**

31058 COLLALTO DI SUSEGANA, TREVISO

TEL. +39 0438841414 ◆ **FAX +39 0438985580** ◆ **E-MAIL: info@masodivilla.it**

Less than an hour outside Venice, with a view towards the foothills of the Alps, this great stone farmhouse stands all by itself on a hilltop within 12 acres of woodland surrounded by vegetable gardens and vines.

Your hosts acquired the property three years ago and have completely restored it, rigorously respecting the original architecture dating back to 1800, and a wing was added in 1920 using only period brick and stone. They are planning fountains with ornamental fish among the bushes on the lawn amid the neat rows of fruit trees and vegetable trellises in the gardens.

The rooms are comfortable and luxurious in a country house style, with warm colors and decorated fabrics arrayed under beamed ceilings. Breakfast is served under the pergola during the warmer months and in the country kitchen in winter, with homemade jams and fruit from their orchard, while your hostess is also willing to cook delicious dinners using her own produce (which can also be purchased by guests on request). This is also the wine growing area of the famous *Prosecco,* which makes an ideal aperitif.

ROOMS: Two twin-bedded rooms and four double rooms, all with their own bathroom and shower. Each room has its own color scheme: blue, yellow, apricot, lilac, and green. There is also a sitting room and library for the use of guests, and an *osteria* dining room with fireplace for private dinners.

AMENITIES:

English and Spanish are
spoken
Private parking
Dinner may be served on
request
Children under the age of two
stay free of charge, and
under the age of ten stay for
half price
Small, well-behaved pets are
welcome

WHERE: Conegliano railway station is 3 miles away, while Venice Airport is 40 miles away. Take highway A27 and exit at Conegliano. Drive toward Susegana, where Collalto is indicated on a sign. From here the green wooden gate of the villa is 3 miles ahead.

CATEGORY: Caffelletto ◆ **RATE:** ○○○ ◆ *Member since 2004*

ASOLO (TV)

INFO: CAFFÈLLETTO, ITALY

TEL. +39 023311814 OR 1820 · FAX +39 023313009 · E-MAIL: info@caffelletto.it

Asolo, reigning on its hilltop and serenely surveying the valley below with Monte Grappa in the background, could be the most magical part of Italy. Asolo has been the resort of the privileged since the seventeenth century and came definitively into its own at the end of the nineteenth. Eleonora Duse, the great romantic actress and muse of Gabriele D'Annunzio, lived, died, and was buried here. Then the English "discovered" Asolo, as they did so many beautiful parts of Italy at the beginning of the nineteenth century, although now it is the Germans who have taken over the role of pioneers.

Asolo itself is small, with all the tortuous walled streets pouring into the delightful central square. Here too there is an exclusive hotel belonging to the same family as Harry's Bar in Venice, the Villa Cipriani, where one can sip Bellini cocktails and eat tiny toasted sandwiches while admiring the beautiful view.

This house couldn't be more romantic. Built in the nineteenth century, it is surrounded by a garden full of roses, bay bushes, cypress trees, and a bank of flowers alternating with the seasons.

Your hostess has traveled all over the world and created this house as a sanctuary to come home to. Both floors have a sitting room, French upholstery, old lace curtains, prints, portraits of ancestors, and antique furniture. With its cozy fireplace and comfortable armchairs, this is a house that you will not want to leave.

Asolo is also close to the legendary Palladian villas of the Veneto region: Villa Barbaro in Maser is five miles away and is home to many splendid frescoes by Veronese, and the Villa Emo at Fanzolo is seven miles away and contains frescoes by Zelotti.

ROOMS: On the first floor there is a twin and a single room both with private bathrooms. On the second floor there is a double, also with private bathroom and French doors that open onto the terrace leading down into the garden. Minimum stay two nights.

AMENITIES:
Children over the age of two are welcome
Pets are not allowed
Parking in the garden
Riding school 3 miles away

WHERE: The nearest airport is in Treviso, 19 miles away, while the airport in Venice is 28 miles miles away. The closest railway station is in Castelfranco, 7 miles away.

CATEGORY: Caffèlletto · RATE: ○○○ · *Member since 1999*

CASTAGNOLE (TV)

VILLA DELLE MERIDIANE · VIA ZARA 3 · 31040 CASTAGNOLE DI PAESE, TREVISO
TEL. AND FAX +39 0422959615 · CELL +39 3391804685
E-MAIL: villadellemeridiane@noiseplanet.com

This handsome country house in Castagnole, two miles away from Treviso, is an ideal point from which to visit the Palladian villas where frescoes by Veronese can be seen. Treviso itself is an elegant city, a treasure trove for the fastidious shopper and famous

for its cuisine and local wines. Your hosts are experts in this field and can give excellent advice on where to dine.

While the villa at Castagnole is not itself by Palladio, it does have traces of frescoes on the facade and a magnificent roof. It dates back to the fifteenth century, although it was extensively restored two centuries later. The bedrooms are furnished with impeccable taste and family antiques. Breakfasts are served in the dining room, with a fireplace, and frequently feature homemade pastries.

ROOMS: There are two rooms: the first, with a private entrance from the garden, is a duplex with a small sitting room, fireplace, and a double room with a bathroom above it; the second room has a double bed and a bathroom.

AMENITIES:
French and some German are spoken
Parking on the premises
Maid service except on holidays
Children under the age of two stay
free of charge

WHERE: The railway station in Treviso is 4 miles away while there is also an airport in Treviso only 3 miles. The airport in Venice is 19 miles away. By car take highway Venezia–Belluno exiting at Treviso Sud. Stay left along the tangenziale, following indications for Treviso and Vicenza. At the end of the tangenziale turn right for Vicenza. Take the first road on the right with signs for Castagnole. Once in town, turn right on Via Grotta just before the church and then right again on Via Zara.

CATEGORY: ✳✳✳✳ · **RATE:** ○ · *Member since 2001*

LANCENIGO (TV)

INFO: CAFFÈLLETTO, ITALY

TEL. +39 023311814 OR 1820 ⋅ **FAX +39 023313009** ⋅ **E-MAIL: info@caffelletto.it**

This charming villa typical of the Veneto region is just outside Treviso, surrounded by parks and shaded by trees. The house is furnished with antiques from the various family homes. The railway station is a short walk from the villa's gates, where the local train to Venice takes about forty minutes. Treviso, the thriving capital of the "joyous and amorous county," with its churches dating back to the thirteenth century and its charming houses accented by frescoes, is only ten minutes away by car.

Day trips are recommended to Asolo, the magical hilltop town and for many years the haunt of expatriates, intellectuals, and English aristocracy. Villa Maser, with its incomparable frescoes by Veronese, and the Villa di Fanzolo are both open to the public and are a short drive away, as is Bassano del Grappa (home of the fiery spirit popular all over Italy, particularly in the north) with its wood-covered bridge dating back to the thirteenth century, and its well-known ceramics factory.

The hosts know every inch of the area and will be happy to advise you on itineraries and gastronomic haunts.

ROOMS: On the second floor there is a double room with a bathroom to share with a single room. In the turret, you have a large room with three beds and a bathroom. On the first floor, there is a sitting room with two beds and a bathroom. Minimum stay two nights.

AMENITIES:

French, English, some German, and some
*   Spanish are spoken*
The hostess loves to cook and will be pleased
*   to entertain her guests for dinner*
A small swimming pool, sauna, and
*   Turkish bath for two are available at a*
*   moderate extra fee*
Private parking
Children under two years of age stay
*   free of charge*

WHERE: The nearest airport is in Venice, 19 miles away, while the Treviso railway station is 4 miles away.

CATEGORY: ✳✳✳✳ ⋅ **RATE:** ◯◯ ⋅ *Member since 1998*

LONGARE (VI)

INFO: CAFFÈLLETTO, ITALY

TEL. +39 023311814 OR 1820 ◆ **FAX +39 023313009** ◆ **E-MAIL: info@caffelletto.it**

Il Monticello is at the epicenter of a circle encompassing all the Venetian cities of art. At eight miles from Vicenza, everything else is within a radius of about thirty-one miles, while Palladio's La Rotonda is only two miles away. The property is on a hill flanked by a forest and surrounded by a park with 200 cherry trees that explode into

blossom in spring and later yield delicious fruit. There are gardens both in front and behind the house where guests may have breakfast among lilac and rosebushes. The house itself is a turn-of-the-century villa built by the grandparents of the present owners. Your hosts live here all year-round with their daughter. Your hostess, an architect, also runs the farming complex.

ROOMS: A short distance from the main villa, the limonaia has a large, romantic double room with a four-poster bed (with the option of a third bed) and a private bathroom. For longer stays, a small, completely renovated house is available on the edge of the property. It has an attractively furnished sitting room with a fireplace and kitchen corner, and on the floor above one double room, one twin room, and a large bathroom (with bathtub and shower). Minimum stay at the limonaia two nights; in the house five nights. The limonaia is only available from March 1 to October 31.

AMENITIES:
English and French are spoken
Private parking
Dinner may be served on request
with organic produce from the
vegetable garden

WHERE: The nearest railway station is in Vicenza, 7 miles away, while the airport in Venice is 37 miles away.

CATEGORY: ✹✹✹✹ ◆ RATE: ☊ ◆ *Member since 2002*

ARCUGNANO (VI)

INFO: CAFFÈLLETTO, ITALY

TEL. +39 023311814 OR 1820 ◦ **FAX +39 023313009** ◦ **E-MAIL: info@caffelletto.it**

This is a typical Venetian country house, eight miles from Vicenza, almost submerged by the green of the surrounding hillsides. The view from the windows sweeps down over the garden, with its multitiered flower beds, pomegranate and persimmon trees,

to the dense woodland and small lake in the distance. In the warmer months guests may breakfast under a pergola of lilac wisteria.

This is a perfect starting point to visit, not only Vicenza, but all the famous Palladian villas nearby. There are three eighteen-hole golf courses within easy distance, while fishermen can cast their lines in the lake below. This is also a wonderful place for walks and mountain biking.

ROOMS: An independent apartment on two floors with private entrance, sitting room, and French windows. On the ground floor, there is a double room with private bathroom (with shower), while on the first floor there is one double and

one twin-bedded room with shared bathroom (with shower and bathtub). A small loft studio with a sofa bed overlooks the sitting room.

AMENITIES:

French and some English are spoken
Private parking
Use of the kitchen may be requested
Children under the age of two stay
free of charge

WHERE: The nearest railway station is in Vicenza, 8 miles away, while the airport is in Verona, 37 miles away.

CATEGORY: ✳✳✳✳ ◦ **RATES:** ○○ ◦ *Member since 2001*

AZ. AGRICOLA MUSELLA CORTE FERRAZZETTE ◆ 37036 ALBERGO, VERONA

TEL. +39 045973385 ◆ FAX +39 0458956287 ◆ CELL +39 3357294627 ◆ E-MAIL: paulo@musella.it

Ten minutes from the center of Verona we are in the wine country of Valpolicella, one of Italy's most prized red wines. The estate extends over eighty-six acres covered in vineyards and woodland where deer run wild and hawks wheel overhead. Old walls, four stone gateways, and a river make up the circumference of the property, which, from a distance, looks like the label of an expensive château wine. It should therefore come as no surprise that the four members of the Pasqua di Bisceglie family are not only eminently hospitable hosts but also produce excellent Valpolicella, Amarone and Recioto wines as well as a fiery grappa.

The various buildings have been ably restored by your hosts and date from the 1500s. Breakfasts are served in a loggia, which commands a beautiful view of the whole estate and opens onto an English lawn studded with age-old olive trees.

ROOMS: Nine rooms, all with private bathrooms (with showers), air-conditioning, central heating, television, small refrigerator, and kettle to make tea or coffee. No two rooms are alike, all furnished with antiques, terra-cotta floors, and beamed ceilings. The Stanza delle Farfalle and Il Brolo are double rooms. Provenza is a single room. In the loft is La Piccionaia, one of the most beautiful rooms in the house, with a double bed and large bathroom. In the building with the red stripes are L'Aia and Le Rose, both with double beds; Le Chicchere, with two single bed; the Golf Room, with a fireplace, double bed, and bathroom (with Jacuzzi and shower); and the Risacca del Mare, with a double bed and a bathroom (with shower).

AMENITIES:

English and Portuguese are spoken
Laundry service is available
Parking nearby
Equipment for bicycling, fishing, or canoeing is available
Children under the age of three will be supplied with folding beds
Small pets are welcome

WHERE: The railway station of Verona Porta Nuova is 6 miles away while the Verona Villafranca airport is 15 miles away. By car from highway A4 Milano–Venezia, exit at Verona Est. Follow the directions for San Martino B.A.; when in the main square, go left at the traffic light and continue until you reach the second-to-last light in San Martino, then turn right toward Ferrazze. After a short distance, the Corte Musella is on the right.

CATEGORY: Caffèlletto ◆ RATE: ○○○ ◆ *Member since 2003*

VERONA–PIAZZA DELLE ERBE

INFO: CAFFÈLLETTO, ITALY

TEL. +39 023311814 OR 1820 ◆ FAX +39 023313009 ◆ E-MAIL: info@caffelletto.it

This bed-and-breakfast is in the loveliest, most central part of Verona, literally around the corner from Piazza delle Erbe, Piazza Dante, and Piazza dei Signori. The little palazzo has four floors is in Via della Trota (Trout Street), a reminder of the days when there was a fish market on the banks of the river behind the house. Today Via della Trota abounds in antique shops, book stores, and little *trattorie*. The two studio apartments available for guests are on the top floor without a lift, but the climb upstairs is worth it for the view of the Roman Arena, Giusti Gardens, and the Torricelle hill. Your hostess is a professional photographer, and has designed the apartments with the flair and taste of an artist. All supplies for a fine breakfast are in the kitchens.

ROOMS: Two light and cozy apartments are on the fourth floor, the first with a hall and dining room, kitchen, little bathroom with shower, and a double room with the option of a third bed. The second is a large studio with a kitchen corner, double bed, and small bathroom with shower. Minimum stay 2 nights.

AMENITIES:

*English and German are
spoken
Parking for an hourly
charge available in
nearby Piazza Isolo
Children under the age of
two stay free of charge*

WHERE: the nearest railway station is less than two miles away, while the Verona airport is 9 miles away.

CATEGORY: ✳✳✳✳ ◆ **RATE:** ◯◯ ◆ *Member since 2004*

NEGRAR DI VALPOLICELLA (VR)

INFO: CAFFÈLLETTO, ITALY

TEL. +39 023311814 OR 1820 • FAX +39 023313009 • E-MAIL: info@caffelletto.it

In the heart of the Valpolicella wine producing area, home of the famous Amarone, this old farmhouse is only six miles from Verona. The house, which has been beautifully restored, is covered in creepers and surrounded by lawns, flowering shrubs, and shady trees under which guests may breakfast in summer.

In the garden is a church dedicated to Santa Maria and first mentioned in historical documents in the year 1212, which is still used by the locals on special feast days. Your host, Matteo—a Renaissance man whose talents range from Internet savvy to making homemade plum cake—personally chose the warm yellows, ochers, and rusts in the elegantly furnished rooms. The rooms are the last word in comfort, including Jacuzzi tubs, air-conditioning, and satellite television. Breakfasts are excellent and abundant with both sweet and savory touches.

ROOMS: There are six rooms. The Suite, with a four-poster bed; Amarone, a twin room with a bathroom (with bathtub); Greta, a triple room with a bathroom (with bathtub); I Due Visi, another triple with a bathroom (with shower); Opera, a double room with a bathroom (with bathtub); Mosaico, a twin room with a sumptuous bathroom (with bathtub and mosaic walls).

AMENITIES:

English and German are spoken
Laundry service is available
Private parking
Car rental available
Small Jacuzzi and swimming pool in
*   the garden*
A charming trattoria at the gates of the villa
All rooms have air-conditioning, telephone,
*   satellite television, small refrigerator,*
*   and safe*
Pets are welcome

WHERE: The nearest railway station is in Verona, 10 miles away, while the Verona Villafranca airport is 14 miles away. By car take highway A22 Brennero—Modena and exit at Verona Nord. Go straight toward the Strada Statale 12 for Valpolicella. At the end of the highway follow the signs for Negrar. Once at Santa Maria turn left at the light. After a short distance turn left again toward Moron.

CATEGORY: Caffèlletto • **RATE:** ○○○○ • *Member since 2002*

SORGÀ (VR)

INFO: CAFFÈLLETTO, ITALY

TEL. +39 023311814 OR 1820 ⬥ FAX +39 023313009 ⬥ E-MAIL: info@caffelletto.it

This villa, built in 1460, has been the country residence of many aristocratic families, including the Gonzaga, Dukes of Mantua. Horseshoe-shaped, the villa embraces a splendid courtyard and garden. The salons contain frescoes by Giulio Romano,

architect and painter to the court of Mantua, commissioned by Muzio Gonzaga, son of the Duke of Mantua. You will find the family charming, welcoming, and eager to introduce you to the villa's surroundings. A half hour from both Mantua and Verona, the villa is ideally situated for visiting these two showpieces of Italian art and culture.

ROOMS: There are six double rooms, all decorated with frescoes and furnished with antiques. They all have private bathrooms.

AMENITIES:

English and German are spoken
Laundry service is available
Dinner is served on request in the
   villa dining room
Children under the age of two stay
   free of charge
Pets are allowed

WHERE: The airport in Verona is 14 miles away, while the nearest railway station is Nogara, 5 miles away.

CATEGORY: Caffèlletto ⬥ **RATE:** ○○ ⬥ *Member since 1998*

INFO: CAFFÈLLETTO, ITALY

TEL. +39 023311814 OR 1820 ◆ FAX +39 023313009 ◆ E-MAIL: info@caffelletto.it

Five minutes from Ponte Rialto, this is a little palazzo dating back to the seventeenth century, with windows crested with the clover motif typical of Venice, tucked away just behind the Campo San Bartolomeo in a quiet, narrow *Rio*, as locals call the tiny alleyways that were once canals and have been bricked over and come tapering to an end at the main waterways.

The palazzo used to belong to the noble Nani family and has been completely restored with a handsome entrance hall and marble staircase. The apartment is on the first floor and guests have an independent entrance. Breakfast is served in the charming dining room with monumental windows overlooking the Rio with watery Venetian sounds echoing up from the small canal. The jams and cakes are made by your hostess, and the fig jam is particularly worth a taste. A mother and daughter team run the bed-and-breakfast with enthusiasm and an attention to detail that is evident everywhere you look, especially in the choice of bed linens and towels, while the mother is an excellent cook and enjoys welcoming friends from all over the world.

ROOMS: An elegant, comfortable suite furnished with family antiques with a double room, a little sitting room with a double sofa bed, and a bathroom with shower. Air conditioning. Minimum stay two nights in low season and three in high season.

AMENITIES:

English, French, and German are spoken
Children under the age of two stay free of charge
Dinner may be served on request
Laundry service is available

WHERE: the railway station is within a couple of miles, while the airport is 9 miles away. Take local *vaporetto* line 82 and get off at the Rialto.

CATEGORY: Caffèlletto ◆ RATE: ○○○–○○○○ ◆ *Member since 2005*

ASOLO VILLA VEGA (TV)

VILLA VEGA B&B · FORESTO DI PAGNANO, 3 · 31011 ASOLO, TREVISO
TEL. +39 042355026 · FAX +39 0423521549 · CELL +39 3358435556
E-MAIL: info@villavega.it

This elegant villa neighbors the legendary Cipriani Hotel on the outskirts of the delightful little medieval hilltop town of Asolo. Though it may not offer the hotel's famous Bellinis and little toasted finger sandwiches for an aperitif, Villa Vega, dating back to the end of the nineteenth century, offers a unique hospitality and shares the same view and lawns fringed with rosebushes. Your hostess also makes a delicious apple pie that is served at breakfast under the centuries-old trees during the warmer months. Asolo is ideally situated to visit the Palladian villas which grace the Venetian countryside all around, and the little town itself, with its medieval castle and ancient Roman baths and theatre, also offers much to the visitor. It is only sixteen miles from Treviso, and there is an 18-hole golf course a short distance away.

ROOMS: On the top floor of the villa there is a double room with bathroom with tub, and a suite including double and single rooms sharing a bathroom with tub. All rooms have air conditioning.

AMENITIES:
English, French, and
  German are spoken
Private parking
Children under the age of
  two stay free of charge
Bicycles and mountain bikes
  are available
Internet connection
  provided

WHERE: The nearest railway station is Castelfranco/Montebelluna, 9 miles away, while the airport in Treviso is 18 miles away.

CATEGORY: ✳✳✳✳ · **RATE:** ○ · *Member since 2004*

VENICE—GHETTO

INFO: CAFFÈLLETTO, ITALY

TEL. +39 023311814 OR 1820 • FAX +39 023313009 • E-MAIL: info@caffelletto.it

Over bridges, down winding alleys, across small squares lined with trees, among strutting pigeons, and around more than one corner from the well-trod tourist path, we are in what was once the ghetto of Venice, in that part of the Venetian labyrinth known as Cannaregio. The studio apartment is on the first floor of this typically Venetian house.

ROOMS: The comfortably furnished apartment comprises a sitting room with a double sofa bed and an armchair (that can be transformed into a single bed for a third guest). The area is divided from the well-equipped kitchen by a long wooden bench. There is a bathroom with a shower. Minimum stay three nights.

AMENITIES:
English is spoken

WHERE: The railway station is 3 miles away while Marco Polo airport is 12 miles away.

CATEGORY: ✳✳✳✳ • **RATE:** ○○ • *Member since 2002*

VENICE–GIUDECCA

INFO: CAFFÈLLETTO, ITALY

TEL. +39 023311814 OR 1820 • FAX +39 023313009 • E-MAIL: info@caffelletto.it

The Giudecca is an island in the Venetian lagoon much loved by Lord Byron, who spent many months here. It is only fifteen minutes from the train station but off the well-beaten tourist path. This part of Venice has a charm all its own: the magnificent facade of the Madonna della Salute rises above the water on the other side of the canal while Palladian churches blend into the neighborhood atmosphere of the Giudecca. This bed-and-breakfast is in a lovely old house built in 1680 and entirely renovated in 1999 by your hostess, Dominique, who is a mine of information about the city and its many haunts. From the inner garden, the scent of roses, basil, mint, sage, lavender, and jasmine wafts onto the tiled patio, where guests may breakfast or drink afternoon tea. The house is three minutes from the vaporetto stop. Harry's Dolci, the pastry and sweets branch of Cipriani, is nearby, as is the famous pizza of Do Mori.

ROOMS: An apartment with a large sitting room/dining room with two comfortable beds, a double room with French windows opening onto the garden, a kitchen, and a bathroom with a shower. Minimum stay three nights.

AMENITIES:
English and French are spoken
Children under the age of two stay free of charge

WHERE: The nearest railway station is fifteen minutes away by vaporetto while the airport is 19 miles away.

CATEGORY: ✹✹✹✹ • RATE: ○○○ • *Member since 2003*

VENICE—SANTA MARGHERITA

INFO: CAFFÈLLETTO, ITALY

TEL. +39 023311814 OR 1820 ⋅ **FAX +39 023313009** ⋅ **E-MAIL: info@caffelletto.it**

The "real" Venice is like a game of snakes and ladders: narrow winding calles (streets) leading over little bridges and opening onto campi (neighborhood squares). This bed-and-breakfast is a typical red Venetian two-story building with green shutters at the end of just such a maze of alleys and bridges, in the Campiello dell'Avogaria, behind the Campo Santa Margherita and Campo San Barnaba. The apartment is on the upper floor, simple but charming with a blue bedroom, a sitting room, and kitchen corner, modern and well-equipped. The apartment is full of light, overlooking the Campiello on the one side and a private garden on the

other. Your hostess meets guests on arrival and departure. You are within easy walking distance of the Accademia, Ca' Rezzonico, and the Madonna della Salute.

ROOMS: A double room with the option of a third and fourth bed, a sitting/dining room with a sofa bed, kitchen corner, and bathroom with shower. Minimum stay three nights.

AMENITIES:
English is spoken
Air-conditioning
Children under the age of two stay free of charge
Small pets are welcome

WHERE: The railway station is under 1 mile away while Marco Polo airport is 12 miles away.

CATEGORY: ✳✳✳ ⋅ **RATES:** ○○○ (2 people); ○○ (3–4 people) ⋅
Member since 2003

VENICE–TINTORETTO

INFO: CAFFÈLLETTO, ITALY

TEL. +39 023311814 OR 1820 · **FAX +39 023313009** · **E-MAIL: info@caffelletto.it**

This typical Venetian sixteenth-century house is on a narrow calle (street) close to the birthplace of Tintoretto, whose paintings can be admired in the nearby church of La Madonna dell'Orto. On the second floor, the rooms are full of light and there is a tiny garden bursting with greenery where guests may breakfast in spring; in the cooler months there is a sitting room/kitchen.

ROOMS: A double room, with the option of a third bed, with a large bathroom (with bathtub), which guests share with their hostess.

AMENITIES:
English, French, and Spanish are spoken
Children over the age of twelve
    are welcome

WHERE: The nearest railway station is a short distance away (10 minutes by foot). The Venice airport is about 12 miles away.

CATEGORY: ✳✳✳✳ · RATE: ○○○ · *Member since 2003*

ALBAREA (VE)

INFO: CAFFÈLLETTO, ITALY

TEL. +39 023311814 OR 1820 ◆ **FAX +39 023313009** ◆ **E-MAIL: info@caffelletto.it**

This historic Venetian villa on the Riviera del Brenta, recently restored to its former splendor, is halfway between Padua and Venice, though it is hard to imagine guests wanting to leave such magical and luxurious surroundings even for a day. The oldest of Venetian villas, the Villa Rizzi dates back to the year 1000 when it was first a church and then a convent—the church with its ceiling of frescoes by the school of Tiepolo and Tintoretto is still open to guests today. This magnificent building has been for generations the residence of the Rizzi family, who still live in a private wing and personally welcome guests. The park is a romantic apotheosis of climbing roses, sylvan statues, and swans that glide on the small lake. Guests may also use the elegant swimming pool. It is easy to slip into this aristocratic lifestyle where tea, served in china cups adorned with the family coat of arms, is proffered by liveried servants at one's beck and call.

ROOMS: Six double rooms, all with their own bathroom with shower, and all sumptuously decorated with family antiques. The bridal suite is particularly appealing. There is a television and minibar in every room. Guests may also use the lofty salons to read and relax or listen to music. Minimum stay two nights.

AMENITIES:
English, French, and German are spoken
Private parking
Swimming pool with sauna and fitness rooms with
*   staff on call for massage and facials*
Cars and bicycles may be rented, while trans-
*   portation can be arranged to ferry guests back*
*   and forth from the railway station or airport*
Golf course and manège nearby
Excursions can be organized by car or by boat to
*   Padua, the villas of the Brenta, or the islands of*
*   Burano or Murano*
Dinner may be served on request

WHERE: The nearest railway station is in Vigonza, less than 1 mile away, while Dolo railway station is 1 mile away and the Venice airport is 7 miles away. By car take highway A4 and exit at Dolo then drive straight to the first traffic light, straight on for a short distance before turning right at the signpost for Albarea. Villa Rizzi is nearby.

CATEGORY: Caffèlletto ◆ **RATE:** ○○○○ ◆ *Member since 2003*

DOLO (VE)

INFO: CAFFÈLLETTO, ITALY

TEL. +39 023311814 OR 1820 · FAX +39 023313009 · E-MAIL: info@caffelletto.it

The Ca' Tron at Dolo is on the famous Riviera del Brenta, where patrician Venetians spent their summers on the riverbanks: a typical Venetian villa from the beginning of the nineteenth century—except for the chapel, which dates back to the original seven-

teenth-century complex destroyed by a fire. The imposing white facade looks out over the garden toward the river. Behind it there is a park with the romantic land-scaping typical of the era, swans floating on the lake, hillocks crested with giant magnolias, pomegranate trees, and cedars of Lebanon.

Inside, the villa is beautifully furnished with family antiques and the original warm and colorful tiled floors. There are two dining rooms, one to the front and one to the back of the villa, one for breakfasts in summer and the other for winter.

The villa has been in the family of your hosts for 200 years. Your hostess is an excellent cook and her strudels, tarts, and plum cakes should be sampled at breakfast, as well as dinner, on request. Every half hour there is a bus for Venice or Padua. This is an ideal starting point to visit both; guests may also rent bicycles and ride along the banks of the Brenta to visit the other famous Venetian villas on the Riviera.

ROOMS: On the first floor there is a double room with a bathroom and a small ter-race overlooking the park. On the floor above, there are two rooms, a double and a single that share a bathroom. Minimum stay two nights.

AMENITIES:
English and French are spoken
Laundry service is available
Private parking
Dinner may be served on request
Children under the age of two stay
  free of charge
Pets are allowed

WHERE: The nearest railway station is in Dolo—Ballò, 3 miles away, while Marco Polo airport is 14 miles away in Venice.

CATEGORY: ✳✳✳✳ · RATE: ○○ · *Member since 2001*

SAMBRUSON DI DOLO (VE)

**BARCHESSA COLLOREDO ◆ VIA BRUSAURA 24 ◆ 30030 SAMBRUSON DI DOLO, VENICE
TEL. +39 041411755 ◆ FAX +39 0415128994 ◆ E-MAIL: barchecollo@libero.it**

The style of this eighteenth-century villa on the Riviera del Brenta is known as a Barchessa. A huge, square inner courtyard paved in terra-cotta surrounded by well-tended lawns is bordered on four sides by a jasmine- and climbing-rose-smothered loggia, beneath green shuttered windows and sloping roofs surrounded by orchards.

The Barchessa Colloredo is only fifteen minutes from Padua and Venice. The more energetic can bicycle along the canal to both. The whole region is a gastronomic treasure trove with restaurants and trattorias specializing in fish dishes within easy reach. Your host is the father of the family who personally makes the jams for breakfast from his wife's fruit trees. He and his son personally look after guests.

ROOMS: A double room with a bathroom (with shower) and a large studio apartment with a double bed, an optional third bed, kitchen corner, and bathroom (with shower). Minimum stay two nights.

AMENITIES:
English, German, and French are spoken
Laundry service is available
Private parking
Children under the age of two stay free of charge
Pets are welcome

WHERE: The nearest railway station is Dolo, less than a mile away, while the airport in Venice is 12 miles away. By car take highway A4 and exit at Dolo–Mirano. Drive into the center of Dolo. At the traffic light near the church, turn left and take the Strada Statale 11 toward Mira and Venice. After a short distance turn right at the car showroom and cross the bridge over the Brenta and drive toward Sambruson and Chioggia until you reach a traffic light. At the T-junction turn left and continue toward the center of Sambruson. Turn right in front of the church onto a dirt road. After a short distance the villa will be on your right.

CATEGORY: ✳✳✳✳ ◆ RATE: OO ◆ *Member since 2002*

PADUA–BRENTELLA

TEL. +39 023311814 OR 1820 ⋄ **FAX** +39 023313009 ⋄ **E-MAIL:** info@caffelletto.it

Although only ten minutes from the center of Padua, Michela's home is more like a farmhouse with cows, horses, and sheep roaming in the courtyard. The house stands next to a historic villa on the banks of the Bacchiglione River. There are a variety of walks and bicycling tours around the property that is on the official route of the Colli Euganei (a famous walking or biking tour of the hills near Padua, with frequent pit stops at pictur-

esque local inns). The hosts are passionate lovers of nature, and organic products they make according to ancient local custom are available for purchase.

ROOMS: The house once belonging to the coachman has been restored and turned into a guesthouse with a large double room on one floor (a third bed can be added on request) and a sitting room/kitchen and bathroom below. Minimum stay two nights.

AMENITIES:
English and Spanish are spoken
Pets are welcome

WHERE: The nearest airport is in Venice, 19 miles away, while the railway station of Padua is 3 miles away. Buses run regularly to and from the center of Padua.

CATEGORY: ✳✳✳✳ ⋄ **RATE:** ○ ⋄ *Member since 1998*

INFO: CAFFÈLLETTO, ITALY

TEL. +39 023311814 OR 1820 ◆ **FAX +39 023313009** ◆ **E-MAIL: info@caffelletto.it**

Villa Pacchierotti was named after the famous tenor who bought the beautiful villa in the second half of the nineteenth century. Ten minutes from Padua, the villa was built in the seventeenth century and acquired in the middle of the 1800s by a family from Trieste, ancestors of the actual owners. It is a typically Venetian villa with three log-

gias, one on top of the other. There are historic outbuildings and an adjoining chapel. Villa Pacchierotti is near the Brenta canal and artificial banks have been constructed to protect it whenever the canal overflows. It stands on the road leading to the walled town of Cittadella and, from there, to Bassano del Grappa, with its famous wooden bridge, where some of Italy's best grappa is made. It is only ten minutes from the splendid Villa Contarini at Piazzola sul Brenta, which is open to the public and should on no account be missed. On a more pedestrian note, Villa Pacchierotti is near the Padua highway and therefore within easy reach of Venice and the other cities of the Veneto region.

ROOMS: A double room with a fireplace and another double room, both with bathrooms and large windows overlooking the park. Minimum stay two nights.

AMENITIES:
Open from January 1 to
*   *June 30 and from October 1*
*   *to December 1*
English is spoken
Parking on the premises
Children under the age of two
*   *stay free of charge*
Pets are not allowed

WHERE: The nearest airport is Venice, 20 miles away, while the railway station is at Padua, 5 miles away.

CATEGORY: Caffèlletto ◆ **RATE:** ○○○ ◆ *Member since 1999*

60   LUVIGLIANO (PD)

INFO: CAFFÈLLETTO, ITALY

TEL. +39 023311814 OR 1820 ♦ FAX +39 023313009 ♦ E-MAIL: info@caffelletto.it

The Villa Pollini, a historic nineteenth-century mansion framed by the Euganean Hills, is eleven miles from Padua. Surrounded by a rambling, romantic garden, the two-story villa is an example of linear elegance, beautifully shaded by centennial cedar trees. The famous composer Cesare Pollini used to spend his summers here and would invite a select group of friends to spend "happy rural and musical days" together in the shade of a gazebo that still stands in a secluded corner of the garden. Today the owners of the villa produce an excellent wine with grapes from the vineyards on the surrounding hills and you are welcome to arrange a visit to the cellars and a wine-tasting session. They also sell honey, grappa, and balsamic vinegar.

The Euganean Hills are crisscrossed by a network of official hiking and mountain-biking routes and Villa Pollini is within the confines of the Regional Euganean Park. Opposite the villa is the magnificent Villa dei Vescovi (Bishop's Palace), a pre-Palladian residence well worth a visit. A short distance away by car are the thermal baths of Montegrotto and Abano Terme, both highly specialized centers for health, beauty, and wellness treatments.

ROOMS: In a wing of the house, there are four delightful independent apartments. Minimum stay two nights.

AMENITIES:
English and French are spoken
Laundry service is available
Parking on the premises
Within a radius of 12 miles there are
*   three eighteen-hole golf courses*
Children under the age of two stay
*   free of charge*
Pets are welcome

WHERE: The nearest airports are Venice and Bologna, both about 31 miles away, while the railway station in Terme Euganee is 5 miles away.

CATEGORY: ✳✳✳✳ ♦ RATE: ○○ ♦ *Member since 1999*

PADOVA–SAN FRANCESCO

VIA DELLA PIEVE, 9 · 35121 PADOVA

TEL. +39 049665463 · FAX +39 0498782533 · E-MAIL: VICOLODELCENTRO@VIRGILIO.IT

This recently renovated, very comfortable, elegant apartment is right in the center of Padova on a quiet side street just around the corner from the Palace of Law (*Palazzo della Ragione*). The apartment is ideal for those seeking a private haven in the heart of the city's historic center and its many attractions. Here the morning market is a buzzing hive of activity, while on Saturdays there is the weekly clothes and flower market in Prato della Valle. Antique stores in what was once the ghetto of Padova are also nearby, and the neighboring Palazzo Zabarella houses important international artistic and cultural exhibitions. Giotto's marvelous frescoes in the Scrovegni Chapel are nearby, as is one of Italy's most famous universities, where Galileo taught in the sixteenth and seventeenth centuries. This is also a perfect base year-round for visiting Padova's famous botanical gardens (*Orto Botanico*) and the Villa Selvatico. For those traveling by train or car, both Venice and Vicenza are less than an hour away, not to mention the many villas of Palladio and other small towns nearby.

In this handsome palazzo, which dates back to the beginning of the eighteenth century, your hosts live on the first floor, while guests have an independent apartment on the ground floor with windows overlooking the garden. All the supplies for breakfast are in the apartment's well-equipped, contemporary kitchen.

ROOMS: An apartment on the ground floor with a hall, a large, sun-filled sitting room with kitchen corner and a double sofa bed, a double room, and a bathroom with shower. Minimum stay 2 nights.

AMENITIES:
English and French are spoken
Children under the age of two stay free of charge

WHERE: The nearest railway station is within a couple of miles, while Venice airport is 25 miles away. By car take highway A4 and exit at Padova Est. Follow the signs for the center and San Antonio Basilica.

CATEGORY: ✳✳✳✳ • **RATE:** ◯◯ • *Member since 2004*

RONCADE – VILLA ARZILLA

INFO: CAFFÈLLETTO, ITALY
TEL. +39 023311814 OR 1820 ◆ **FAX +39 023313009** ◆ **E-MAIL: info@caffelletto.it**

In the heart of the Veneto region, with easy access to wherever you want to go, this charming country house dating back to the sixteenth century is on the banks of the Sile River. Only nine miles from Treviso and sixteen miles from Venice, Villa Arzilla is ideally located for those who wish to explore the famous Palladian Villas and Venice itself. The garden surrounds the swimming pool and is lined by orchards of fruit trees. A shady terrace, where breakfasts are also served in the warmer months, overlooks the river and is the perfect place to relax in summer, while for more active guests there are games, ping-pong and bowling facilities elsewhere. Your hosts are Venetians, and will gladly organize cultural and sporting tours and events, including canoeing on the river or boat trips to Venice and the vicinity.

ROOMS: Two apartments—the first has a large salon/dining room with kitchen and two double rooms sharing a bathroom with tub, while the second is a large studio with kitchen corner and bathroom with shower. Minimum stay two nights.

AMENITIES:
English and French are spoken
Swimming pool
Children under the age of two
   stay free of charge
Pets are welcome
Laundry service available on
   request

WHERE: the nearest airport is in Venice, 5 miles away, while the nearest railway station is in Altino.

CATEGORY: ✳✳✳✳ ◆ RATE: ○○ ◆ *Member since 2004*

SAN MARTINO DI VENEZZE (RO)

INFO: CAFFÈLLETTO, ITALY

TEL. +39 023311814 OR 1820 ⋅ FAX +39 023313009 ⋅ E-MAIL: info@caffelletto.it

This estate has been in the family for six centuries, although the original castle was destroyed long ago. Today's red brick manor house stands at the end of an avenue of ancient lime trees. The guest apartments are in a separate building, which your host has just finished restoring, leaving intact the spirit of both the era

and the area, with old terra-cotta floors, stone fireplaces, and bedrooms that combine period charm with modern comforts. The estate is between twenty minutes and one hour's distance from Venice, Ferrara, Padua, the fishing port of Chioggia, Vicenza, Verona, Ravenna, the Po Delta, and the abbey of Pomposa.

ROOMS: In the main house there are thirteen double rooms, each with its own bathroom and air-conditioning. Three small houses are also available, each with a large sitting room with a fireplace, and a kitchen where guests will find the necessary elements for both breakfast and dinner; on the floor above there are two delightful, sunny bedrooms, each with its own television and private bathroom. Minimum stay four nights.

AMENITIES:
*Open from April 1 to
November 4
English is spoken
Parking on the premises
Swimming pool
A half hour away by car is an
eighteen-hole golf course
There is a bathroom for
handicapped guests
Dinner may be served on request
Children under the age of two
stay free of charge
Pets are welcome*

WHERE: The Venice airport is 31 miles away, while the Rovigo railway station is 5 miles away.

CATEGORY: ✳✳✳✳ ⋅ **RATE:** ○ ⋅ *Member since 1999*

TAGLIO DI PO (RO)

CA' ZEN 4 · 45019 TAGLIO DI PO, ROVIGO

TEL. AND FAX +39 0426346469 · CELL +39 3398688715 · E-MAIL: mary.adelaide@virgilio.it

This eighteenth-century manor house sits in the midst of parkland sloping down toward the river on the banks of the Po Delta. The villa has two wings looking out over gardens, while behind the house there is a wide rectangular terrace paved in seasoned terra-cotta, which is a perfect place to have tea on a sunny afternoon. The interior features antique Venetian furniture and elegant wall hangings and upholstery. You will be welcomed by the lady of the house, Elaine, who is Anglo-Irish and has a keen interest in the surrounding beauty of the Po Nature Reserve and Park. She can recommend bicycle rides and bird-watching trails.

Elaine's home is near Adria with its Archaeological Museum; Chioggia, the delightful fishing port with its canals and the largest fish market in Italy; and Pellestrina, romantically surrounded by water and only accessible by boat—all of which are about twenty minutes away—and Ferrara with its ducal palaces, walled gardens, and quiet waters is only an hour's drive away. This area is rich in restaurants specializing in fish dishes. Amateur fishermen can rent canoes or boats to take to fishing haunts. Ca' Zen has its own private stables, three paddocks, and an open-air manège. Dressage and show-jumping stages are organized by the riding instructor, Alfredo Marcelli, who has a lifetime of experience with horses.

ROOMS: Accommodation consists of a suite with a double room and a single room (with a bed in the French Empire style and a bathroom), as well as a single room with

its own bathroom. The style and atmosphere of these rooms are in keeping with the rest of the house, transporting guests into the luxury and mood of country-house living in the nineteenth century.

AMENITIES:
Open from March to October
English and French are spoken
Horseback riding

WHERE: The nearest airport is in Venice, 40 miles away, while the railway station is Adria, 11 miles away.

CATEGORY: Caffèlletto · RATE: ○○ · *Member since 1998*

Friuli–Venezia Giulia

Friuli and Venezia Giulia are considered a single region although they share little more than their names—both "Friuli" and "Giulia" come from the name of Julius Caesar's Forum Iulii—and to a certain extent their history. Bordered by Austria and Slovenia, Friuli–Venezia Giulia is the most centrally located European region of Italy and was, for many centuries, part of the Austro-Hungarian Empire.

The region is geographically varied with vast flatlands to the south, Adriatic beaches to the east, and hills covered with vineyards that lead gradually to the Alps in the north. Ethnically, the Friulani descend from the Celts, whose language is still alive in local dialects. There is little of the "O Sole mio" cliché about the people of this region; however, the Friulani are undoubtedly Italian in their love of good food and wine. One of the best wine-producing areas in Italy is to be found in the hills south and east of Cividale: Tocai, Sauvignon, Pinot Grigio, and Pinot Chardonnay are the

best-known whites, together with Picolit, the famous dessert wine, while the reds are Cabernet, Merlot, and Refosco.

The capital of Friuli is Udine, a city, like its inhabitants, serious and hardworking. Trieste, on the other hand, is the epitome of Venezia Giulia. Trieste was once the main port of the Austro-Hungarian Empire, and Emperor Franz Joseph's brother, Maximilian, had a residence there and the mingling of the two cultures is evident.

THE LOCAL RECIPE

The cuisine of Friuli is different and simpler than it is in the nearby Veneto region. Polenta is the main dish of almost every meal. The yellow cornmeal mixed with water is slowly cooked until it becomes thick and creamy. It is served with cheese, meat, vegetables, or simply drowned in melted butter. The local Prosciutto San Daniele has a special sweet flavor due to the pigs' free-range existence.

Veal Goulash
Ingredients (serves 4)

2 cups veal stewing meat, cut into
    small cubes
2 cups coarsely chopped onion
1/4 cup butter
1 cup broth
2 bay leaves

1 tbsp. chopped fresh thyme
2 tbsp. paprika
1 cup sour cream
1 clove of garlic
1 tsp. grated lemon rind
salt and pepper to taste

Place the butter, veal cubes, and chopped onion in a pan and sauté until golden. Add the bay leaves, thyme, paprika, and garlic. Simmer on low heat for about 2 hours, moistening with the broth. Discard the bay leaves and garlic and mix in the sour cream and lemon rind. Season with salt and pepper. Serve hot with steamed whole potatoes on the side.

GORIZIA

PALAZZO LANTIERI B&B ✦ **PIAZZA SANT'ANTONIO 6** ✦ **34170 GORIZIA**
TEL. +39 0481536740 ✦ **FAX +39 0481533284** ✦ **CELL +39 3392435562** ✦
E-MAIL: contatto@palazzo-lantieri.com

One thousand feet from the border of Slovenia, Gorizia is also near the beaches of Grado, the rocky coasts of Trieste and Istria, and just over an hour from some of Italy and Austria's leading ski resorts. But the charm of Palazzo Lantieri is reason enough to visit this part of the world. An imposing palazzo on the city's main square, it is the most historically important landmark in Gorizia. Centered around a cobbled inner courtyard that looks onto a splendid garden in bloom with roses and fruit trees, the Palazzo Lantieri has a timeless grace. It is easy to imagine ladies in period crinolines pruning the roses or children bowling their hoops between the flower beds. A noble residence since the 1300s, Palazzo Lantieri has welcomed illustrious travelers over the centuries, from emperors to popes to the likes of Goethe, Goldoni, and Casanova. This noble tradition of hospitality is still maintained today by your hosts. The interconnected salons overflow with priceless antiques mirrored in the highly polished

wood floors. The bedrooms all overlook the garden and have a distinct old-world elegance; the only modern touch is the state-of-the-art plumbing. Breakfast is served on a beautiful terrace whose wrought-iron stairway leads down to a rose garden; during the winter months breakfast is served in a charming dining room.

ROOMS: A romantic suite with a double room and a single room with shared bathroom (with shower), and a twin room with private bathroom (with shower). Discounts are available for stays exceeding two nights.

AMENITIES:
English, French, German, and Spanish are spoken
Private parking
Dinner may be served on request
Concerts, receptions, gala evenings, and cultural
events can be organized
Children under the age of two stay free of charge;
children between the ages of two and ten
receive a 50 percent discount

WHERE: The nearest railway station is 1 mile away in Gorizia, while the Trieste airport is 15 miles away. By car take highway A4 and exit at Villesse. Follow the directions for Gorizia where the Palazzo will be clearly indicated by signs.

CATEGORY: Caffèlletto ✦ **RATE:** ○○ ✦ *Member since 2003*

LIGURIA

Liguria is a small stretch of mountainous land along the northwest coast of Italy, beginning at the Tuscan border and curving upwards toward France's Côte d'Azur. Shielded from northern winds by the Alps and the Apennines, Liguria has one of the mildest climates in Europe, and is home to the earliest inhabitants of the Italian peninsula. In the nineteenth century, sufferers of tuberculosis would come to winter along the Riviera where bright bougainvillea cascades down the walls all year-round. Liguria was also the favorite haunt of Shelley and Byron and, later, of D.H. Lawrence and Ezra Pound. At least two classic works, *Frankenstein* and *The Scarlet Pimpernel,* were written here.

The most spectacular resort area, the Riviera di Levante, includes Genova (Genoa), Portofino, the Cinque Terre, Lerici, and Tellaro. One of Italy's most memorable drives, along the coastal road from Chiavari through Zoagli, Rapallo, and Santa Margherita to Portofino, runs past languidly elegant turn-of-the-century villas.

In contrast, life for the Ligurians has been a struggle since time immemorial. Dependent on the sea for their livelihood, these peace-loving people were a constant prey to pirates. To grow grapes and olives and basic crops, the Ligurians literally had to carry soil by boat or on their backs and slather it onto the rock face, creating a style of terraced agriculture unique in Europe and found elsewhere only in parts of China and Peru; it is best seen here along the coast of the enchanting Cinque Terre.

Perhaps for this reason the people of Liguria are hardworking, relatively sober folk with a reputation, especially in Genoa, for being thrifty. Ever of seafaring stock, the Ligurians gave the world Christopher Columbus.

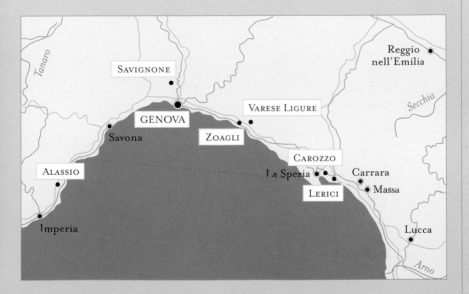

THE LOCAL RECIPE

Liguria's is a unique "surf and turf" cuisine. The excellent fish is often prepared with an extraordinary variety of vegetables from inland. Traditionally, many different kinds of wild herbs are used for stuffing, omelettes, or even deep-frying. For example, borrago leaves stuffed with anchovy filets are coated in flour and beaten egg, then fried. Or take the magnificent capon magro, in which layers of poached fish fillets are alternated with bread slices, herbs, and vegetables, topped with chunks of lobster, and drizzled with light and fruity Ligurian oil. Pesto sauce was "invented" here using the highly fragrant local basil leaves to create a sauce for trofie pasta. Walnut sauce served with pansotti, a kind of ravioli, is also delicious.

Condiggion (Sailor's Bread Salad)
Ingredients (serves 4)

4 matzos

2 ripe, yet firm tomatoes

2 tbsp. grated bottarga (dried tuna roe)

2 tbsp. chopped basil

4 anchovies

1 tbsp. capers

olive oil, garlic, vinegar, and salt to taste

Rub the matzos with garlic and soak them lightly in water and vinegar. Break them into 4 pieces and place in a salad bowl, alternating with the chopped tomatoes and the rest of the ingredients. Dress with abundant olive oil, sprinkle with basil, and serve as an appetizer or salad.

ALASSIO (SV)

VILLA DELLA PERGOLA ◆ **VIA PRIVATA MONTAGÙ 9/1** ◆ **17021 ALASSIO, SAVONA**
TEL. +39 0182640414 ◆ **FAX +39 0182554969** ◆ **CELL +39 03332789305**
E-MAIL: villapergola@tin.it

The Villa della Pergola or Villa Hanbury is left over from the days at the end of the nineteenth century when the English aristocracy colonized the Ligurian coast. Drawn by the balmy temperatures and the joys of gardening in a climate where trees and plants grew at such a rapid pace, Sir Daniel Hanbury, the original owner of the villa, found it necessary to employ fourteen gardeners. On gently descending terraces covering five acres, every conceivable kind of Mediterranean bush and flower can be found in abundance, from swaying palms to magnolias, carob, and jacaranda trees.

The villa itself is pure colonial style, with its vaguely oriental roofs and rose brick facade decorated with a William Morris–style trompe l'oeil motif. The groun- floor rooms all open onto a loggia, and the bedrooms onto a wide veranda running the whole length and breadth of the villa, supported by dainty white columns and commanding incomparable views of the Gulf of Ponente.

Ambassadors, members of the English aristocracy, and the Royal Family, have all stayed at Villa Hanbury, and when the English fleet docked at Alassio, Sir Daniel would give sumptuous receptions (he employed six cooks). The present owners have done everything to preserve the "*Enchanted April*" atmosphere of the villa.

Villa della Pergola is a little less than an hour from Genoa and perfectly situated to visit the many beautiful spots on the Ligurian coast. There are daily cruises to Portofino and the island of Gallinara, which can be seen from the villa's windows.

R O O M S : In the main villa there are three large bedrooms with double and twin beds, all with fireplaces and French windows opening onto a veranda (all with bathtub or shower). In the Pergolino there is a large suite with two double beds. There are also two double rooms, each with private bath. Minimum stay two nights.

AMENITIES:
English is spoken
Laundry service is available
Private parking
Children under the age of five stay free of charge and those
under thirteen receive a 50 percent discount
All bedrooms have a small refrigerator and television

WHERE: The nearest railway station is 3 miles away in Alassio, while there are airports in Villanova, 9 miles away, and Genoa, 37 miles away. By car take the Genoa–Ventimiglia highway and exit at Albenga. Follow the signs for Alassio. At Alassio head for the railway station.

CATEGORY: **Caffèlletto** ◆ RATE: ○○○○ ◆ *Member since 2000*

GENOA–NERVI

INFO: CAFFÈLLETTO, ITALY

TEL. +39 023311814 OR 1820 · **FAX +39 023313009** · **E-MAIL: info@caffelletto.it**

This delightful bed-and-breakfast on the hillside below Nervi is nine miles from the center of Genoa. From the main street, stone steps lead down to a romantic lane and the three-story house, which dates back to the 1400s. Recently restored, the walls are washed in bright colors and the terrace, where guests may breakfast, overlooks the sea. Alternatively, on rare rainy days, there is a charming dining room. The house has been furnished with highly original good taste and is an uplifting place to stay. The lane, known here as a creusa, leads down to an oceanfront promenade and the well-tended beaches of Nervi with its sparkling sea. Nervi is a culturally and socially thriving town and during the summer months there is always plenty to do. Your host is a very

affable and amusing gentleman who will be delighted to offer his suggestions.

ROOMS: One double and one single room, both with private baths (one with bathtub and one with shower), although not en suite. Guests may also use the scenic living room, whose French windows open onto a lovely terrace. Minimum stay two nights.

AMENITIES:

English is spoken

Private parking

Dinner may be served on request

Children over the age of twelve are welcome (the quaint steep staircases make the house unsuitable for smaller children and the elderly or infirm)

WHERE: The nearest railway station is in Genoa–Nervi, less than a half mile away, while the airport in Genoa is 6 miles away.

CATEGORY: ✳✳✳✳ · **RATE:** ○○ · *Member since 2003*

GENOA–BRIGNOLE

INFO: CAFFÈLLETTO, ITALY

TEL. +39 010586529 ◆ CELL +39 3397469307 ◆ E-MAIL: icapricci@lycos.it

Conveniently located in the center of town near the Brignole railway station, this charming and pastoral bed-and-breakfast is an ideal sollution for tourists and travelers who wish to visit the various trade fairs in Genoa, such as the Salone Nautico. Comfortably furnished and possessing the staid decor of the period, this palazzo dates back to the beginning of the last century. Elegant breakfasts are served in the formal dining room.

ROOMS: One double, one twin, and one single room; two bathrooms, one with shower and tub, the other with tub only.

Genoa, 12 miles away.

AMENITIES:

English, French, and Spanish
  are spoken
Internet access in every room
Satellite television in the sitting room
Laundry service is available
Children under the age of two and pets
  are regretfully not allowed

WHERE: The nearest railway station is in Genoa–Nervi, 3 miles away, while the airport is in

CATEGORY: ✳✳✳✳ ◆ **RATE:** ◯◯ ◆ *Member since 2001*

SAVIGNONE (GE)

"A O SOÂ" B&B ◆ **LOCALITÀ BROGLIO 11** ◆ **16010 SAVIGNONE, GENOVA**
TEL. AND FAX +39 010936884 ◆ **E-MAIL: a.crosa@tin.it**

Only twelve miles from the center of Genoa, tucked into a hollow among the Ligurian Apennines, the village of Savignone is 1,650 feet above sea level. This charming coun-

try house stands above the main square of Savignone at the edge of the village. It still belongs to the patrician descendants of the feudal lords of Savignone.

Both architects, your hosts restored this nineteenth-century house to its original appearance, while your hostess personally created the design of the fabrics in the bedrooms. The lawns are shaded by trees and fragrant with rosebushes. Breakfasts include the delicious potato focaccia typical of the area. The fashionable beach of Paraggi is forty minutes away, and all around are restaurants serving Ligurian cuisine.

ROOMS: Two twin rooms, which can become double on request (with bathroom and shower). On the upper level is a suite with a double room, two single rooms, a small sitting room with a sofa bed, and a bathroom with bathtub. Closed from December 15 until January 10, as well as the month of February. Minimum stay two nights.

AMENITIES:
English, French, and Spanish are spoken
Laundry service is available
Private parking
No smoking
Children over the age of ten are welcome
Well-behaved pets are welcome

WHERE: The nearest railway station is in Busalla, 5 miles away, and the airport in Genoa is 15.5 miles away. By car take highway A7 Milano—Genoa and exit at Busalla. Turn left and follow the signs for Savignone until you arrive in the center of the village where your hosts will pick you up.

CATEGORY: ✳✳✳✳ ◆ RATE: ○ ◆ *Member since 2002*

ZOAGLI (GE)

INFO: CAFFÈLLETTO, ITALY

TEL. +39 023311814 OR 1820 ✦ FAX +39 023313009 ✦ E-MAIL: info@caffelletto.it

This villa, dating back to the early 1900s, is surrounded by parks sloping down to the sea on the splendid coastline, which curves around Genoa and beyond. Tall trees and lush vegetation line the path from the guest apartment down to the private beach. The wide terrace overlooks the gulf of Portofino and from the ports of Rapallo or Chiavari, boats leave to visit this famous resort, as well as for Porto Venere, San Fruttuoso, and Cinque Terre.

ROOMS: An independent apartment with large living and dining rooms, a well-equipped kitchenette, a sofa bed for two, as well as two double and twin rooms, each with their own bathroom and shower. Minimum stay three nights; seven nights in July and August.

AMENITIES:
English is spoken
Private parking
Private access to beach
Eighteen-hole golf course at Rapallo

WHERE: The nearest railway station is Zoagli, 1 mile away, while the airport in Genoa is 25 miles away.

CATEGORY: ✳✳✳✳ ✦ RATE: OO ✦ *Member since 2003*

VARESE LIGURE (SP)

GUMO B&B ◆ **GUMO 69** ◆ **19028 VARESE LIGURE, LA SPEZIA**
TEL. +39 0187842282 ◆ **E-MAIL: ilgumo@tin.it**

This pretty, raspberry-colored house, smothered in Virginia creeper, is perched on a hillside with a view over rolling pasturelands as far as the eye can see. The estate sits on sixty-seven acres in the Vara Valley dedicated to organic farming and sheep, some of which graze under the windows. The farmhouse is two hundred years old and lovingly restored by your hosts who live here all year-round. They are among the few inhabitants of this beautiful area, ideal for trekking and mountain biking. In the fall people come from all over Liguria to look for the many types of mushrooms growing through the leaves on the forest floor. It is during this season that the vines on the pergola in front of the house are fragrant with the scent of uva fragola, an oval-shaped grape that tastes and smells like strawberries and makes an excellent dessert wine.

The house is near the small town of Varese Ligure, where there is a swimming pool, tennis court, and horseback riding school. Varese Ligure is called a rotunda because of its circular shape and is famous for the annual opera performances held here on August 15. Cassego is two miles away, with its country museum, while Maissana, a well-known archaeological site, is five miles away.

ROOMS: The guest house is connected to your hosts' home and in summer guests may breakfast together with the family under a grape arbor. Breakfast is always a celebration with delicious homemade jams, pastries, and honey. Though it remained a country house, it has all the modern comforts. Two doubles and one twin room with a bathroom, living room, and kitchenette. Minimum stay two nights.

AMENITIES:
Open from March 30 to November 30
English, French, and Greek are spoken
Laundry service is available
Parking on the premises
A feast of Lucullan proportions with specialties of the region, is laid out for guests who stay a week
Children under the age of two stay free of charge
Pets are welcome

WHERE: The railway station in Sestri Levante is 17 miles away, while the nearest airport is in Genoa at 50 miles away. Take highway A12 Genoa–Livorno and exit at Sestri Levante. Follow signs for Varese Ligure and then for Passo di Cento Croci until you find signs for Gumo.

CATEGORY: ✳✳✳✳ ◆ **RATE:** ○ ◆ *Member since 1999*

CAROZZO (SP)

INFO: CAFFÈLLETTO, ITALY

TEL. +39 023311814 OR 1820 ♦ **FAX +39 023313009** ♦ **E-MAIL: info@caffelletto.it**

Carozzo is a pretty little village on a hill over-looking the Gulf of La Spezia, the famous Gulf of Poets, particularly of Shelley and Byron. On the cusp between Liguria and Tuscany, it is an ideal starting place from which to visit both. In summer the sea is only ten minutes away. Ferries go regularly to Portofino and to the five fishing villages of the Cinque Terre. The marble mines of Carrara are only nine miles away and for the duration of the month of August there is an antique fair, La Soffitta nella Strada (Attic in the Street), at Sarzana.

Your hostess is Polish, lived in Germany where she worked as a psychologist, and has since moved to Italy. Breakfasts are German in charac-ter, with cheeses and hams served in the warmer months on the terrace overlooking the gulf.

ROOMS: An apartment with a living room and sofa bed and French windows open-ing onto the garden, a small double room with a bathroom (with both shower and bathtub). Guests have access to the kitchen. Open from October 30 until May 1.

AMENITIES:
Open from January 2 to December 20
English, French, German, and Polish are spoken
Private parking

WHERE: The nearest rail-way station is in La Spezia, approximately 6 miles away, while the airport in Pisa is 43 miles away.

CATEGORY: ✳✳✳ ♦ **RATE:** ○○ ♦ *Member since 2001*

ARENZANO (GE)

INFO: CAFFÈLLETTO, ITALY

TEL. +39 023311814 OR 1820 · FAX +39 023313009 · E-MAIL: info@caffelletto.it

Here at Arenzano, six miles from Genoa, everything from breakfast to the evening aperitif at sundown on the terrace will have a splendid view of the sea. Your hostess, whose three grown children were all born here, says that she never ceases to be spellbound by this spectacular panorama of the Ligurian coastline and the Mediterranean scrub that grows on the steep coast and makes its way down to the sea. The villa is relatively modern, with giant windows in a residential complex hidden away among maritime pines with access to a private beach. There is a swimming pool in the garden, and golf, tennis, and horseback riding facilities are all close at hand.

ROOMS: One double, one twin, and one single; two bathrooms, not en suite, one with shower and tub, the other with tub. Children under the age of two, as well as pets, are regretfully not allowed.

AMENITIES:
English, French, and some German
Children under two stay free
Private parking
Swimming pool, pool room, laundry

WHERE: The railway station is in Arenzano, 3 miles away, while the Genoa airport 9 miles away.

CATEGORY: ✳✳✳✳ · RATE: OO · *Member since 2004*

EMILIA–ROMAGNA

Emilia–Romagna is located in northern-central Italy. To the east, it borders on the Adriatic Sea (where Rimini and other resorts lie), while to the south and west it hits the Apennine mountain range. The Apennines kept Emilia–Romagna and Tuscany apart for centuries and, perhaps for this reason, they remain two different regions to this day. While Tuscany has an austere rolling landscape covered in olive trees and vineyards, Emilia–Romagna is a flat, low-lying plain, irrigated by four different rivers. It is a fertile landscape with ample farmhouses and verdant fields where cattle graze—it's no accident that the most popular local dish is tortellini bathed in cream sauce and Parmesan cheese.

The main cities are Ferrara, Modena, Parma, Piacenza, Reggio nell' Emilia (Reggio Emilia), and the capital city, Bologna. Also nearby is Ravenna, the so-called Capital of Mosaics, and Faenza, home of the Museo delle Ceramiche (Museum of Ceramics).

This is a prosperous region and, for centuries, people here have not only been patrons of the arts—to which the cities are a testament—but have also invested their riches in palaces, country villas, and entertainment, as witnessed by the beautiful Farnese theater in Parma. Above all, however, they have concentrated on food: Parma is world-famous for its cheese but also for its ham, Modena offers unsurpassed balsamic vinegar, and spaghetti alla bolognese (spaghetti with meat sauce) is one of the best-

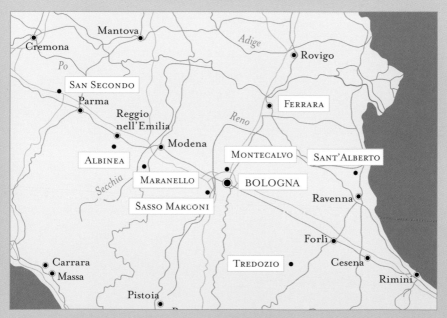

known Italian dishes abroad. Emilia–Romagna also produces many different wines, the most famous of them being Lambrusco.

Bologna's twenty-five miles of portici (porticoes)—uninterrupted covered arches along the sidewalks—suggest that the people of Emilia–Romagna have always been enthusiastic shoppers and, for car enthusiasts, there's always the Ferrari factory of Maranello.

THE LOCAL RECIPE

Lasagna, tortellini, and spaghetti alla bolognese were all born here. Although they are now popular throughout the world, there's nothing like the real thing. Don't forget to visit the producers of Parma ham and Parmesan cheese, you won't regret it.

Fettuccine with Fresh Vegetables
Ingredients (serves 4)

2 cups fresh fettuccine
1 carrot
1 celery stalk
1 small onion
1 zucchini
1/4 cup butter
2 tbsp. coarsely chopped fresh basil

Wash and trim the vegetables. Cut them into julienne strips. Place the butter in a skillet and sauté the vegetables over medium heat until they are crisp and glossy, about seven to eight minutes. Boil the fettuccine until al dente, drain, and add to the vegetables. Mix and transfer into a dish. Sprinkle with basil.

BARCO DI BIBBIANO (RE)

CORTE BEBBI B&B ◆ **VIA SPALLANZANI 119** ◆ **42021 BARCO DI BIBBIANO, REGGIO EMILIA**
TEL. +39 0522243056 ◆ **FAX +39 0522246183** ◆ **E-MAIL: info@cortebebbi.it**

Corte Bebbi is on the outskirts of a little village on the ancient Via Emilia, eight miles from Reggio Emilia and eleven miles from Parma. This walled enclave, with buildings grouped around a courtyard and garden, dates back to the seventeenth century and is a beautiful example of the rural architecture of the period and the region. Your hosts, who live here year-round, are descendants of the original owners, the noble Bebbi family, and have personally restored the property, installing every possible comfort in the best of taste. Furnished with family antiques, the walls are painted in bright, cheerful colors. Breakfasts are quite a feast, served in the dining room in winter and in the garden during the warmer

months. There is a small pool in the garden, surrounded by a well-manicured lawn dotted with fruit trees. This part of Italy is a gastronome's delight, with prosciutto of Parma, Parmesan cheese, traditional balsamic vinegar, and the local Lambrusco wine.

ROOMS: Five elegant double rooms, all with bathroom with shower, television, and air-conditioning. A pool room and sitting room with television and library are all to be found adjacent to the sunny veranda.

AMENITIES:
English, French, German, and Russian are spoken
Private parking, swimming pool, horseback-riding
Children under the age of two stay free of charge
Golf course, sauna, Jacuzzi, and solarium

WHERE: The railway station and the airport in Parma are both 9 miles away. By car take the Autostrada del Sole A1 and exit at Parma Ovest. Drive toward Fontanellato, then Albareto, after which you will find the house called Il Galù.

CATEGORY: Caffèlletto ◆ **RATE:** ○○○○ ◆ *Member since 2003*

ALBINEA (RE)

VILLA ARNÒ B&B ◦ **VIA VITTORIO EMANUELE II 50** ◦ **42020 ALBINEA, REGGIO EMILIA**
TEL. +39 0522598035 ◦ **FAX +39 0522347721** ◦ **E-MAIL: castudio@tin.it**

Albinea is a village on a hillside above Reggio Emilia and this bed-and-breakfast is majestically situated where the town ends and the countryside begins. Surrounded by parks studded with magnificent trees, this is a nineteenth-century villa built in the neoclassical style, with an imposing entrance supported by columns of Napoleonic proportions. Your host has traveled far and wide and now lives here all year-round. He is particularly well informed about the city of Reggio Emilia, less than six miles away, and its surroundings, as well as about the local wines—above all the famous Lambrusco, a favorite of Pavarotti—and the equally famous cuisine. The

continental-style breakfast features, among other things, the local focaccia called "erbazzone" and Parma ham.

ROOMS: One double room with its own bathroom on the first floor and a room with twin beds on the ground floor, also with a private bathroom. There is also a small suite with a double and single room sharing a bathroom with shower. A discount will be given for stays exceeding three days.

AMENITIES:
English and French are spoken
Private parking

WHERE: The nearest railway station is Reggio Emilia, 6 miles away, and Bologna's airport is 43 miles away. By car take highway A1 and exit at Reggio Emilia. Drive toward the center. When in Viale Isonzo, continue until Porta Castello. Turn right into Viale Umberto. At the second traffic light, after less than a mile, turn left for Albinea and then at the next light, right, still following directions for Albinea. After 4 miles you'll see the villa on the left.

CATEGORY: **Caffèlletto** ◦ RATE: ○○ ◦ *Member since 2003*

MARANELLO (MO)

INFO: CAFFÈLLETTO, ITALY

TEL. +39 023311814 OR 1820 ∘ FAX +39 023313009 ∘ E-MAIL: info@caffelletto.it

Maranello is famous for two things: making Ferraris and, like the rest of Emilia–Romagna, its cuisine. Your hosts, a charming and affable couple, will be happy to recommend nearby restaurants. Modena, home of aceto balsamico (balsamic vinegar), is at a short distance and the city of Bologna is about twenty-five miles away.

The house itself, in the center of a large garden, has been restored with particular attention to detail and is furnished with taste and flair. Guests are housed in the annex, a smaller version of the main house with a large sitting room with fireplace and a dining room where your hostess personally serves abundant and stylishly presented continental breakfasts.

ROOMS: An annex on two floors with a small basement recreation room is available. On the ground floor, there is a large sitting room with fireplace, a dining room, and a large bathroom. On the first floor, there is one double room with a bathroom in the hallway as well as a large double room that can be made into a twin on request. The

latter has an overhead loft with two beds that can be made into a double. These two rooms may use the bathroom on the floor below. Minimum stay two nights.

AMENITIES:
French is spoken
Garage with space for two cars, otherwise parking on the premises is available
Depending on your hostess's commitments, dinner may be served on request
Children under the age of two stay free of charge

WHERE: The railway station in Modena is 9 miles away while Bologna's airport is 25 miles away.

CATEGORY: ✳✳✳✳ ∘ **RATE:** ◯◯ ∘ *Member since 2002*

BOLOGNA–HISTORIC CENTER

INFO: CAFFÈLLETTO, ITALY

TEL. +39 023311814 OR 1820 ◆ FAX +39 023313009 ◆ E-MAIL: info@caffelletto.it

At the heart of Bologna's historic center, this imposing palazzo dates back to the sixteenth century and is just around the corner from the famous Via Galliera, and five minutes from the Piazza Maggiore. Your hostess is an antique dealer and has restored and furnished the apartment as if it were a showroom. On the third floor (there is no elevator), the large windows look out over the courtyard so that, despite its central location, the apartment is exceptionally quiet.

ROOMS: There is a large sitting room with tall ceilings covered with frescoes and two sofa beds. In the overhead loft, there is a large double room with two beds and a bathroom with a shower.

AMENITIES:
French and some English are spoken
Children under the age of two stay free of charge
Small pets are welcome

WHERE: The railway station is nearby while Bologna's airport is 9 miles away.

CATEGORY: Caffèlletto ◆ RATE: ○○ ◆
Member since 2002

MONTECALVO (BO)

INFO: CAFFÈLLETTO, ITALY

TEL. +39 023311814 OR 1820 · FAX +39 023313009 · E-MAIL: info@caffelletto.it

This large property surrounded by lawns, woodland, and pastureland is on a hillside above Bologna, only six miles from the city. Once a stable, the house was completely restored and renovated in 1992. It is now a handsome country house with rose-washed walls dominating a large lawn and, in the distance, the vineyards and orchards belonging to your hosts. The property has been in the family for generations and the house is attractively furnished with family antiques, in patrician country-house style. While the owners used to come only on weekends they now live here all year-round. Breakfasts are served in the kitchen and dining room in winter, or under the loggia in summer, with local honey and jams made from their organically grown fruit. Montecalvo, Ferrara, and Ravenna are all nearby.

ROOMS: There are three rooms available for guests. Two doubles are on the second floor accessible by an elevator, and include a small sitting room with fireplace and satellite television, and a bathroom (with bathtub). The third, a twin room, is a little larger, with a bathroom (with shower). In the attic, there is a double room with a sofa bed, sitting room, and bathroom (with shower). Closed from December 19 until February 9, as well as the month of August. Minimum stay two nights.

AMENITIES:
English and French are spoken
Laundry service is available
Private parking
Basic fitness center on the ground floor
Pets are welcome if they can stay in a kennel

WHERE: The nearest railway station is in Bologna, 6 miles away, while Bologna's airport is 12 miles away.

CATEGORY: ✳✳✳✳ · RATE: ○○ · *Member since 2002*

MONZUNO (BO)

LODOLE LOC. LODOLE 325 ◆ 40036 MONZUNO, BOLOGNA
TEL. +39 0516771189 ◆ CELL +39 3356811306 ◆ E-MAIL: INFO@LODOLE.COM

This mountain retreat is delightfully situated on a green hillside with a splendid view over one of the many wooded valleys of the Apennine mountain range. The house is a typical stone farmhouse on which skilful restoration has just been completed, and the garden, which promises certain beauty, is still in its infancy. Your hostess serves breakfast in the mezzanine sitting room. This is the perfect place to escape the stresses and strains of city life, although it is close enough to Bologna for guests visiting the city on business.

ROOMS: There are six rooms of which five have double beds and one twin beds, all different from each other and named astronomically: Dawn, Sun, Sky, Stars, Sunset, and Moon. All are furnished with antiques and have large bathrooms with shower. Guests may also use the sitting room.

AMENITIES:
English is spoken
Laundry service is available
Private parking
Children under the age of two stay free of charge

WHERE: The railway station and airport of Bologna are both 12 miles away. By car take the Autostrada del Sole AI and exit at Sasso Marconi. Take road 325 towardVado, Firenze. After 2 miles drive through the small village of Cinque Cerri, turn left onto a small road leading to the Locanda dei Cinque Cerri.

CATEGORY: ✳✳✳✳ ◆ **RATE:** ○○○○ ◆ *Member since 2003*

PIUMAZZO (MO)

AZ. AGRITURISTICA IL RICCIO E LA VOLPE ◦ **VIA MUZZA CORONA 165** ◦ **41010 PIUMAZZO, MODENA**
TEL. +39 051332886 ◦ **FAX +39 059931232** ◦ **CELL +39 3393628312**

One should definitely visit Piumazzo, especially in springtime when all the fruit trees are in blossom. Il Riccio e la Volpe (the Hedgehog and the Fox), housed the farmers who looked after the fruit trees and lived here with their families, until two years ago when your young hostess set to work to prepare the house for guests. The house has the original oxblood facade typical of the area, as well as beams and terracotta floors made locally. Fruit from the orchards is present on the breakfast table in the form of delicious jams and tarts, and a rich repertoire of salami, hams, and sausages are always at hand. Modena is famous not only for its balsamic vinegar but for some of the best restaurants.

ROOMS: One double bedroom, three rooms with twin beds, and two single bedrooms. All have their own bathroom with shower. Each room is decorated in a different motif. There is a televidion in every room.

AMENITIES:
English, French, and Spanish are spoken
Children under the age of two stay free of charge
Small pets are welcome

WHERE: The Modena railway station is 10 miles away, while the Bologna airport is about 18 miles away.

CATEGORY: ✳✳✳ ◦ **RATE:** ○ ◦ *Member since 2002*

TREDOZIO (FO)

**TORRE FANTINI · VIA SAN MICHELE 47 · 47019 TREDOZIO, FORLÌ
TEL. +39 0546943403 · FAX +39 051332692**

Torre Fantini is a farmhouse that was once a tower built to defend the local family of Fantini. It is pink and white like all the buildings of the family and above the door is a young rooster, part of the family's coat of arms. The house has recently been renovated, leaving the old terra-cotta floors and beamed ceilings intact while furnishing it with nineteenth-century antiques. This house is unique in that breakfasts are prepared by a professional chef, Mr. Gentilini, who owns Mulino di San Michele in Tredozio, once an old mill, now one of the more sought-after restaurants of the area.

The Torre Fantini is about nineteen miles from Faenza, the Italian city renowned for producing pottery called faience. It is a beautiful little city where artisans, covered in white dust from the potter's ring and kiln, ride bicycles down the narrow streets and where it is possible to buy copies of the plates made for noble patrons centuries ago (these can be seen today in the city's museum). Ravenna, with its splendid Byzantine mosaics of empresses, is only one hour away by car. Brisighella on a nearby hilltop seems like it could be a medieval version of Disney World, with its illuminated clock that seems far too big for the tower. At Brisighella, La Grotta restaurant is recommended. The narrow streets have special covered passages for donkeys, once the principal mode of transportation.

Tredozio is famous for the park and gardens of Palazzo Fantini built in the late 1700s. In the inner courtyards both classical and jazz concerts are held in summer and the park and gardens are members of the Italian Gardens Association and can be visited together with your hosts, who have also founded a country museum with historic implements used in agriculture in the surrounding countryside.

ROOMS: Four bedrooms each with its own bathroom. We especially liked the room on the first floor with its own fireplace and the attic room known as the "swallow's nest." A suite for four people has its own bathroom (with shower) and small kitchen; satellite television is also available.

AMENITIES:
English and French are spoken
Laundry service is available
Parking on the premises
Hunting when in season
Children under the age of two stay free of charge
Pets are welcome

WHERE: The railway station in Faenza is 19 miles away, while the nearest airport is in Bologna, 53 miles away. Bus service to and from Faenza and Tredozio is available. By car from the center of Faenza follow the directions for Modigliana and Tredozio. At Tredozio take the Via San Michele, in the direction of Lutirano. Torre Fantini is number 47.

CATEGORY: ✳✳✳✳ · **RATE:** ○ · *Member since 1999*

TUSCANY

Tuscany needs little introduction—its rolling landscape, expanses of vines and olive groves, rows of cypress trees, and ochre-colored farmhouses make it one of the loveliest regions in Italy. The cities of most interest to visitors are Florence, Siena, Pisa, Lucca, and Arezzo with a host of small villages and hilltop towns in between.

Tuscany was colonized by the Etruscans between the seventh and the fourth

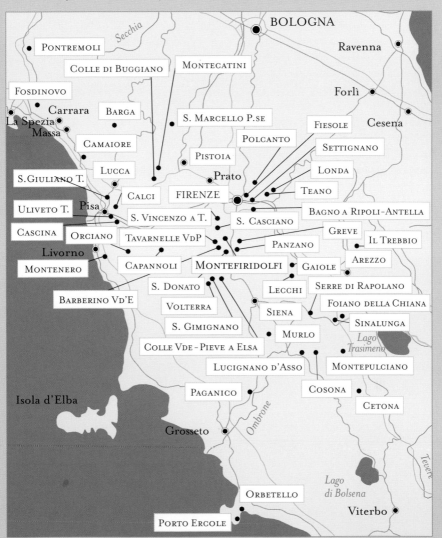

centuries B.C. There are still many traces of this mysterious civilization, which D.H. Lawrence maintained was the true precursor of modern Italy and today's Italians, whose "inner carelessness" is in sharp contrast to the militarized might of ancient Rome. From Etruscan times date a number of sulfurous springs, the most famous being the blue waters of Saturnia and the Montecatini Terme, an old-fashioned spa with palatial hotels and elegant watering holes.

Tuscany is bordered by the Apennines in the northeast and by the Apuan Alps in the northwest, where the famous Carrara marble—the raw material used for many of Michelangelo's works—was quarried. To the west lie the Tyrrhenian Sea and miles of stretching coastline beginning above Massa in the north and straggling down past the popular resorts of Forte dei Marmi and Viareggio. The coastline continues through the Maremma area, the wild landscape between Livorno and Grosseto where white, long-horned cattle are raised, down to the jet-set meeting points of Porto Ercole and Porto Santo Stefano. The Tuscan archipelago, including the island of Elba, is also part of the region.

Tuscany is famous not just for its art, but also for its artisans, an infinite variety of whom are found in Florence—a legacy of the Medici court. Alabaster craftsmen are clustered in Volterra, those of crystal in Colle Val d'Elsa, glass in Empoli, marble in Pietrasanta, ceramics in Montelupo, straw in Signa, terra-cotta in Impruneta, and basket weaving in Pontassieve.

Tuscany is also renowned for its wines—not just Chianti, but Brunello di Montalcino, Vino Nobile di Montepulciano, and Vernaccia di San Gimignano—and the robust cuisine that accompanies them. Another Tuscan specialty is extra-virgin olive oil. The people of Tuscany are ironic, parsimonious, iconoclastic, and difficult to impress. Since the time of Dante Alighieri, however, they have been known to be the most cultured and civic-minded of Italians.

THE LOCAL RECIPE

Tuscan food is not as inventive and sensual as in other parts of Italy, but its appeal, based on an ancient peasant culture and the quality of local produce, particularly the olive oil, is outstanding. It is olive oil that gives the final touch to the simple but delicious soup Pappa col Pomodoro (tomato and country-bread soup), for example.

Milk-braised Pork Loin

Ingredients (serves 4)

2 pounds boneless pork loin

2 tbsp. butter

3 tbsp. olive oil

2 cups milk

3 cloves of garlic

1/4 cup wine vinegar

1 bay leaf

1 sprig of rosemary

salt and pepper to taste

Rub the meat with salt and pepper and place it in a Dutch oven greased with butter and oil. Sauté until golden brown on all sides. Pour the vinegar into the pan and let evaporate. Add the garlic cloves, rosemary, bay leaf, and milk. Cook on a low flame for about one hour, until the meat is very tender. The sauce should appear well reduced and have a slightly curdled appearance. Cut the pork loin into thin slices and pour the milk sauce over the meat.

PONTREMOLI (MS)

VILLA EMILIA ✦ **LOC. VERSOLA 4** ✦ **54027 PONTREMOLI, MASSA CARRARA**
TEL. AND FAX +39 0187836455 ✦ **E-MAIL: info@villaemilia.com**

Pontremoli is the capital of Lunigiana, a lesser-known region of Italy overlapping Tuscany and Liguria. Lunigiana gets its name from Luni, the city founded by the Romans in 177 B.C., but its origins are far older. Scattered over the region are primitive statues with rectangular bodies and half-moon—shaped heads left over from a Bronze Age civilization. It is however very close to what we call civilization today, such as the autostrada and the airport of Pisa, fifty miles away.

The Lunigiana has played a leading role in the history of Italy, and every hilltop has a castle left to tell the tale. Dante even mentions the region in his *Divine Comedy*. Literary tradition is still strong here and the internationally famous book prize, the Premio Bancarella, is awarded every year on July 16. Pontremoli has excellent judges and three of their prizewinners have gone on to win the Nobel Prize, starting with Ernest Hemingway in 1953.

The local cuisine is also very interesting, characterized by flat, thin testaroli pasta, mushrooms that grow thick on the ground in the woods of the Lunigiana, and chestnut flour that is made into frittelle (fritters). Locally made cheeses and cold cuts are the perfect accompaniment to the genuine wines of the region.

The Villa Emilia is five miles away from the medieval town of Pontremoli, built in the 1920s in the middle of a large garden with views all around of woodlands, medieval stone farmhouses, and the slopes of the Apennines. Breakfasts can be served either in the warm country kitchen with its marble fireplace and oxblood-red walls or outside on the patio overlooking the terraced vineyards and fields.

ROOMS: There are four bedrooms, three doubles and one twin with two bathrooms. The Green Room, painted in a vivid sage, has its own balcony with a view. Minimum stay two nights.

AMENITIES:
*Open from June to September. Other periods of
   the year are also possible on request
English and Spanish are spoken
Children over the age of two are welcome
Pets are not allowed*

WHERE: The railway station in Pontremoli is 6 miles away while the airport in Pisa is 50 miles away. By car take highway A15 Parma—La Spezia and exit at Pontremoli. Follow the directions for Parma until the crossroads for Molinello. At Molinello follow directions for Casalina-Versola.

CATEGORY: ✳✳✳✳ ✦ **RATE:** ○ ✦ *Member since 2000*

FOSDINOVO (MS)

VIA MONTECCHIO 16 ◆ 54035 FOSDINOVO, MASSA

TEL. +39 0187693244 ◆ CELL +39 3283170624 ◆ E-MAIL: danibern@freemail.it

On the edge of Liguria, this charming bright villa is near the town of Sarzana, not far from Cinque Terre and the beautiful port of Tellaro. The sandy beach at Marinella is only two miles away. The house is pleasantly and comfortably furnished with antiques. Guests may breakfast under the loggia or at a communal wooden table in the kitchen. There is a large vegetable garden and homegrown produce is featured for breakfast. Picnic lunches are also possible.

ROOMS: A double which can become a twin on request with the option of a third child's bed, with a bathroom (with shower) in the corridor. The room is furnished with antiques and has a beamed ceiling, original terra-cotta floor, and two windows overlooking the garden.

AMENITIES:
French and a little German
are spoken
Private parking
Dinner may be served on request
Children under the age of two stay
free of charge
Pets are welcome

WHERE: The nearest railway station in Sarzana is under a mile away, while the airport in Pisa is 31 miles away. By car take highway A12 and exit at Sarzana. Follow the directions for Pisa on the Aurelia for just over a mile. Guests will be picked up at the corner of Viale Malaspina, a short distance from the house.

CATEGORY: ✳✳✳✳ ◆ **RATE:** ○ ◆ *Member since 2002*

LUCCA–HISTORIC CENTER

INFO: CAFFÈLLETTO, ITALY

TEL. +39 023311814 OR 1820 • **FAX +39 023313009** • **E-MAIL: info@caffelletto.it**

This apartment, in a fifteenth-century palazzo on one of the main streets of the historic center of Lucca, is a real find for anyone wishing to visit one of Tuscany's most beautiful cities. The palazzo was built by a close relation of the Arnolfinis, the couple immortalized in the famous *Arnolfini Wedding Portrait* (1434) by Jan van Eyck. Your host

is a professor of art history who lives in the main part of the palazzo among priceless antiques and beneath frescoed ceilings. The one-room apartment available for guests is simply furnished but with considerable charm.

ROOMS: A large, sunny studio apartment with dining and sitting room area, kitchen corner with dishwasher and microwave, single beds, and a large bathroom in green and white Carrara marble. Minimum stay three nights.

AMENITIES:
English, French, and German are spoken
Laundry service is available
Television and stereo

WHERE: The Lucca railway station is a short distance away, while the airport in Pisa is 13 miles away.

CATEGORY: Caffèlletto • **RATE:** ◯◯ • *Member since 2002*

LUCCA–GATTAIOLA

INFO: CAFFÈLLETTO, ITALY

TEL. +39 023311814 OR 1820 ◆ FAX +39 023313009 ◆ E-MAIL: info@caffelletto.it

Lucca is one of the most beautiful cities in Tuscany. Its has close to 100 churches and two-and-a-half miles of massive seventeenth-century ramparts and walls so wide that the tops of the walls have been turned into tree-lined avenues—thoroughly awe-inspiring. As Henry James put it, Lucca is a "circular lounging place of a splendid

dignity." Lucca, however, does not have anywhere near 100 hotels or guest houses, so it is comforting to know that ten minutes from the center of town, there is the Villa il Nonno, where you will receive a warm welcome all year-round.

The rooms have a beautiful view on all sides and guests can gather in the evenings in front of the fireplace in the main sitting room. The house belonged to the grandparents of the current owners and they take great pride in its upkeep and in their hospitality.

ROOMS: One double room (with bathtub and shower) and a small dressing room. Another double room with bathroom and dressing room has a small adjoining studio and four windows looking out over a splendid view of olive trees, cypresses, and a Romanesque church. A third double room also with dressing room and private bedroom, very light and airy. Minimum stay two nights.

AMENITIES:

Open from April 1 to September 30
French and some English are spoken
Laundry service is available
Parking in the garden
Dinner may be served on request
The owners can arrange an efficient taxi service

WHERE: The railway station in Lucca is 2 miles away while the airport in Pisa airport is 12 miles away.

CATEGORY: ✳✳✳✳ ◆ **RATE:** ◯◯ ◆ *Member since 2000*

LUCCA–LA CAPPELLA

LA CAPPELLA B&B ◆ **VIA DEI TOGNETTI 469, CECCUCCIO** ◆
55060 FRAZ. LA CAPPELLA, LUCCA
TEL. +39 0583394347 ◆ **FAX +39 0583395870** ◆ **E-MAIL: lacappella@lacappellalucca.it**

This large house, once a convent, is called La Cappella after a chapel that dates back to the days when weary pilgrims rested here on their way from Santiago de Compostela to Rome. At only four miles from Lucca, the roofs of the city can be seen from La Cappella's windows, beyond the citrus trees and climbing plants in the garden lead-

ing down to the pool.

Your hosts, who live here all year-round, have personally renovated the eighteenth-century house in the sober, patrician style of Tuscan country homes, characterized by terra-cotta floors and well-chosen pieces of period furniture. Guests also have private sitting rooms with wide windows and a fireplace. Breakfast, abundantly English in style, is served in a delightful kitchen/dining room, which opens onto the garden.

ROOMS: On the first floor of the villa there are two double rooms and two twin rooms, each with their own bathroom (with bathtub). On the top floor are three completely independent apartments. The first has a large sitting room with a kitchen corner and a sofa bed for two and a double room with a bathroom (with shower). The second and the third have two bedrooms, one double and one twin, two bathrooms (with showers), a sitting room with kitchen corner and a sofa bed. Minimum stay two nights for the rooms, three days to a week for the apartments, depending on the season.

AMENITIES:
Open all year except for the Christmas holiday
English and French are spoken
Laundry service is available
Private parking
Swimming pool
Children under the age of two stay free of charge

WHERE: The nearest railway station is Lucca, 5 miles away, while the airport in Pisa is 25 miles away. By car take highway Florence–Mare and exit at Lucca, following indications for the center. Turn left in front of the city walls following the signs for Camaiore. Cross over the bridge on the Serchio River and turn right. You will pass through the town of Monte San Quirico, a yellow sign for Mutigliano–Pieve Santo Stefano, a bar, a post office, a grocery store, and right after it a small square. Take the road on the right of the square, toward La Cappella. Drive around the church and go uphill until you see the sign for the house on the left.

CATEGORY: Caffèlletto ◆ **RATE: ○○○** ◆ *Member since 2002*

FATTORIA MANSI BERNARDINI ⬩ **VIA DI VALGIANO 34** ⬩
55018 SEGROMIGNO IN MONTE, LUCCA
TEL. +39 0583921721 ⬩ **FAX +39 0583929701** ⬩ **E-MAIL: fmbsas@tin.it**

This is not so much a bed-and-breakfast as an exclusive enclave in eighteenth-century parkland extending over 247 acres and surrounded by olive trees. The main villa dates back to 1500 and is still the residence of a member of the Mansi Bernardini family, who also supervises hospitality throughout the estate. What were once peasant cottages, conservatories for lemon trees in winter, hay barns, and dovecotes, have all been

transformed into villas for guests, each with their own garden and pool. Guests of Caffèlletto may stay in the Casa Maria surrounded by an English lawn with a panoramic view from the pool and a beautiful patio with a barbecue for breakfasts and a fresco dining. Il Fienile di Bianca (Bianca's Hay Barn), on the other hand, looks out over an olive grove, while the sitting room opens onto the garden and the pool.

ROOMS: In Casa Maria there are three double rooms and two twin rooms all with their own bathrooms (with showers), air-conditioning, telephone, a sitting room, and a dining room/kitchen that opens onto the patio. Il Fienile di Bianca has two double rooms and one twin, all with their own bathrooms (with showers), air-condi-

tioning, satellite television, stereo, and a sitting room/kitchen. Minimum stay two nights.

AMENITIES:

English, French, and German are spoken
Laundry service is available
Private parking
Swimming pool and tennis court
Dinner may be served on request
Children until the age of two stay
free of charge

WHERE: The nearest railway station is Lucca, 9 miles away, while the Pisa airport is 25 miles away. By car take highway A1 Florence–Mare and exit at Capannori if you come from the east or from the west. Follow signs to Segromigno in Monte.

CATEGORY: **Caffèlletto** ⬩ **RATE:** ○○○ ⬩ *Member since 2003*

98

BARGA (LU)

INFO: CAFFÈLLETTO, ITALY

TEL. +39 023311814 OR 1820 ◦ **FAX +39 023313009** ◦ **E-MAIL: info@caffelletto.it**

Barga is a little town on a hill nineteen miles from Lucca, which borders on the area known as "La Garfagnana," famous for its mushrooms, Pecorino cheese, and faro, a delicious grain first planted by the Romans and still used in soups today. Giovanni Pascoli, one of Italy's most beloved poets, lived in Castelvecchio, four miles from Barga, where he wrote *I Canti di Castelvecchio* (The Songs of Castelvecchio), considered one of his

great masterpieces. His house, with its pastoral stillness, is well worth a visit.

This house is a real villa with stone gateposts and an avenue lined with sculpted box hedges leading up to the front door. Built in the mid-eighteenth century, it was purchased two hundred years later by your hostesses' family. Furnished with aristocratic elegance born of centuries of gracious living, the rooms look out over the Apuan Alps as well as the property's gardens, which yield fresh roses and dahlias for every room.

Your hostesses are two sisters, one of whom lives in the villa all year-round. For riding enthusiasts there is a manège next to the house. Barga itself has a beautiful cathedral, a fifteenth-century Franciscan convent, and a delightful theater called "Dei Differenti" dating back to the eighteenth century.

ROOMS: Two twin rooms, one blue and one yellow, both with their own bathroom, and two other communicating rooms both with two beds (the green and the pink rooms)—one with a bathroom with a bathtub and the other with a shower. Minimum stay three nights.

AMENITIES:

Open May 1 to September 30
English and French are spoken
Laundry service is available
Parking on the premises
Horseback riding school
Transportation for guests to and from the railway station and
    the airport can be arranged
Children under the age of two stay free of charge

WHERE: The nearest railway station is in Fornaci di Barga, 20 miles away, while the airport in Pisa is 37 miles away.

CATEGORY: **Caffèlletto** ◦ RATE: OO ◦ *Member since 2001*

CAMAIORE (LU)

VILLA LA BIANCA ✦ VIA NUOVA 41–47, VADO ✦ 55041 CAMAIORE, LUCCA
TEL. AND FAX +39 0584984657 ✦ +39 0584985720 ✦ E-MAIL: info@villalabianca.com

"Villa La Bianca is a balm to my unquiet mind—until I discovered it, it was far from my thoughts, as how could I ever have imagined it? Whether you arrive on foot or by car, the moment you enter you are captivated. . .in no other place have I such a desire to return, drawn by the place and what happens there, as at Villa La Bianca."

This is how Luigi Veronelli, Italy's leading gastronome, describes Villa La Bianca—these few words sum up the magic of the place. A farmhouse dating back to the late eighteenth century, it has been transformed into a romantic country hotel in a unique natural setting, framed by the Apuan Alps. The Riviera of Versilia, with its beaches and throbbing nightlife, is nearby. Villa La Bianca is the perfect starting point from which to visit the Tuscan towns of Lucca, Pisa, and Florence. Once belonging to

a famous writer, the villa has become over the years a refuge for poets and the intelligentsia and it is still, as your hosts put it: "Your home for as long as you wish to stay, for a day or for a month. To enter here means to turn your back on the past and discover a new dimension." During their stay guests may like to sample special dishes to complement excellent wines at the wine and oil emporium and restaurant, La Brilla.

The rooms in the central part of the villa are furnished in a romantic style, each with different furniture and color schemes. The apartments in the guest houses have preserved their peasant heritage, and the park and swimming pool are both entirely at guests' disposal.

ROOMS: Two junior suites, two smaller suites, and two double rooms, all with private bathrooms. Closed January and February. Minimum stay two nights.

AMENITIES:
English, French, and Spanish are spoken
Laundry service is available
Parking on the grounds
Private swimming pool
Dinner may be served on request
Children under the age of two stay free of charge
Well-behaved pets are welcome

WHERE: The nearest railway station is in Viareggio, 7 miles away, while the airport in Pisa is 13 miles away. From Rome by car take highway A1 and exit at Florence Nord, then take highway A11, exiting at Viareggio. Follow the directions for Camaiore and Vado and then the signs for Villa La Bianca. From Milan take highway A1 and exit at Parma Ovest, then the A15 until La Spezia, then the A12, exiting at Viareggio.

CATEGORY: **Caffèlletto** ✦ RATE: ○○○ ✦ *Member since 2000*

SANTA LUCIA DI CAMAIORE (LU)

LOCANDA AL COLLE, FRAZIONE SANTA LUCIA 103 ◆ 55041 CAMAIORE, LUCCA
TEL. +39 0584915195 ◆ FAX +39 0584917053 ◆ E-MAIL: locandaalcolle@interfree.it

The view from the hills above Camaiore and Viareggio and the coastline of Versilia seems to go on forever. On the proverbial clear day you can see as far as Porto Venere (Port of Venus). This old stone farmhouse covered in climbing plants follows the contours of the hillside with a panoramic

view of the sea. The house has been furnished in excellent taste with a mixture of styles creating a harmonious whole. Breakfast, served in the garden, features homemade muesli and warm croissants from the oven. The seaside is five miles away, and Pietrasanta with its marble workshops is close by, as is Lucca and the entire Lunigiana region.

ROOMS: On the first floor there is a double room with a queen-size bed and a bathroom (with bathtub), with a view reaching as far as the horizon and Porto Venere. Two doubles each with a bathroom (with shower). On the ground floor there is a little sitting room and two bedrooms, one double and one twin, both with bathrooms and an independent entrance. Minimum stay two nights.

AMENITIES:
Open from March 15 to October 31
English, French, Spanish, and some Portuguese are spoken
Private parking
Guests may have a professional massage on request

WHERE: The nearest railway station is in Viareggio, 5 miles away, while the airport is in Pisa, 15 miles away. By car take highway A11 or A12 and exit at Viareggio Nord. Follow the signs for Camaiore. At the third traffic light turn left for Via Dietro Monte. Drive uphill until you see the sign for the bed-and-breakfast.

CATEGORY: ✳✳✳✳ ◆ RATE: ○○ ◆ *Member since 2001*

SAN MARCELLO PISTOIESE (PT)

INFO: CAFFÈLLETTO, ITALY

TEL. +39 023311814 OR 1820 • FAX +39 023313009 • E-MAIL: info@caffelletto.it

This enchanting turn-of-the-last-century villa in a large park shaded by giant conifers is in the Tuscan Apennines, above the town of Pistoia and on the way to the

skiing resort of Abetone. The reception rooms are entirely frescoed in the style of the period, with delicate friezes framing walls of a periwinkle blue. Breakfast is served in the frescoed dining room with French windows opening onto the park. The villa has always been in your hosts' family and today it is the thirty-year-old heir who looks after guests. Just one hour from Lucca and half an hour from Pistoia, the house is also forty-five minutes from the spa of Bagni di Lucca.

ROOMS: On the ground floor there is a double room with bathroom (with bathtub). On the floor above a large airy double room with its own bathroom (not en suite), and a terrace, as well as a suite composed of a double room and a twin room with shared bathroom. Minimum stay two nights.

AMENITIES:

English and French are spoken
Private parking
Swimming pool
Laundry service is available
Children under the age of two stay
*   free of charge*

WHERE: The nearest railway station is 8 miles away in Pracchia, while the airport is in Florence 40 miles away.

CATEGORY: ✳✳✳✳ • RATE: ○ • *Member since 2002*

MONTECATINI ALTO (PT)

INFO: CAFFÈLLETTO, ITALY

TEL. +39 023311814 OR 1820 ◆ **FAX +39 023313009** ◆ **E-MAIL: info@caffelletto.it**

The Montecatini Terme, Italy's most popular thermal baths, need no introduction, but not everybody is familiar with the medieval village of Montecatini Alto. A funicular linking the resort to its older counterpart is still in use. Much frequented at the turn of the last century by illustrious habitués of the spa, such as Giuseppe Verdi,

Montecatini Alto offers spectacular views of the valleys below its lofty abode. The Casa Albertina is on the edge of the village with a view over the surrounding countryside and Montecatini Terme. It is here, in the 1300s, that Ugolino Simoni, the physician who first quantified the healing properties of the thermal waters, was born. The nucleus of the house dates back to 1200 although there have been many additions and modifications over the centuries. With pale pink walls, it stands in a little garden where breakfast is served in the warmer months. Guests will be delighted to find bacon, eggs, and fresh orange juice served by your host. It is he who has so expertly transformed the house into a comfortable bed-and-breakfast. He is also well versed in the various properties of the thermal baths and their curative powers.

ROOMS: Two doubles on the ground floor with French windows that open onto the garden. Both have private bathrooms with showers. On the floor above, a double with a bathroom (with shower but not en suite), plus a double and a single room that share a bathroom. Minimum stay two nights.

AMENITIES:
English is spoken
Special elevator for handicapped guests
Children under the age of two stay free of charge
Pets are welcome

WHERE: The nearest railway station is at Montecatini Terme, 1 mile away, while the airport in Florence is 28 miles away.

CATEGORY: ✳✳✳✳ ◆ RATE: ○○ ◆ *Member since 2003*

COLLE DI BUGGIANO (PT)

INFO: CAFFÈLLETTO, ITALY

TEL. +39 023311814 OR 1820 • FAX +39 023313009 • E-MAIL: info@caffelletto.it

Colle di Buggiano is a beautifully preserved medieval hamlet dating back to 1238. Sitting on a hilltop surrounded by olive groves and only three miles from the

Montecatini Terme, it is ideally situated for guests who wish to "take to the waters" in this historic spa town, also famous for its shops, which are even open on Sundays. The Pescia Valley is renowned all over the world for its flowers and it is here that dealers come from far and wide while casual visitors can also take home a mimosa bush or a lemon tree. Your hosts, an architect and his wife, have expertly restored their house in the hamlet, carefully preserving the original terra-cotta floors and eighteenth-century frescoes. Cars are not allowed on the ancient paving stones of Colle di Buggiano and the silence is absolute, broken only in springtime by nesting swallows. Breakfast is served in the limonaia—the conservatory for lemon trees—or, in the cooler months, in a splendid kitchen with a fire at its wide hearth.

ROOMS: On the first floor there are two double rooms, both with bathrooms (with showers). Le Rondini (The Swallows) has a double bed, which can be divided on request, a vaulted ceiling covered with frescoes, and a sofa bed. Le Lance (The Lances) has a double bed and private bathroom. On the second floor there are four doubles, each with a private bathroom.

AMENITIES:
English and French are spoken
Laundry service is available
Guests may use a kitchen corner in the limonaia
Children under the age of two stay free of charge
Small pets are welcome

WHERE: The nearest railway station is in Montecatini, 2 miles away, while the airport is in Florence, 28 miles away.

CATEGORY: **Caffèlletto** • RATE: ○○ • *Member since 2001*

FLORENCE–BATTISTERO

RESIDENZA DEI PUCCI ◆ **VIA DEI PUCCI 9** ◆ **50122 FLORENCE**
TEL. +39 055281886 ◆ **FAX +39 055264314** ◆ **E-MAIL: residenzapucci@interfree.it**

One block away from the Piazza del Duomo, the Via dei Pucci takes its name from the family of designer Emilio Pucci, whose vast palazzo extends down one side of the street. The bed-and-breakfast is in an elegant nineteenth-century palazzo, which has recently been restored, and the rooms have been attractively furnished with antiques, no two the same. The wherewithal for breakfast can be found on a tray in every room. Although more like a residence than a traditional bed-and-breakfast, the atmosphere is welcoming and the young women at the reception desk are very willing to be of assistance.

ROOMS: Eleven double rooms (which can be made into twins on request) and a suite, all with their own bathroom (with shower).

AMENITIES:
English and French are spoken
Private parking at extra cost
Air-conditioning and telephone
 in every room
Small pets are welcome

WHERE: The railway station in Florence is a half mile away, while the airport is 6 miles away.

CATEGORY: Caffelletto ◆ **RATE:** ○○○ ◆ *Member since 2003*

FLORENCE−CERTOSA

I PARIGI ◆ **VIA LUIGIANA 12** ◆ **50125 FLORENCE**
TEL. +39 0552048483 ◆ **FAX +39 0552286959** ◆ **E-MAIL: info@iparigi.com**

The Certosa (charterhouse or monastery) is on a hill surrounded by rolling country-side, scattered cottages, and vineyards, where the streets of Florence dwindle and what we think of as the "real" Tuscany begins. The Certosa is in an ideal location for traveling north to Bologna or south to Rome on the Strada Chiantigiana, the historic road winding through olive groves to the heart of Chianti, twenty-five minutes away. I Parigi is also fifteen minutes from the center of Florence.

I Parigi, named after the fifteenth-century owners of this imposing villa, is at the end of a characteristically narrow Florentine street with walls on either side and olive trees and cypresses peering over the top. The villa's rambling old buildings are dominated by a medieval tower complete with turrets. The oldest part of the villa dates back to the fourteenth century. I Parigi has belonged to the present owners since 1918. Marco, one of the owner's sons, welcomes guests. Ample breakfasts are served in a small dining room in winter and in the garden during the warmer months; more English than continental, these are enriched with cold cuts and local cheeses.

The villa is a short walking distance from the Certosa, which is still inhabited by monks and is well worth a visit. Paths lead off into the countryside for walkers and mountain bikers. The pool has an uninterrupted view of the Tuscan hills and is surrounded by lawns and a delightful country garden with mossy terra-cotta pots, lemon trees, and bees buzzing in the lavender. The family makes its own wine and oil.

ROOMS: In the newer nine-teenth-century wing on the second floor there are four double rooms with air-conditioning, each with its own bathroom. The rooms are cheerful and furnished in crisp colors with hand-painted headboards. Each room has its own color scheme, a well-stocked refrigerator, and satellite televi-sion. On the first floor there is an apartment with a small private garden, a sitting room with sofa bed, a double room, bathroom, and kitchen. In the fourteenth-century tower there are three deluxe air-conditioned bedrooms with satellite television. A double suite also with air-conditioning and satellite television has been made out of the very top of the tower that commands a panoramic view.

AMENITIES:
English, French, and German are spoken
Parking on the premises
Private pool
Credit cards are accepted
Children under the age of five stay free of charge
Small pets are welcome

WHERE: The railway station in Florence is 4 miles away while the airport is 7 miles away. By car from highway AI exit at Florence–Certosa and proceed in the direction of Florence. Just before the sign for Galluzzo take Via Luigiana, a street winding upward on the right; you will find I Parigi at the top on the left.

CATEGORY: Caffèlletto ◆ **RATE:** ○○○ ◆ *Member since 2000*

FLORENCE–DUOMO

RESIDENZA GIOTTO ✦ **VIA ROMA 6** ✦ **50123 FLORENCE**
TEL. +39 055214593 ✦ **FAX +39 0552648568** ✦ **E-MAIL: residenzagiotto@tin.it**

The Residenza Giotto is so called because it is literally a stone's throw from the Campanile (Giotto's splendid Gothic bell tower) and, in at least three of the bedrooms, propped up on their pillows, guests may gaze out of their windows at Brunelleschi's dome. This bed-and-breakfast is on the top floor of Palazzo Ginnasi-Rostagno. During the warmer months, breakfast is served on a delightful terrace from where the Baptistery and the Cathedral seem near enough to touch. Guests will also find all they need for breakfast in their rooms.

ROOMS: Six double rooms (which can be made into twins on request) furnished with antiques, with private bathrooms (with showers).

AMENITIES:
English and French are spoken
Private parking at extra cost
Air-conditioning and telephones with Internet connection in each room
Elevator
Small pets are welcome

WHERE: The railway station is a short distance away and Florence's Peretola airport is 6 miles away.

CATEGORY· **Caffelletto** ⟩ RATE. ○○○ ✦ *Member since 2003*

FLORENCE–NORD

INFO: CAFFÈLLETTO, ITALY

TEL. +39 023311814 OR 1820 · **FAX +39 023313009** · **E-MAIL: info@caffelletto.it**

Villa la Sosta is a charming, cocoon-like bed-and-breakfast set in one of Florence's most exclusive residential areas. The Via Bolognese is in fact the oldest thoroughfare to cross the Tuscan Apennines. From the ancient gate of San Gallo at Ponte Rosso in the city center, the road goes up the Florentine hills and continues on upward to the Futa Pass as far as Bologna.

This villa dates back to the nineteenth century. Once part of a larger property on

the Montughi Hill, it is surrounded by a beautiful garden with cypresses and fruit trees. Here, under an arbor, abundant breakfasts are served in the summer months, while in winter guests may breakfast in the elegant dining room. The ancient tower has been converted into a loft with a magnificent view, where guests may watch television, listen to music, and relax. Villa la Sosta is an ideal starting point to visit Florence (it is only a ten-minute bus ride to the city's historic center) and its surroundings, while enjoying a quiet and congenial atmosphere, "a home away from home." Daily trips can be arranged for guests to the Chianti wine region, as can wine tastings in a few of the better-known cellars.

ROOMS: Three quiet and airy double rooms, one triple, and one room for four persons, each with its own bathroom and private entrance. Some of the rooms are furnished with family antiques.

AMENITIES:
English and Spanish are spoken
Private parking
Children under the age of two stay
* free of charge*

WHERE: The nearest railway station is 4 miles away while the airport is 9 miles away.

CATEGORY: ✳✳✳✳ · **RATE:** ❍❍❍ · *Member since 2003*

FLORENCE–PIAZZA DONATELLO

INFO: CAFFÈLLETTO, ITALY

TEL. +39 023311814 OR 1820 · FAX +39 023313009 · E-MAIL: info@caffelletto.it

This quiet apartment is on the first floor of a handsome palazzo built at the beginning of the nineteenth century, located just off one of the wide avenues that lead away from the historic center of Florence (just a fifteen-minute walk away). The apartment originally belonged to the grandparents of the present owner, who personally serves breakfast to guests. The rooms are comfortable and convenient.

ROOMS: A large double room with a bathroom (with bathtub) and the possibility of adding two single beds; a double room with a small terrace and bathroom (with shower); a double with a bathroom (with shower) and a view over the garden. Minimum stay two nights.

AMENITIES:
French is spoken
Parking on the premises
Dinner may be served on request
Children under the age of two
 stay free of charge
Well-behaved pets are welcome

WHERE: The nearest railway station is Florence's Santa Maria Novella, less than a mile away, while the airport is 9 miles away.

CATEGORY: ✳✳✳✳ · **RATE:** ○ · *Member since 2001*

FLORENCE–PIAZZA SANTA CROCE

LE STANZE DI SANTA CROCE B&B ◆ **VIA DELLE PINZOCHERE 6** ◆ **50122 FLORENCE**
TEL. +39 0552001366 ◆ **FAX +39 0552008456** ◆ **E-MAIL: lestanze@viapinzochere6.it**

Via delle Pinzochere (literally, Street of the Bigots) is a typically narrow Florentine alleyway leading to the Piazza Santa Croce. The Church of Santa Croce is the pantheon of illustrious Florentines and dominates a neighborhood square where children chase pigeons, students strum guitars, and senior citizens doze on benches. It is also around the corner from Vivoli's, the most beloved gelateria in Florence. Other leading attractions are a five-minute walk away. Recently restored, this bed-and-breakfast is on three floors with a terrace where breakfast is served year-round. Your hostess prides herself on her breakfasts, which include fresh fruit, juices, and homemade jams, as well as Tuscan cold cuts and cheese.

ROOMS: Two double rooms and two twin rooms, each with a private bathroom (with shower). The bedroom in the loft has its own private bathroom with Jacuzzi, though

it is not en suite. No two rooms are the same and each one is named after a different church bell of Florence.

AMENITIES:
English is spoken
Air-conditioning, telephone,
and safe in every room
Children under the age of two
stay free of charge

WHERE: The Florence railway station is a short distance away, while the airport is 6 miles away. Via delle Pinzochere is to the left of Piazza Santa Croce, facing the church.

CATEGORY: ✳✳✳✳ ◆ **RATE:** ○○○ ◆ *Member since 2003*

FLORENCE—PIAZZA SIGNORIA

VIA DEI MAGAZZINI 2/4 ◆ 50100 FLORENCE
TEL. +39 0552399546 ◆ FAX +39 0552676616 ◆ CELL +39 03483210565
E-MAIL: info@inpiazzadellasignoria.it

With bedrooms overlooking Florence's most famous square, the Piazza della Signoria, this bed-and-breakfast looks more like a film set. One can easily imagine a movie star waking up under the awnings of her Renaissance bed to an open window with a view over the square and the back of Michelangelo's *David*.

The interiors are splendidly furnished with antiques, canopy beds, richly patterned upholstery, and coffered ceilings. Wood floors give the rooms an additional touch of elegance. Your hosts are a family with three children who have put a lot of enthusiasm into the project, and it shows. Breakfast is served in a delightful dining room, or in your suite.

ROOMS: Each room is named after a famous Florentine. On the first floor there are four doubles, with an extra bed available in two of them. On the second floor there are five doubles, two of which are adjoining (one has a bathroom with shower and the other a Jacuzzi), while in one bedroom an extra bed is available. All rooms have private baths. On the fourth floor there are three apartments: Umberto has a living room with a sofa bed and kitchen corner, bathroom (with shower), and one double bedroom with a loft with room for another bed. Giulio has a living room with kitchen corner, sofa bed,

and one double room with a bathroom (with shower). Matteo has a living room with kitchen corner and two double rooms each.

AMENITIES:

English and French are spoken
Private parking at extra cost
Bicycles can be rented
Air-conditioning, satellite television, telephone, safe, and hair dryer in every room
Your hosts have a special agreement with a fitness and beauty center with a swimming pool less than a mile away
Children under the age of two stay free of charge

WHERE: The nearest railway station is less than a mile away in Santa Maria Novella, while the airport is 6 miles away.

CATEGORY: Caffèlletto ◆ **RATE:** ○○○○ ◆ *Member since 2001*

FLORENCE–SANTA CROCE

INFO: CAFFÈLLETTO, ITALY

TEL. +39 023311814 OR 1820 ◦ FAX +39 023313009 ◦ E-MAIL: info@caffelletto.it

In the 1400s, this palazzo belonged to the de Benci family, whose daughter, Ginevra, was immortalized by Leonardo da Vinci. The present owners have been living here for over a century. The apartment is literally around the corner from the Church of Santa Croce, the Florentine pantheon of great Italians from Dante Alighieri to Galileo Galilei. It is also near Vivoli's, Florence's best-known gelateria. Your charming hosts will be delighted to help guests find their way around all the other landmarks of the city within easy walking distance. The apartment is pleasantly furnished with bright blue wrought-iron beds. Guests may utilize the kitchen for breakfasts and dinners.

ROOMS: An apartment on the first floor with an entrance hall, sitting room with sofa bed, a large bedroom with two beds, with the option to add a third; a smaller bedroom with two beds; two bathrooms; and a kitchen.

AMENITIES:
English and French are spoken
Parking is available at extra cost
Children under the age of two stay
  free of charge

WHERE: The nearest railway station is Florence's Santa Maria Novella, less than a mile away, while the airport is 6 miles away.

CATEGORY: ✳✳✳✳ ◦ **RATE:** ◯◯ ◦ *Member since 2001*

FLORENCE–CORSO ITALIA

INFO: CAFFÈLLETTO, ITALY

TEL. +39 023311814 OR 1820 • **FAX +39 023313009** • **E-MAIL: info@caffelletto.it**

Anyone fortunate enough to find tickets for the Florence music festival, Maggio Musicale, each May, could not find a better location than opposite the Teatro Comunale. This bed-and-breakfast is also conveniently around the corner from the city park, ideal for a morning jog along the river, and only ten minutes by foot from the

Duomo, a walk that passes the main shopping streets of Florence and follows the river toward Ponte Vecchio.

The apartment is on the first floor of this nineteenth-century, elegantly furnished, and welcoming palazzo. Your hosts are two young sisters who follow every detail, from fresh flowers in each room to replenishing the books in the library, with the utmost care, and are only too happy to pass on hints for shoppers and gastronomes visiting Florence. Breakfast, including homemade tarts and jams, is served in the comfortable little breakfast room.

ROOMS: Five rooms: the Green Room is a double with the option of a third bed; there are two double Blue Rooms; one Red Room with a queen bed and two twin beds; and the Yellow Room has two twin beds with the option of a third bed. All rooms are equipped with a private bathroom with shower.

AMENITIES:
English is spoken

WHERE: The central railway station is less than a mile away, and only 10 minutes on foot, while the Florence airport is 4 miles away.

CATEGORY: ✳✳✳✳ • **RATE:** ○○○ • *Member since 2004*

SIENA–CORSIGNANO

INFO: CAFFÈLLETTO, ITALY

TEL. +39 023311814 OR 1820 · **FAX +39 023313009** · **E-MAIL: INFO@CAFFELLETTO.IT**

This is serious Chiantishire, located in a tiny village near Siena surrounded by vines and olive groves punctuated by cypress trees. Some of the most famous Chianti Classico wines come from these slopes, and your hosts themselves produce forty thousand bottles from their 54-acre vineyards. From the windows of the villa and guesthouses scattered all over the property there are charming vistas of the domes and spires of

Siena. The air is fragrant with lavender and rosemary, and the scent of roses fills the gardens surrounding the guesthouses. Breakfasts are served in the Limonaia, where in winter the huge terracotta tubs with lemon tress used to be stored. Here, too, guests may dine or participate in cooking classes.

ROOMS: Eleven apartments of various sizes for two, four, and six guests in the four farmhouses on the property: Fattoria, Forno, Villa, and Casale. The most elegant are in the Villa apartment.

AMENITIES:
English and French are spoken
Parking on the grounds
Swimming pool
Children under the age of two
 stay free of charge
dinner served on request
Pets are welcome

WHERE: The nearest railway station is 6 miles away in Siena, while the Florence airport is 43 miles away.

CATEGORY: ✳✳✳✳ · **RATE**: ○○ · *Member since 2004*

FLORENCE–FORTEZZA DA BASSO

RESIDENZA JOHANNA I + VIA BONIFACIO LUPI 14 + 50129 FLORENCE

TEL. +39 055481896 + FAX +39 055482721 + E-MAIL: LUPI@JOHANNA.IT

RESIDENZA JOHANNA I + VIA DELLE V GIORNATE 12 + 50129 FLORENCE

TEL. AND FAX +39 055473377 + E-MAIL: CINQUEGIORNATE@JOHANNA.IT

The Johanna Residence I, on the second floor of a handsome palazzo in the center of Florence dating back to the nineteenth century, was a pioneer in what has become an exciting new trend in hospitality, providing a home-away-from-home in elegant surroundings at a price that is affordable for everyone. Johanna Residence II has now opened its doors just around the corner from the Fortezza da Basso, the congress, exhibition, and international fair center in Florence. It is a small villa on two floors dating back to the beginning of the last century opening onto a garden. Both residences have sunny, elegant, quiet rooms with cheerful fabrics and all the charm and atmosphere of a private house. This impression is reinforced by the friendly and hospitable way in which guests are welcomed on arrival.

ROOMS: The Johanna Residence I has eleven bedrooms, including some double and twin rooms, all with their own bathroom. The Johanna Residence II has six large and sunny rooms, all with their own bathroom and TV. Three rooms have air conditioning, and the others have a ceiling fan. In each room guests will find breakfast with a kettle for coffee in the morning, tea at five in the afternoon, and a tisane before bed. Arrival by seven o'clock in the evening is kindly requested. Pets are, regretfully, not welcome.

AMENITIES:
English and French are spoken
Private parking at Johanna I
Garden at Johanna II
Children under the age of two stay
 free of charge

WHERE: The railway station is just round the corner, while the airport is about 6 miles away. For Johanna II Residence take Via dello Statuto from the Fortezza da Basso and the fourth street to the right is Via delle V Giornate.

CATEGORY: ✳✳✳✳ + **RATE:** ○○ + *Member since 2005*

FLORENCE–VIA SAN GALLO

RESIDENZA JOHLEA ◆ **VIA SAN GALLO 76 E 80** ◆ **50129 FLORENCE**
TEL. +39 0554633292 ◆ **FAX +39 0554634552** ◆ **E-MAIL: johlea@johanna.it**

This is not one but two bed-and-breakfasts so near to the Duomo that it seems close enough to touch, especially from the delightful terrace belonging to one of the apartments. Built in the late nineteenth century, both houses have been tastefully restored and decorated in cool pastels and antique furniture. Both establishments have their own reception area and sitting room for guests. The wherewithal for breakfast is in every room.

ROOMS: Twelve bedrooms—two single rooms, seven double or twin rooms, three triples. All bathrooms are in marble or handmade tiles. Check-in is between 4:00 and 7:00 PM.

AMENITIES:
English, French, and German are spoken
All rooms have telephone, television set,
air-conditioning, safe, outlet for computer,
and hair dryer
Children under the age of two stay
free of charge

WHERE: The Santa Maria Novella railway station is less than a mile away, while the Florence Peretola airport is 6 miles away. By car from Milan take highway AI and exit at Florence Nord and follow signs to Fortezza da Basso and Piazza Libertà. By car from Rome exit at Florence Sud and follow directions for Piazza Libertà. Once in Piazza Libertà, go toward the center taking Via Cavour (tell the police officers you are going to Residenza Johlea). Once in Piazza San Marco, turn right on Via Arazzieri, then right again onto Via San Gallo; the residences are at number 76 and 80 black (as opposed to the red numbers which are used by stores).

CATEGORY: ✳✳✳✳ ◆ **RATE:** ○○ ◆ *Member since 2002*

FIESOLE (FI)

LE CANNELLE B&B • VIA A. GRAMSCI 52/54 • 50014 FIESOLE, FLORENCE
TEL. +39 0555978336 • FAX +39 0555978292 • E-MAIL: info@lecannelle.com

It is wonderful to be in Florence but sometimes, especially in summer, it can be even better to admire this beautiful city from above. Here in Fiesole at Le Cannelle bed-and-breakfast you can do just that. Florence is fifteen minutes away on bus number 7, down a hillside lined with villas and punctuated by olive groves and rows of cypresses. Le Cannelle is just a stone's throw from the main square of Fiesole and has recently been completely restored. The house dates back to the 1500s when it was probably a convent. Breakfast is served daily by your hostesses, two young sisters whose father is responsible for the expert restoration.

ROOMS: On the first floor, there is a room for three with a bathroom (with bathtub) and a double room with a bathroom (with shower). On the second floor, there is a double room with a bathroom (with shower), a single room with a bathroom (with shower), and a large double room with an overhead loft with two other beds and a bathroom (with bathtub). Three of the rooms have views over the hills of Fiesole.

AMENITIES:
English is spoken
Laundry service is available
Air-conditioning, telephone, and television set in
*   every room*
Suggested arrival time between 12:00 noon and
6:00 pm
Children under the age of two stay free of charge

WHERE: The nearest railway station is Florence 9 miles away, while the airport is 12 miles away. By car take highway A1 and exit at Florence Sud, then follow indications for the Stadio and then for Fiesole. Le Cannelle is 600 feet past the main square in Fiesole.

CATEGORY: ✳✳✳✳ • RATE: ○○
Member since 2001

CAMAIORE VILLA IL COLLETTO (LU)

VILLA IL COLLETTO ◆ **VIA COLLETTO ZACCONI, 31** ◆ **55041 CAMAIORE, LUCCA**
FAX +39 05842531191 ◆ **CELL +39 335365654** ◆ **E-MAIL: info@ilcolletto.com**

Camaiore is in a particularly attractive part of Tuscany, with rolling hills facing the fashionable seascape of Versilia near the fascinating marble mines where Michelangelo came to select the massive monoliths destined to become a *Pietà* or the famous *David*. This white-washed villa, surrounded by tall trees and an English garden, has welcomed many famous guests in the century since it was built, including Giacomo Puccini and the famous Italian actress Eleonora Duse.

Your hostess is from Rome but has chosen to live with her daughter in this wonderous part of Italy year round. Breakfast is served under a gazebo in the garden in the warmer months and in a pleasant breakfast room in winter. The bedrooms all have an individual charm: two have balconies overlooking the Apuan Alps, another is decorated in the Art Nouveau style, and all are furnished with antiques.

ROOMS: One single room with balcony and bathroom with shower in the corridor. Three double rooms; one with its own bathroom with tub, the second is a large room with dressing room and bathroom with shower, and the third has a balcony and bathroom with shower in the corridor. There is also one room with twin beds and Art Nouveau furniture and a bathroom with shower. Closed from January 7 to 31.

AMENITIES:
*English, French, and Spanish
  are spoken
Guests may use the sitting room
  and library with fireplace
Swimming pool installed in
  2004
Private parking
Children over the age of twelve
  are welcome
Pets (depending on size and sex,
  as there are three dogs at the
  villa) are also welcome*

WHERE: The nearest railway station is 7 miles away in Viareggio, while the Pisa airport is 15 miles away. By car exit from the Firenze Mare highway at Camaiore and follow signs for Camaiore. At the entrance to the town you will see signs for Il Colletto.

CATEGORY: Caffèlletto ◆ **RATE:** ○○—○○○ ◆ *Member since 2004*

POLCANTO (FI)

CASA PALMIRA ✦ **VIA FAENTINA 4/1, LOC. FERIOLO, POLCANTO**
50030 BORGO SAN LORENZO (FLORENCE)
TEL. AND FAX +39 0558409749 ✦ **E-MAIL: palmira@cosmos.it**

Fiesole is a hilltop town above Florence much favored by the Anglo-Florentines in the nineteenth century. Today's Florentines, and many tourists, flock up the hillside on hot summer evenings to have a gelato at one of the outdoor cafés. With its Roman theater—where film and music festivals are held every summer—and its incomparable view

of Florence from the convent of San Francesco, Fiesole possesses the charm typical of Tuscan hilltop towns.

At five miles from Fiesole and ten from Florence, Casa Palmira is an expertly restored old hay barn. It is part of a rural complex, with a tower dating back to the eleventh century that once stood guard over a thoroughfare leading from medieval Florence to the Apennines. The house is in a lovely setting, surrounded by green fields and woodlands. The garden with its wide lawn and shady pergola has a vegetable garden where Assunta, your hostess, finds inspiration for her excellent meals. She will also prepare picnic baskets for guests planning excursions further afield. Assunta and Stefano have restored and decorated their house with engaging simplicity. There is a large sitting room/kitchen with a fireplace where guests may choose to commune.

ROOMS: There are six rooms, two doubles, one single, and three with twin beds. A third bed can be added on request. All have private baths and are furnished with old-fashioned charm, with crisp curtains and bedspreads. Minimum stay three nights.

AMENITIES:

Open from March 10 to January 10
Laundry service is available
Private parking
Mountain bikes
Dinner may be served on request and guests can also
 barbecue in the garden
English and French are spoken
Children under the age of two stay free of charge
Pets are not allowed

WHERE: The Florence railway station is 9 miles away, while the nearest airport is in Florence, 13 miles away, . By car take the road to Fiesole. When in the main square of Fiesole take the Via dei Bosconi toward Olmo. After five miles take the road for Borgo San Lorenzo at the crossroads. After less than a mile later turn right at the sign for the Ristorante Feriolo; on your left you will see Casa Palmira.

CATEGORY: ✳✳✳✳ ✦ **RATE:** ○ ✦ *Member since 1998*

SAN QUIRICO (SI)

AZ. AGRICOLA IL RIGO ⬥ **LOC. CASA BIANCA** ⬥ **53027 SAN QUIRICO D'ORCIA, SIENA**
TEL. +39 0577897291 ⬥ **FAX +39 0577898236** ⬥ **E-MAIL: ilrigo@iol.it**

This mellow old stone manor house on a hill is a mile from San Quirico, a medieval village in the heart of the Val d'Orcia, the lush valley south of Siena. A kaleidoscope of colors, with rolling green hillsides in spring, yellow ripening wheat in summer, or purple clover alternating with fields of sunflowers, this is perhaps the most poetic landscape in Tuscany. The patchwork of fields changes with the seasons, bordered with broom in spring and scattered with poppies in summer. The view from the house spans out splendidly, giving a nice view of the papal enclave in nearby Pienza. Surrounded by fields, the house is built around a delightful inner courtyard and is at the centre of an estate that has been in the hands of the same family since the seventeenth century. This is an organic farm, and since 1989 the family also extends hospitality to guests in simple, cheerful rooms decorated with antique country furniture. Breakfast features homemade cakes and tarts on a long table in a cozy and inviting atmosphere. Your hosts are also very happy to welcome guests for dinner, especially on the evening they arrive, which has become a tradition in this house of unusual old world charm. They can also organise hiking excursions through the countryside and cooking lessons in July as well as musical soirees with both classical and other musical genres.

ROOMS: The Casa Bianca has eight double or twin-bedded rooms all with their own bathroom including shower. One suite on the first floor has a double room and a twin-bedded room, both sharing a bathroom. In the Bacoca cottage there are seven double rooms, one of which can be made into twin on request, all with their own bathroom with shower. Minimum stay 2 to 3 nights. Closed from January 10 to 31.

AMENITIES:

English, French, and Spanish are spoken
Children under the age of two stay free of
  charge
Dinner may be served on request
Private parking
Small pets are welcome

Where: The nearest railway station is in Buonconvento 7 miles away, while the Florence airport is 68 miles away. By car take the Firenze/Siena superstrada and exit at Siena Ovest. Continue toward the Via Cassia SS 2 to Buonconvento and San Quirico. A mile after San Quirico turn left for Il Rigo.

CATEGORY: ✳✳✳✳ ⬥ **RATE:** ◯◯ ⬥ *Member since 2004*

FIESOLE INCANTO (FI)

L'INCANTO DI FIESOLE ◆ **VIA SAN CLEMENTE, 5** ◆ **50014 FIESOLE, FIRENZE**

TEL. +39 055597507 ◆ **FAX +39 055598779** ◆ **E-MAIL: booking@incantodifiesole.it**

Incanto means spell, and guests may well feel spellbound by the good fortune that has brought them to this hillside above Fiesole covered in olive groves with a view over the city of Florence below. Once a manor house with its own private chapel, the Fiesole Incanto dates back to the fifteenth century. Just a half mile from Fiesole and about six miles outside Florence, it is both ideally situated to visit the city and to escape from it when the day's sightseeing is done and nothing could be better than to relax by the pool. Furnished in excellent taste, visitors to Florence will find this a very pleasant place to stay.

ROOMS: Four double rooms (the most romantic room also has a fireplace) all have their own bathroom with shower, and two suites are available: Le Rose has a four-post bed, single sofa bed, and bathroom with shower, while Il Golf has a large room with double bed in the overhead gallery, a little sitting room with two single sofa beds, and a large bathroom with tub. Minimum stay two nights.

AMENITIES:
English is spoken
Private parking
Swimming pool
Children under the age of two stay free of charge
Small pets are welcome

WHERE: The nearest railway station is seven miles away in Florence, while the Florence airport is 10 miles away. By car, take highway A1 and exit at Firenze Sud. Follow the indications for Stadio and Fiesole. In the main square of Fiesole go straight uphill until after a half mile you will see the sign for Incanto di Fiesole.

CATEGORY: ✳✳✳✳ ◆ **RATE:** ◯◯–◯◯◯ ◆ *Member since 2004*

ANTELLA (FI)

INFO: CAFFÈLLETTO, ITALY

TEL. +39 023311814 OR 1820 ◆ **FAX +39 023313009** ◆ **E-MAIL: info@caffelletto.it**

The Villa "Il Colle" is on a hillside above the little town of Antella, with a spectacular view of Florence, only four miles away. The villa, which dates back to the fourteenth century and is near an even older monastery, is surrounded by cypress trees and olive groves. Your hosts have only just finished restoration work and the bedrooms reserved for guests are suitably luxurious.

ROOMS: One suite with a double bed (with the option of a third bed) and a bathroom (with bathtub and shower). Two double or twin rooms, the Margherita (Daisy) and the Peonia (Peony), both with bathrooms (with showers) that can also be rented as single rooms. The Violetta (Violet) room, a double with a bathroom (with Jacuzzi and shower). Minimum stay two nights.

AMENITIES:

English and French are spoken

Laundry service is available

All rooms have air-conditioning and satellite television

Guests may make full use of the cloister gardens, a billiard room, and a cellar for wine tasting

Telephone/Internet service

Transportation on request to and from the railway station or airport

Four miles away is the famous Ugolino golf club

Children over the age of eight are welcome

WHERE: The nearest railway station is in Florence, 6 miles away, while the airport is 7 miles away.

CATEGORY: Caffèlletto ◆ **RATE:** ○○○ ◆ *Member since 2003*

MIGLIARINO (PI)

FATTORIA DI MIGLIARINO ◆ VIALE DEI PINI ◆ 56010 MIGLIARINO, PISA
TEL. AND FAX +39 050803170 ◆ E-MAIL: info@fattoriadimigliarino.it

The Fattoria di Migliarino is on a 7,410-acre estate belonging to a famous family of Italian patricians. A bucolic oasis on the Tyrrhenian coast only four miles from Pisa, fifteen from Lucca, and eight from Torre del Lago (of operatic Puccini fame), it is itself famous for its *pineta*, a statuesque forest of maritime pines, each one hundreds of years old and bent into dramatic poses by the winds from the sea. On the estate guests may ride in the grounds, play tennis, go sailing, canoeing, fishing, or mountain biking, while the beaches of the coast of Versilia are a short distance away. There are four 18-hole golf courses within a radius of thirty miles.

The Fattoria is a handsome building dating back to the end of the nineteenth century surrounded by a large garden with swimming pool. The word *fattoria* means farm, and your hosts are a young couple with four children who raise livestock and cultivate and sell agricultural products in addition to welcoming guests. Their Capanna del Benessere offers beauty treatments and products. Generously proportioned breakfasts are served in the large sunny dining room furnished, like the rest of the Fattoria, in a style typical of a Tuscan country house.

ROOMS: On the first and second floors are four double rooms, one triple, one with four beds, and a single, all with their own bathroom with shower. On the ground floor is a large sitting room with fireplace, a television room with satellite, and a dining room. Entirely independent apartments in various sizes are also available. Minimum stay two nights.

AMENITIES:
English and French are spoken
Private parking
Swimming pool
Children under the age of two stay free of charge
Dinners may be arranged for small groups
Pets are welcome
The products of the Fattoria are for sale at a
  special discount for guests

WHERE: The nearest railway station is 6 miles away in Pisa, while the Pisa airport is 7 miles away. By car take highway A11 and exit at Pisa Nord. Drive toward Pisa, and after a half mile turn right at the light, drive under the railway bridge, and after 800 yards turn left after the Carabinieri station along the Via del Mare. Continue for 300 yards, and after a right bend in the road you will see the entrance to the Fattoria.

CATEGORY: ✳✳✳✳ ◆ RATE: ○○ ◆ *Member since 2004*

SAN CASCIANO–VILLA IL POGGIALE (FI)

VIA EMPOLESE 69 50026 · SAN CASCIANO VALDIPESA, FLORENCE
TEL. +39 055828311 · FAX +39 055829429 · E-MAIL: villailpoggiale@villailpoggiale.it

Villa Il Poggiale is the ultimate dream for lovers of Tuscany, a sixteenth-century villa with a beautiful garden surrounded by olive groves, vineyards, rows of cypress trees, and ocher-colored farmhouses—all this at twenty minutes from Florence and a little more than thirty from Siena. The villa belongs to the Associazione delle Dimore Storiche (Historical Mansion Association). The owners (who spent their childhood here) have done wonders during the lengthy restoration: they wanted to retain the original charm of their home but also offer their guests all the amenities—the Poggiale is more like a private house than an hotel. It is a Tuscan villa with family antiques, an

elegant but very warm ambiance, spacious and quiet bedrooms, and memorable breakfasts. These feature a large buffet, which includes Tuscan specialties such as fresh ricotta cheese, the local focaccia, prosciutto, and homemade brioche. The loggia looks out onto a formal garden, while the swimming pool area is in the olive grove, which, in turn, is surrounded by enchantingly landscaped gardens.

ROOMS: Nineteen doubles, three apartments, and two suites. All bedrooms are spacious, most of them vast; some have frescoed walls and ceilings and a couple of them have fireplaces. Each room has its own refrigerator, computer outlet, electric kettle, and a tea and coffee tray. The views are either of the garden, the olive grove, or the central courtyard with the old well and fragrant creepers. Bathrooms have been decorated with thorough attention to detail, all with handmade tiles, while some retain their original frescoes. Closed in February.

AMENITIES:
English, French, and some German and Spanish are spoken
Private parking
Swimming pool
Children under the age of two stay free of charge

WHERE: The railway station in Florence is 11 miles away, while the airport is 13 miles away. By car from highway A1 exit at Firenze Certosa. From here, take the highway to Siena. Exit at San Casciano, just before the village turn right following the sign for Empoli-Cerbaia. You will find Il Poggiale on your left after a mile or so.

CATEGORY: Caffèlletto · **RATE:** standard rooms ○○○; superior rooms ○○○○
Member since 2003

MONTEFIRIDOLFI (FI)

INFO: CAFFÈLLETTO, ITALY

TEL. +39 023311814 OR 1820 • FAX +39 023313009 • E-MAIL: info@caffelletto.it

At about five miles from San Casciano Val di Pesa, this one-time convent dating back to the fourteenth century is in the heart of Chianti Classico. Situated on a hill at ten minutes by foot from the little village of Montefiridolfi, the view over the surrounding landscape is like the backdrop of a Renaissance painting, crested with cypresses,

striped with vines, and dotted with gingerbread cottages, hamlets, and church towers. A stairway leads up to the apartment from the inner cloister with an ancient well in the center. The floors are paved with the original seventeenth-century terra-cotta tiles; the ceilings are beamed and the windows overlook the surrounding countryside and the convent roof. Simply furnished, the apartment is very welcoming and comfortable. Your hostess lives here by herself and will be delighted to inform guests about the local landmarks. Halfway between Florence and Siena, close to Greve, the capital of Chianti, this is also an ideal place to visit San Gimignano and Volterra, and at four miles away, the magical hamlet of Badia a Passignano.

ROOMS: A comfortable double room with a writing desk and the possibility of adding a child's bed. Bathroom with shower.

AMENITIES:
English and German are spoken
Depending on your hostess's
  commitments, dinner may be
  served on request
Children under the age of two stay
  free of charge

WHERE: The nearest railway station is in Florence, 13 miles, while the airport in Florence is 15 miles away.

CATEGORY: ✳✳✳✳ • RATE: ○○ • *Member since 2002*

SAN DONATO (FI)

INFO: CAFFÈLLETTO, ITALY

TEL. +39 023311814 OR 1820 ◆ **FAX +39 023313009** ◆ **E-MAIL: info@caffelletto.it**

A stream still runs by this old mill built in 1600 and surrounded by woodland. Your hosts happened on it, fell in love with it, and have restored it into an elegant and romantic bed-and-breakfast in the heart of Chianti. Both Siena and Florence are only twenty minutes away. Your host is an excellent cook and nothing could be more inviting after a day spent sight-seeing than a plate of her homemade pasta by candlelight. In the garden, with its roses, climbing plants, and flowers in terra-cotta pots, is a swimming pool.

ROOMS: Three doubles all with their own bathrooms (with showers) and an independent entrance from the garden. Two independent and elegant apartments for two to four people with a private terrace. Hidden away in the woods is a third apartment, Il Mulinetto, with a sitting room with fireplace and kitchen corner, a bathroom (with shower), and a double room in the overhead gallery opening to a terrace, the ultimate

romantic hideaway. Minimum stay two nights for the rooms, seven nights for the apartments.

AMENITIES:
English and French are spoken
Dinner may be served on request
Private parking
Swimming pool
Children over the age of twelve are welcome

WHERE: The nearest railway station is Florence's Santa Maria Novella, 20 miles away, while the Florence Peretola airport is 25 miles away.

CATEGORY: Caffèlletto ◆ **RATE:** ○○ ◆ *Member since 2002*

INFO: CAFFÈLLETTO, ITALY
TEL. +39 023311814 OR 1820 ◆ FAX +39 023313009 ◆ E-MAIL: info@caffelletto.it

Greve is the heart and soul of Chianti. Its main square is filled with colorful stalls and equally colorful expatriate locals on market days, offering tastings of the local wines, and its famous butcher selling sausage smoked on the embers. Like rays of the sun, all

the roads leading out of Greve wind into the Tuscan countryside, along roads flanked by cypress and olive trees and wild irises in the springtime. Here, less than a mile away from Greve, is Corte di Valle and three typical Tuscan cottages in a garden merging into the landscape for guests of the bed-and-breakfast. Your hosts live here all year-round and serve English breakfasts in the dining room below. This farm produces wine, oil, its own grappa, and saffron from the Tuscan hills.

ROOMS: In the main house there are eight rooms, of which one is a suite with a terrace. All of the rooms have their own bathrooms (with showers). In one of the houses there are two independent apartments and, in the other, six double and twin rooms each with private bathrooms (with showers).

AMENITIES:
English is spoken
Swimming pool
Restaurant for guests
All the rooms have satellite television
It is possible to visit the farm and
  purchase produce

WHERE: The nearest railway station is Florence's Santa Maria Novella, 12 miles away, while the airport in Florence is 19 miles away. By car the farm is on the SS 222, the famous Strada Chiantigiana. From the highway, exit at Florence Sud. Once at Greve, continue following signs to Località Le Bolle on the SS 222. From the Firenze–Certosa exit follow the signs for Tavarnuzze, then Il Ferrone, until you reach Le Bolle.

CATEGORY: **Caffèlletto** ◆ RATE: ○○○ ◆ *Member since 2001*

SAN GIULIANO TERME (PI)

INFO: CAFFÈLLETTO, ITALY

TEL. +39 023311814 OR 1820 ◆ **FAX +39 023313009** ◆ **E-MAIL: info@caffelletto.it**

This one-time farmhouse transformed into an elegant and comfortable country house is two miles from Pisa on the Aurelia, the old Roman road built by Marcus Aurelius for his legions to tramp up and down the peninsula to conquer the world. Unfortunately it is still a thoroughfare today and legions are still tramping, albeit on wheels. In the plush interior of the guest house, with its well-chosen antiques or in the garden where there is a pool. The positive factor is that guests are well connected to the road network taking them to Lucca, Montecatini, Livorno, and Viareggio, while the beaches of Pisa are only two miles away and can be reached by bicycle across the fields. Breakfasts can either be served by your hosts, or stocked in the refrigerator in the guests' kitchen.

ROOMS: A large and very comfortable apartment next to the hosts' villa. On the first floor there is a large sitting room with a fireplace, kitchen, and small bathrooms. On the second floor there are two bedrooms both with their own bathrooms. Even the bathrooms have an irresistible style. Minimum stay two nights.

AMENITIES:

English and French are spoken
Private parking
Dinner may be served on request
Videos and stereo are at guests' disposal
Children under the age of two stay free of charge

WHERE: The nearest railway station is in Pisa, 4 miles away, as is the airport.

CATEGORY: ✳✳✳✳ ◆ **RATE:** ○ ◆ *Member since 2001*

CALCI (PI)

INFO: CAFFÈLLETTO, ITALY

TEL. +39 023311814 OR 1820 ● FAX +39 023313009 ● E-MAIL: info@caffelletto.it

A few miles from Pisa, surrounded by the Pisan mountains, is the Valgraziosa, the wide and lush "Gracious Valley," so called by the Carthusian monks who settled here in the fourteenth century. There is still a Charterhouse at Calci, near the medieval

hamlet of Montemagno, where Pope Eugenio III was born. Here, just outside the village is the villa, built in the eighteenth century, with a view over the valley toward the sea.

Your hosts come from an old and noble family who chose this relatively unknown corner of Tuscany, not only as their home, but to share with their friends. Their hospitality includes not only comfortable rooms and delicious breakfasts by the fireplace, but also fascinating conversations on art and history—your hosts' son has written an interesting guide to the Charterhouse at Calci—and friends in far-flung outposts of the world. The family motto "pour bien voir," to see clearly, could well sum up a stay in this exceptional house in this unusual part of Tuscany.

Pisa and its leaning tower are only seven miles away, while there is a splendid tower designed by Brunelleschi at Vicopisano; on Mount Verruca, the ruins of the fortress and abbey of the Archangel Saint Michael is well worth a visit. The coast of Versilia is a short distance by car and, for hiking enthusiasts, there is the whole range of the Pisan mountains.

ROOMS: One double and one twin room, each with a bathroom. Alternatively there is a small suite with a double room, a single room (with the option of an extra bed), and a bathroom. Guests may also avail of a large sitting room.

AMENITIES:
English and French are spoken
Swimming pool
Children under the age of two stay
*   free of charge*
Pets are not allowed

WHERE: The airport and railway station are both in Pisa, 7 miles away. The villa can be reached from Pisa by bus.

CATEGORY: ✳✳✳✳ ● **RATE:** ○ ● *Member since 1999*

ULIVETO TERME (PI)

INFO: CAFFÈLLETTO, ITALY

TEL. +39 023311814 OR 1820 ✦ FAX +39 023313009 ✦ E-MAIL: info@caffelletto.it

This historic Tuscan villa, six miles from Pisa, is located next to the famous spa of Uliveto, which is home to one of Italy's most prestigious mineral waters. The villa was built in the 1400s and still has its original frescoes and floors. It stands in a beautiful Italian garden, with lemon trees in terra-cotta urns and lawns surrounding a shady gazebo. Your hostess provides breakfast and conversation in the dining room. Ideally situated to visit Pisa and its surroundings, the villa is also next to the park that belongs to the spa, which offers a swimming pool and tennis courts.

ROOMS: A romantic suite with a large double room and a balcony overlooking the garden, sitting room with fireplace, and bathroom (with shower). Minimum stay two nights.

AMENITIES:
English and French are spoken
Private parking
Dinner may be served on request
Children under the age of two stay free of charge

WHERE: The nearest railway stations are Cascina or Pisa, each 6 miles away, while the airport is in Pisa, 7 miles away.

CATEGORY: **Caffèlletto** ✦ RATE: ⃝⃝ ✦ *Member since 2003*

ORCIANO PISANO (PI)

INFO: CAFFÈLLETTO, ITALY

TEL. +39 023311814 OR 1820 ✦ **FAX +39 023313009** ✦ **E-MAIL: info@caffelletto.it**

In the countryside not far from Pisa, this bed-and-breakfast was once a farm perched on a hilltop surrounded by fields. It has been ably and tastefully restored by your hosts, who are originally from Milan, and stands in a typically Mediterranean garden with flowering bushes in terra-cotta vases. Guests may breakfast on a well-tended lawn in the warmer months, enjoying fresh fruit from the trees in the garden. There is a swimming pool, while the rocky beaches of Castiglioncello are twelve miles away, and a breeze from the sea tempers even the most torrid of days.

ROOMS: Two romantic double rooms (the Blue and the Pink Rooms) each with its own bathroom (one with shower, the other with bathtub). There is also an annex for two to three people with a private entrance from the garden, a living/dining room with kitchen corner on the first floor and a double room on the floor above with a bathroom (with shower). Minimum stay two nights for the rooms, three nights for the apartment.

AMENITIES:
English is spoken
Private parking
Swimming pool open for four hours
  every day
Children over the age of ten are wel-
  come

WHERE: The nearest railway station is in Livorno, 9 miles away, while the airport is in Pisa, 15 miles away.

CATEGORY: Caffèlletto ✦ **RATE:** ○○ ✦ *Member since 2003*

CAPANNOLI (PI)

INFO: CAFFÈLLETTO, ITALY

TEL. +39 023311814 OR 1820 ◆ **FAX +39 023313009** ◆ **E-MAIL: info@caffelletto.it**

In the midst of a rather bland Tuscan landscape, this is more like a town house in a Renaissance city than a country house. The facade is covered with frescoes of trompe-l'oeil arches opening onto faux vistas. The interior is furnished with the patrician elegance of a Florentine palazzo. A wing of the house was once the residence of Diego Martelli, important Maecenas of the Macchiaioli painters—artists who thought that patches (macchia) of color were the most significant element of painting.

The house is well situated for visits to the western part of Tuscany: San Gimignano is twenty-five miles away, Volterra is nineteen miles away, and the seaside is less than an hour away. Your hosts have only just started opening their house to guests and are giving it their all. All you need for breakfast can be found in the kitchen of the guests' apartment.

ROOMS: A large apartment with a sitting room with a wide fireplace and a sofa bed, a double room with a four-poster bed, and a bathroom (with shower); twin-bedded room with private bathroom (with shower). Upstairs is a delightful dovecote with a single room. Halfway up the stairs is a tiny but charming bathroom. Minimum stay two nights.

AMENITIES:
Some English is spoken
Private parking on request
Air-conditioning
Children under the age of two stay free of charge
Pets are welcome

WHERE: The nearest railway station is in Pontedera, 6 miles away, while the airport in Pisa is 19 miles away.

CATEGORY: **Caffèlletto** ◆ RATE: ○○ ◆ *Member since 2002*

CASCINA (PI)

INFO: CAFFÈLLETTO, ITALY

TEL. +39 023311814 OR 1820 + FAX +39 023313009 + E-MAIL: info@caffelletto.it

Here in a village near Pisa we are only four miles from the Leaning Tower. This is a large nineteenth-century country house, spacious, with high ceilings, recently restored, and lavishly redecorated. In the back, there is a rambling garden with fruit

trees and a swimming pool. Guests have part of the garden to themselves. Your hosts are both doctors whose children have left home, leaving them plenty of room for guests. Ideally situated to visit Pisa, Lucca, Montecatini, and Volterra, this house offers the relaxation and quiet of a country house within easy reach of all the activities of the Tuscan region.

ROOMS: A double room with private bathroom at the center of the house. Next to the house is a large apartment, completely independent, with a large sitting room with French windows opening onto the garden, a dining room and well-equipped kitchen, and a small double room with a bathroom (with bathtub). On the floor above, there is another large sitting room, as well as a double room and a twin room that share a bathroom. Minimum stay two nights.

AMENITIES:

English and French are spoken
Laundry service is available
Parking on the premises
Swimming pool
Dinner may be served on request
Children under the age of two stay
  free of charge

WHERE: The nearest railway station is in Pisa, 3 miles away, while the Pisa airport is 4 miles away.

CATEGORY: Caffèlletto + **RATE:** ○○ + *Member since 2001*

MONTEVERDI MARITTIMO (PI)

INFO: CAFFÈLLETTO, ITALY

TEL. +39 023311814 OR 1820 ✦ **FAX +39 023313009** ✦ **E-MAIL: info@caffelletto.it**

Surrounded by 27 acres of parkland and the rolling hillsides of Mediterranean woodlands in the heart of Tuscany's Maremma region is a splendid villa belonging to the renowned sculptor Rolando Stefanacci, who has decided to throw open his remarkable residence to guests. The artist has created an open-air sculpture museum on the grounds. Dating back to the sixteenth century, this enormous villa, which in France would be called a chateau, is typically Florentine in style, towering majestically at the end of an avenue bordered by woodland and lined with sculptures by the artist. Beautifully restored, it is furnished in the style of the period and populated by yet more works by the artist, whose atelier on the grounds is open to visitors. The marble staircase is lined with hunting trophies, while breakfast is served in the sixteenth-century dining room.

The swimming pool is reminiscent of the follies of ancient Rome, with a mosaic floor depicting the exploits of Ulysses under marble arcades. Caffèlletto guests may stay on the top floor of the villa in rooms with marble bathrooms, and also have access to the drawing room and tower with its huge windows and a spectacular view on all sides spanning out to the sea.

ROOMS: One large double room and a triple room each have their own bathroom with shower, a suite with a double room and a single room with queen-size bed share a bathroom, and a single has its own bathroom with tub in the corridor. There is also a ninteenth-century billiards room. Minimum stay 2 to 3 nights.

AMENITIES:
Private parking
Swimming pool
Children under the age of
  two stay free of charge
A baby bed is available
Dinner may be served on
  request

WHERE: The nearest main railway station is in Cecina, 15 minutes away, while the Pisa airport is an hour away.

CATEGORY: **Caffèlletto** ✦ **RATE**: ○○○ ✦ *Member since 2004*

**VILLA EUGENIA • VIA DI MONTENERO 442/444 • 57128 MONTENERO, LIVORNO
TEL. +39 0586579077 • CELL +39 03387243893 • E-MAIL: cherimoi@tiscalinet.it**

Livorno, or Leghorn as the English call it, is one of the unsung corners of Italy. In the nineteenth century, when it was an important port and seaside resort, it was all the rage, especially among the English. It is still well worth a visit today, and here on a hilltop at Montenero is the perfect place to stay, in this nineteenth-century villa with the sea and the city at your feet.

The villa has always belonged to your hostess's family. Today, mother and daughter personally tend to their guests' every need, ensuring that the rooms are both comfortable and welcoming. Here the old terra-cotta floors are waxed to perfection and the family antiques gleam with the patina of centuries. All the windows have a view of the sea in the distance; light and airy they are full of the scent of maritime pines. Breakfast is served on the panoramic terrace.

From Livorno, ferryboats leave for Elba, Sardinia, and Corsica. Livorno itself has a "Venice" quarter on the banks of canals lined with antique stores and gift shops.

At the end of July there is a feast in the streets that lasts ten days; the covered Bontalenti market is open all year-round. Livorno is famous for its local cacciucco, or bouillabaisse, and close to the market hall the Antico Moro restaurant serves the best in the city. Although off the regular tourist beat, Livorno is very vital and active, especially at night when a number of bars and cafés have live music.

ROOMS: Two doubles with one bathroom. The greenhouse in the park has been restored and transformed into an independent apartment that features a double bedroom, sitting room with fireplace, and sofa bed for two people, as well as a private bathroom and well-equipped kitchen corner.

AMENITIES:
English and French are spoken
Private parking
Children under the age of two stay free of charge

WHERE: The nearest railway station is Livorno, 2 miles away, while the airport is in Pisa, 9 miles away. By car take highway Firenze—Pisa—Livorno and exit at Livorno Centro—Grosseto. Follow the directions for Grosseto and exit at Montenero. Follow the signs for the Sanctuary of Montenero on the left and drive on straight for about two miles until you find an API gas station. Take a left and drive up to Montenero, then right toward Le Casine. At the Conad supermarket, turn right and continue for about 300 feet. The road will go down and then up again until you arrive at the gates of Villa Eugenia.

CATEGORY: ✳✳✳✳ • RATE: ○ • *Member since 2001*

AREZZO–GRAGNONE

INFO: CAFFÈLLETTO, ITALY

TEL. +39 023311814 OR 1820 • **FAX +39 023313009** • **E-MAIL: info@caffelletto.it**

What better starting point for a tour of the masterpieces of Piero della Francesca than the Villa I Bossi, a short distance from Arezzo and not far from Sansepolcro and the hilltop town of Cortona? The villa itself, a jumble of cinnamon-colored roofs, arched windows, and chimneys, with a private chapel nestled in an olive grove, dates back to the sixteenth century and has been recently restored by the owners, members of an aristocratic family that has lived here for centuries. One of their ancestors fought in Napoléon's campaigns and brought back with him many of the furnishings that reflect that illustrious period. The family, husband and wife and three children, produces an excellent olive oil stored in cellars with origins dating back to the Middle Ages. Your hostess, Francesca, is dynamic and pleasant, and often serves breakfast for guests in the garden on sunny mornings.

The garden is typically formal and Italian with sculpted box hedges, lemon trees in terra-cotta vases, and majestic magnolias, with a swimming pool discreetly invisible

from the villa windows, surrounded by lawns. Inside, the walls are covered with frescoes and lined with portraits of family ancestors. The main salone has a marble fireplace (the work of Benedetto da Maiano), and the sort of intimidating antique furniture on which guests seat themselves somewhat gingerly.

ROOMS: The bedrooms available for Caffèlletto guests are the Green Room, with a magnificent bed in green damask with golden curlicues around the headboard and doors painted in trompe l'oeil, and the Yellow Room, which has walls embellished with exquisite stucco and the original faux marble finish. Another room has twin wrought-iron beds with flowered bedspreads, and yet another is a double room opening onto a small veranda. All have private bathrooms and a third bed can be added to some of the bedrooms. There is also an apartment available with a double room, sitting room, and kitchen corner. Guests may use the salone, which leads into two of the bedrooms and the charming study, with eighteenth-century prints on the frescoed walls and a piano. In a cottage close to 300 feet from the main villa there are six recently restored rooms. Minimum stay one night.

AMENITIES:

English and French are spoken
Laundry service is available
Parking on the premises
Use of private pool and garden, volleyball court, and outdoor table tennis
Private telephone lines for guests
Children under the age of two stay free of charge
Pets are welcome

WHERE: The Arezzo railway station is 4 miles away, while the airport in Florence is 31 miles away.

CATEGORY: Caffèlletto (the rooms); ✳✳✳✳ (the apartment) • **RATE:** ○○
• *Member since 2000*

IL TREBBIO (AR)

POGGIO D'ACONA · 52010 SUBBIANO, AREZZO
TEL. AND FAX +39 0575487252

The Trebbio manor house could not be in a more typically Tuscan area. Nestled in one of the most picturesque valleys of the Casentino region, the Trebbio is only a short distance from the birthplace of Michelangelo and of Piero della Francesca. Less popular, but nonetheless fascinating, this region remains an eloquent testimony to

the work of Piero della Francesca, one of the most intriguing artists of the Quattrocento. His incomparable fresco cycle depicting the Legend of the True Cross in the church of San Francesco in Arezzo took fifteen years to restore and can now be seen in all its glory. His Madonna del Parto (Madonna of the Delivery) at Monterchi and his Resurrection in the Pinacoteca Comunale Sansepolcro, which the English art critic Sir Kenneth Clark pronounced "the most beautiful painting in the world," are also important stops for those interested in the history of art.

The Trebbio manor house is built of old stone, beautifully restored in harmony with the original structure, while introducing every possible comfort for guests. All the rooms have a private bathroom, and there is a large common sitting room with a wide fireplace, beams, and cheerfully upholstered sofas and chairs. The rooms all have breathtaking views—the perfect way to start the day—and breakfast is more like brunch with homemade cakes, jam, and ricotta cheese still warm from the dairy of the shepherd nearby.

Federico and Caterina Bellucci, your hosts, will welcome you with warmth and enthusiasm and are happy to organize your days—whether you're looking for an artistic itinerary or are more interested in sports, of which there is no lack: soccer, volleyball, golf, canoeing, and horseback riding are all a short distance from Trebbio.

ROOMS: There are four bedrooms, all with private bathrooms.

AMENITIES:
English and French are spoken
Laundry service
Private parking
Children under the age of two stay free of charge
Pets are welcome

WHERE: The Calbenzano railway station is 2 miles away, while the nearest airport is in Florence 62 miles away. By car take highway A1 Milano—Napoli and exit at Arezzo; follow signs for Arezzo then for Subbiano. Two miles after the village of Subbiano, turn right for Poggio d'Acona, then right again for Chitignano. After a quarter-mile, you will find Il Trebbio.

CATEGORY: ✳✳✳✳ · RATE: ○ · *Member since 1998*

FOIANO DELLA CHIANA (AR)

LA LODOLA B&B + VIA PIANA 19 + 52045 FOIANO DELLA CHIANA, AREZZO
TEL. +39 0575649660 + FAX +39 0575642521 + E-MAIL: lalodola@laxari.com

La Lodola is an eighteenth-century country house in the Val di Chiana, in the heart of Tuscany, fifty minutes from Siena, twenty from Arezzo, and forty from Perugia, just over the border in Umbria. The house is outside the village of Foiano. Although it faces the road, there is a large garden in the back with rose-bushes and fruit trees. All bedrooms look out over the garden.

The house is furnished with well-chosen period pieces, as your hostess is an antiques dealer. The breakfast room, which also has a fireplace, features a striking old marble sign salvaged from a bar facing demolition. Your hosts personally restored the old farmhouse with the help of one of their sons, Paolo, who is an architect.

ROOMS: There are five rooms. On the first floor a double room with a bathroom (with shower) and French doors opening onto the garden. On the second floor there is a double room with a large bathroom (with bathtub), two doubles (with showers), and a suite on two levels, with a double room and a third bed—comfortable and with a nice view.

AMENITIES:
English and French are spoken
Laundry service is available
Private parking
Swimming pool
Dinner may be served on request for a group of four or more
Television set, telephone, and Internet are available
Children under the age of two stay free of charge
Pets are welcome

WHERE: The nearest railway station is 16 miles away in Arezzo. The airport is in Florence, 56 miles away. By car take highway Firenze–Roma and exit at Val di Chiana. Follow directions for Foiano della Chiana, from there proceed toward Pozzo della Chiana; at the end of the village of Foiano, La Lodola is on the left.

CATEGORY: Caffelletto + **RATE:** ○○○ + *Member since 2001*

PALAZZO BRUCHI B&B ✦ **VIA PANTANETO 105** ✦ **53100 SIENA**

TEL. AND FAX +39 0577287342 ✦ **E-MAIL: masignani@hotmail.com**

Anyone who wants to visit Siena as a real insider should stay in this fifteenth-century palazzo around the corner from Piazza del Campo. A staircase sweeps up from the entrance hall to the rooms, which are light, airy, and furnished with family antiques. Wide windows look out over the inner courtyard and the hills around Siena, which inspired Lorenzetti and much of the art of the Trecento. In the rooms guests will find all they need for breakfast. Your hostess and her daughter are always on hand to help with friendly advice during your stay.

ROOMS: On the second floor are two double rooms, the Frescoed Bedroom and the Blue Room, both with bathrooms (with showers) en suite. Opening onto the courtyard on the ground floor are two more double rooms and a single, each with bathrooms (with showers). There is an optional extra bed for all rooms.

AMENITIES:
English and French are spoken
Children under the age of five stay free of charge

WHERE: The nearest railway station is less than a mile away, while the airport in Florence is 31 miles away. By car exit at Siena Sud; Via Pantaneto is 700 feet after the entrance to Porta Romana. In Porta Romana there is plenty of parking space.

CATEGORY: **Caffèlletto** ✦ **RATE:** ⭕⭕ ⭕⭕⭕ ✦ *Member since 2003*

SIENA–SANTA REGINA

FRANCES LODGE ◆ **STRADA DI VALDIPUGNA 2** ◆ **53100 SIENA**
TEL. AND FAX +39 0577281061 ◆ **E-MAIL: info@franceslodge.it**

Only two miles from Siena, Frances Lodge offers stunning views of the city, especially at sunset, when Torre del Mangia stands out against a technicolor sky. The large windows of the limonaia (lemon conservatory) look out over the garden, with its lemon trees in centennial terra-cotta vases, old roses, and rampant wisteria. In summer breakfast is served either here or under the loggia overlooking the attractively landscaped pool, which seems as if it were hewn out of the hillside. Guests can jog for one mile through the vineyards without ever leaving the estate before returning to an ample breakfast more reminiscent of brunch. Frances is an enthusiastic hostess. She makes fig and lemon jams and will be delighted to suggest itineraries to many towns and local attractions, such as Pienza, Montalcino, San Gimignano, or lesser-known but equally beautiful Bagno Vignoni with its thermal baths, the Sant' Antimo Abbey, or the panoramic roads that wind through the Crete Senesi.

ROOMS: There are three double rooms, each with its own personality: one Moroccan in style with bright-colored bedcover and cushions, the last two all in white. Includes dryer, satellite television, video, and refrigerator wellstocked with fresh fruit. Minimum stay two nights.

AMENITIES:
English and French are spoken
Private shaded parking
Private swimming pool and solarium
Mountain bikes at guests' disposal
Car rental available

WHERE: The railway station of Siena is one mile away, while Florence airport is 45 miles away. By car take the Firenze–Siena highway toward Arezzo and exit at Siena Est. Continue toward Siena until you arrive at the Due Ponti. First right toward Santa Regina and then, after the railway crossing, turn right following directions for Valdipugna. After a few hundred yards there is a sign for Frances Lodge.

CATEGORY: Caffèlletto ◆ **RATE:** ○○○○ ◆ *Member since 2000*

SAN GIMIGNANO (SI)

IL CASOLARE DI REMIGNOLI ◆ **LOC. REMIGNOLI 26** ◆ **53017 SAN GIMIGNANO, SIENA**
FAX +39 0577950104 ◆ **CELL +39 3486615984** ◆ **E-MAIL: info@remignoli.com**

With a breathtaking view from its swimming pool over the towers of San Gimignano, this bed-and-breakfast is a restored hay barn dating back to the turn of the nineteenth century. Your young host, Lorenzo, divides his time between greeting guests and growing saffron, a form of commerce in which the inhabitants of San Gimignano have been active since the Middle Ages. Seven minutes from San Gimignano, twelve miles from Volterra, and equidistant from Siena and Florence, the Casolare di Remignoli is on one of the most beautiful roads in Tuscany, winding in hairpin swoops of asphalt through vines and fields crested with cypress trees. It is ideally situated for visiting Tuscany and the countryside of Chianti.

ROOMS: Five doubles, all with their own bathrooms (with showers).

AMENITIES:
English, French, and German are spoken
Private parking
Large swimming pool
All rooms have air-conditioning, telephone, and satellite television
Pets are welcome

WHERE: The nearest railway station is Poggibonsi, 4 miles away, while the airport in Florence is 25 miles away. By car take highway A1 Milan–Roma and exit at Firenze–Certosa. Then take the Siena "superstrada" and exit at Poggibonsi Nord. Follow the signs for San Gimignano. Pass the Superal supermarket, and after just over a mile, turn right for Ulignano. Continue straight for 500 yards, then turn left for Casaglia-Remignoli. After 3 miles you will find Il Casolare di Remignoli on your left.

CATEGORY: ✳✳✳✳ ◆ **RATE:** ○○ ◆ *Member since 2003*

PIEVE A ELSA (SI)

INFO: CAFFÈLLETTO, ITALY

TEL. +39 023311814 OR 1820 • FAX +39 023313009 • E-MAIL: info@caffelletto.it

Colle Val d'Elsa is a hilltop town halfway between Florence and Siena and about half an hour along Tuscany's most spectacular country roads from both. It is the crystal

capital of Italy and the little town is full of factory outlets and showrooms selling its wares. It also has more than one excellent restaurant, the most famous being Arnolfo in the northern part of town. There are plenty of opportunities for walking and horseback riding in the Elsa valley, while those keen on mountain biking can do so all the way to the heart of Chianti from Pieve. Colle Val d'Elsa is also a very short distance from San Gimignano. The owner is carrying on a tradition of hospitality at La Piccola Pieve that goes back centuries. Her old stone house, which dates back to 1200, once offered assistance to pilgrims on their way to Rome.

Much care has gone into the furnishing and embellishing of La Piccola Pieve, both inside and out. Sweet-scented bushes cover the walls, while the gazebo in the middle of the lawn is smothered in lavender, rosebushes, and Tuscan heather. Inside there are two sitting rooms, one with beamed ceilings and a large fireplace, the walls lined with books and prints, the other with comfortable armchairs and sofas where guests can relax and listen to music. The bedrooms, too, are comfortable, and the bathrooms quite luxurious, each furnished in a different style. The hostess serves breakfast every morning. Among the offerings are typical local specialties such as crostini (toasted country bread with fresh tomato and basil).

ROOMS: On the first floor there are two communicating rooms, a double and a twin, which share a bathroom (ideal for a family or two couples) while on the floor above are two more double rooms, each with its own bathroom. Minimum stay three nights.

AMENITIES:
French, English, Spanish, Portuguese, and some
  German are spoken
Parking in the garden
Children under the age of two stay free of charge

WHERE: The nearest railway station is in Poggibonsi, 6 miles away, while the station in Siena is 12 miles away. The airport in Florence is 28 miles away.

CATEGORY: ✳✳✳✳ • **RATE:** ○○ • *Member since 2000*

COLLE VAL D'ELSA (SI)

INFO: CAFFÈLLETTO, ITALY

TEL. +39 023311814 OR 1820 · **FAX +39 023313009** · **E-MAIL: info@caffelletto.it**

Not only is Colle Val d'Elsa the crystal-manufacturing capital of Italy, with a magical ancient upper town, it is also approximately twenty minutes by car from Siena and forty from Florence. This particular bed-and-breakfast is just outside the town in the middle of the countryside, with a view of the towers of San Gimignano, six miles away. The old stone farmhouse creeping with ivy is surrounded by olive trees and orchards and has been restored and furnished with affectionate zeal by your hostess, who spoils her guests with linen sheets, silver cutlery, and—not surprisingly—Colle Val d'Elsa crystal glasses. Guests may use the local golf club or borrow mountain bikes (you'll notice that enthusiasts flock to test their skills on the surrounding hills and dales).

ROOMS: Two doubles with independent entrances. The first-floor room has a bathroom (with shower), the option of a third bed, and opens out onto the garden. The other, on the second floor, has a large bathroom (with bathtub). In the annex, there is also a twin room with kitchen corner and bathroom. Minimum stay two nights.

AMENITIES:
English and French are spoken
Laundry service is available
Private parking
Children under the age of two stay free of charge
Small pets are welcome

WHERE: The nearest railway station is Poggibonsi, 5 miles away, while the airport in Florence is 25 miles away.

CATEGORY: ✳✳✳✳ · **RATE:** ⭘⭘ · *Member since 2002*

GAIOLE IN CHIANTI (SI)

**BORGO ARGENINA B&B · ARGENINA 30 · 53013 GAIOLE IN CHIANTI, SIENA
TEL. +39 0577747117 · FAX +39 0577747228**

An avenue of cypresses leads up to the medieval hamlet of Argenina, so called because of its position on the "argine," the border between the wine-producing regions of Chianti and Berardenga. After years of neglect, the houses of Argenina were bought by a Neapolitan designer who has restored them to their former glory. Some of these houses are available for guests and have been furnished in a Provençal style in perfect harmony with the village and the surrounding countryside. The Castle of Brolio, for centuries the seat of the Ricasoli family, is open to the public, who can walk along the castle walls and admire the crisscross patchwork of vines and olives all around. There are many small trattorias in the area. In the fall you can enjoy fresh olive oil that seeps onto

toasted peasant bread. Gaiole is on the beautiful winding Strada Chiantigiana between Florence and Siena and is at a perfect distance for visiting both.

ROOMS: Seven doubles each with private bathrooms, telephone, and refrigerator. All the rooms have magnificent views.

AMENITIES:
Open from March 1 to November 10
English and French are spoken
Laundry service is available
Parking is available in the village
There is a riding school and thermal baths nearby
Children over the age of twelve are welcome

WHERE: The nearest railway station is in Siena, 9 miles away, while Florence's airport is 40 miles away. By car take highway A1 and exit at Firenze—Certosa. Take the highway in the direction of Siena and exit at Siena Est. Then take the Strada Statale 408 for Gaiole in Chianti. After 9 miles follow the signs for Borgo Argenina.

CATEGORY: Caffèlletto · **RATE**: ○○○ · *Member since 1999*

GAIOLE IN CHIANTI IL POGGERINO (SI)

IL POGGERINO B&B&MORE ◆ **LOC. POGGIO SAN POLO, 3** ◆ **53013 GAIOLE IN CHIANTI, SIENA**

TEL. AND FAX +39 0577746154 ◆ **E-MAIL: cal-tur@tiscali.it**

If you close your eyes and imagine a house in Chianti, it will probably look like Il Poggerino. In the heart of the wine growing area, near Radda and Castellina, the house looks down over the vineyards of the castles of Ama and San Polo in Rosso with the usual backdrop of olive groves, cypresses and a coppice of oaks.

Your hosts were originally from Lombardy but fell in love with this old stone farmhouse the moment they saw it, and have now transformed one of the wings into a guest house with its own independent entrance and a swimming pool hidden away at the bottom of the garden among olive groves and Mediterranean scrub with fragrant borders of lavender and rose bushes. The four children take turns in helping their mother receive guests and prepare irresistible breakfasts and brunches featuring local products and homemade cakes and jams served either in the little sitting room or under the pergola in the warmer months.

With Siena only thirty minutes away by car and Florence and San Gimignano just under an hour away, the house is ideally suited for sightseeing around Tuscany, and guests will also have every opportunity to taste the local wines from the cellars and savour Tuscan cuisine in the little *trattorie* that punctuate the entire region. For nature lovers there are endless possibilities for walks or bicycle tours in the surrounding countryside.

ROOMS: One suite with an independent entrance from the garden with a double room which can become twin on request, bathroom with shower, sitting room with sofa bed for two, TV, and mini fridge. Available from March 15 until December 15. Minimum stay two nights.

AMENITIES:
English, French, and Spanish are spoken
Private parking
Swimming pool
Bicycles available for rent
Laundry service is available
Dinner or snacks may be served on request
Shuttle service to and from railway station or airport
Children under the age of two stay free of charge

WHERE: the nearest railway station 15 miles away in Siena, while the airport in Florence is 40 miles away. By car from the North, take highway A1 and exit at Firenze-Certosa, then take the superstrada and exit at San Donato and drive towards Radda in Chianti where at La Croce you will find the SP 114. Turn right after 3 miles. From the South, from Siena and Montevarchi, take the SP 408 and after 11 miles turn onto the SP 114 and after 3 miles turn left.

CATEGORY: ✳✳✳✳ ◆ **RATE**: ◯◯ ◆ *Member since 2001*

SERRE DI RAPOLANO (SI)

PALAZZO BIZZARRI, D'ELCI VIA MATTEOTTI 5 ◆ 53040 SERRE DI RAPOLANO, SIENA
TEL. +39 0577704765 ◆ CELL +39 3487848761 ◆ E-MAIL: civitellig@jumpy.it

Serre is a medieval fortified village that was founded in the year 800 by the Byzantine Empire in order to ward off the Longobards. It is halfway between Chianti and the so-called "Crete Sienese," the rolling hills of Siena. This beautifully restored house, the Palazzo Bizzarri D'Elci, was bought by your hosts, a young couple with a daughter. It is eighteen miles from Siena, fifty-six miles from Florence, and eighteen miles from Arezzo. The main part of the house is a tower dating back to the year 1200 with an old walled garden. When your hosts bought the palazzo they also acquired the original furniture, curtains, crockery, and linens—all too perfect to change. A great stone fireplace dominates the kitchen, while breakfasts—featuring only organically grown products—are served in the sitting room.

ROOMS: A double room in an alcove with frescoes with a seventeenth-century bed and bathroom (with shower); a suite with a double room, a four-poster bed, small sitting room with a single sofa bed, and a large bathroom (with bathtub and shower). Guests may also use the large drawing room with fireplace, a small study, and a sunny loggia.

AMENITIES:
French is spoken
Children over the age of twelve are welcome

WHERE: The nearest railway station is in Asciano, 3 miles away, while the airport in Florence is 56 miles away. By car take highway A1 Firenze—Roma and exit at Val di Chiana. Turn right onto the Siena—Bettolle highway toward Siena and exit at Serre di Rapolano. Drive ahead to the city center. Park the car in Piazza XX Settembre from which Via Matteotti starts; Palazzo Bizzarri is on Via Matteotti, number 5.

CATEGORY: Caffèlletto ◆ **RATE:** ○○ ◆ *Member since 2001*

SINALUNGA (SI)

PODERE MENCOINI ⬩ **CASELLA POSTALE 52, I** ⬩ **53048 SINALUNGA, SIENA**
TEL. AND FAX +39 0577660132 ⬩ **E-MAIL: mencoini@inwind.it**

A country road winds up the hillside through a typically Tuscan landscape, shaded by oak trees, until it reaches this sun-mellowed brick house surrounded by olive groves. A medieval farmhouse, only a couple of miles from Sinalunga, the Podere Mencoini

is ideally situated at the crossroads between Tuscany and Umbria and is the perfect starting place to visit both. Once a simple manor house inhabited by those who used to be called peasants, the property was bought and restored by an English architect at the end of the 1980s. The lawns, lavender and rosemary bushes, creepers, and flower beds have a characteristically English flair. The interiors owe more to their present owners, who are contagiously in love with their Podere (farmhouse) and make an excellent olive oil from the two hundred trees growing on the estate. Sinalunga, three miles away, has everything one needs in terms of banks and shops, as well as a lively weekly market on Tuesdays, a swimming pool, and tennis courts. One of the most famous—and expensive—restaurants in Italy is La Locanda dell'Amorosa at Sinalunga, where courtyard concerts are held in the summer.

ROOMS: There are six doubles all with private bathrooms, simply and comfortably furnished. Some of the rooms open out onto the gardens. Closed from October 24 until March 27. Minimum stay two nights.

AMENITIES:
English, French, and German are spoken
Private parking
Swimming pool
Your host can arrange car and bicycle rentals
Children are welcome
Pets are not allowed

WHERE: The railway station is in Sinalunga, 3 miles away, while the airport is in Florence, 59 miles away. By car take highway A1 Milano–Roma, exit at Val di Chiana and take the highway to Siena for 25 miles. Here you will see on your left a big oak tree with a sign for the Podere Mencoini. Follow the dirt road for just under a mile.

CATEGORY: ✳✳✳✳ ⬩ **RATE:** ○○ ⬩ *Member since 1999*

MURLO (SI)

PODERE MONTORGIALINO ◆ **53016 MURLO, SIENA**
TEL. AND FAX +39 0577814373 ◆ **E-MAIL: info@montorgialino.com**

Only twelve miles from Siena, the Podere (farmhouse) of Montorgialino blends perfectly with the scenery. The old stone walls are the golden brown hue of the soil, where cypresses and olive groves, woods and undergrowth, and pin oaks and arbutus bushes grow. Geraniums and petunias offer splashes of bright color among the browns and greens, and the swimming pool is a veritable oasis.

Your hosts are a young couple with a young son. They only recently bought this property, built upon the site of a medieval church dedicated to Santa Margherita, and have decided to live here all year-round. They serve breakfast to guests in their own dining room or under the cool shade of the pergola.

ROOMS: All rooms have private entrances. There are three doubles, all with private bathrooms, television sets, and well-stocked refrigerators. There are also two apartments, the first with a double room, a bathroom, a sitting room, and a kitchen; and the second, with two double rooms, one single, a kitchen that doubles as a living/dining room, and an overhead loft with a sofa bed and a bathroom. Closed January 16 to February 19.

AMENITIES:
English and French are spoken
Parking on the premises
Private swimming pool
Dinner may be served on request
Pets are welcome

WHERE: Siena is 12 miles away and both Pienza and Montalcino are a short distance away. The railway station is in Buonconvento, 7 miles away, while the airport in Florence is 50 miles away. From Siena follow the Cassia road toward Rome until you come to a right turn for Vescovado di Murlo. From Vescovado take the road toward Buonconvento. After 2 miles there is a dirt road on the right with signs for Montorgialino.

CATEGORY: Caffèlletto ◆ **RATE: ○○○** ◆ *Member since 2000*

MONTEPULCIANO (SI)

CASALE DI POGGIANO ◆ **VIA DI POGGIANO 21** ◆ **53045 POGGIANO, SIENA**
TEL. +39 0578716446 ◆ **FAX +39 0578715231** ◆ **CELL +39 3282599729**
E-MAIL: casale-poggiano@libero.it

Montepulciano is the medieval home of the Vino Nobile, one of Tuscany's most noble wines. "Questo vino ha odore, calore e sapore", (This wine has bouquet, color, and flavor) said the Farnese Pope, Paul III .

Two miles from Montepulciano, this house with its simple facade covered in creepers has a spectacular view of the hilltop town from its garden of roses and flower beds. The rooms are attractively furnished and full of light. Few hosts are as enchanting as Montepulciano's, who prepares ample breakfasts featuring eggs on a "pillow" of bacon and freshly baked cakes every day. The house is ideally situated to visit the valley of the Orcia River, including the papal town of Pienza, San Quirico, Monticchiello, Montalcino, and the Abbey of Sant'Antimo.

ROOMS: One suite with two doubles that share a bathroom, and two doubles each with private bathrooms. In winter breakfast is served in the sitting room by the fireplace.

AMENITIES:
Open all year, except for New Year's Eve
French is spoken
Private parking
Pets are welcome

WHERE: The nearest railway station is in Chiusi, 15 miles away, while the airport is in Florence, 93 miles away. By car take highway AI Firenze–Roma and exit at Val di Chiana for those coming from the north, or at Chiusi for those coming from the south. Follow the signs for Montepulciano.

CATEGORY: ✳✳✳✳ ◆ **RATE:** ○○ ◆ *Member since 2001*

MONTEPULCIANO–
FATTORIA SAN MARTINO (SI)

VIA DI MARTIENA 3 ◆ 53045 MONTEPULCIANO, SIENA

TEL. AND FAX +39 0578717463 ◆ E-MAIL: sanmartino@montepulciano.com

In the heart of the Val d'Orcia, on a hilltop in the wine-producing country of Montepulciano, this farmhouse is an oasis of organic, biologically uncontaminated nature. The building itself and the furniture are examples of "bio-architecture"; even the electricity is monitored to exclude magnetic fields. Breakfasts benefit from the rigorously organic produce of your hosts' twelve acres of land, with homemade bread, jams, yogurt, and vegetarian cuisine. Your hosts themselves are a fascinating couple whose lifestyle, guests find, is wonderfully contagious.

ROOMS: Three large (each about 450 square feet), elegant, and colorfully decorated double rooms (the doors were once part of the local theater). The beds can be made into twins on request. Each room has a private bathroom (with shower).

AMENITIES:
English, German, French, and
  Dutch are spoken
Laundry service is available
Private parking
Swimming pool
Dinner may be served on request
Children under the age of two stay
  free of charge
Pets are welcome

WHERE: The nearest railway station is in Chiusi/Chianciano, 12 miles away, while the airport in Florence is about 62 miles away. By car take highway Firenze–Roma and exit at Chianciano. Continue toward Montepulciano. Here, turn right at the Esso Petrol Station and drive toward the bus station. Turn into Via di Martiena and, after the tennis court, take the first left, a dirt road, and follow the wooden signs toward the Fattoria San Martino.

CATEGORY: Caffèlletto ◆ **RATE:** ○○○ ◆ *Member since 2003*

LUCIGNANO D'ASSO (SI)

INFO: CAFFÈLLETTO, ITALY

TEL. +39 023311814 OR 1820 ◆ FAX +39 023313009 ◆ E-MAIL: info@caffelletto.it

Lucignanello takes the art of bed-and-breakfasts to a new level. This is not one villa, but a whole village housing guests in an atmosphere halfway between a Renaissance condominium, a lived-in museum, and the stage set of a period film. The crest over the stone archway leading into the old streets of the village is that of the Piccolomini family, who have given Italy two popes and were feudal patrons for centuries in this most beautiful and least-trodden part of Tuscany, the Val d'Asso. Not far away is Pienza, named after Pope Pius II Piccolomini, who was born here and who commissioned architect Bernardo Rossellino to transform this medieval town into an experiment in Renaissance urban planning. An hour away is Montepulciano, with its fourteenth-century palazzi dwarfing the narrow streets, and where, in many cellars, you can taste the Vino Nobile di Montepulciano. Around Montalcino, the famous Brunello wine is produced. The Abbey of Sant'Antimo just outside this town is one of the most awe-inspiring sights in Tuscany. The La Chiusa restaurant at Montefollonico is a short drive away for a memorable meal, and Siena itself is a comfortable day trip.

The Piccolomini family still owns this hamlet and has restored each of the houses preserving the original beams and terra-cotta floors, but introducing twentieth-century comfort as well as beautiful fabrics for the curtains and upholstery. The second swimming pool overlooks the valley.

ROOMS:

Casa Amedeo: In the large entrance hall there are two single beds. A spiral staircase leads to another large sitting room and dining room/kitchen where a huge fireplace dominates a whole wall. The two bedrooms, one double and one twin, each have their own bathroom (one with shower, the other with bathtub). As in the other three apartments, Casa Amedeo can house four to six guests.

Casa Remo: This house has a huge living/dining room/kitchen with an imposing fireplace. Three steps down lead into the two bedrooms, a double room with a bathroom (with shower) and a twin with bathroom (with bathtub). This is one of three houses with ornate frescoes covering the walls.

Casa Clementina: The hall with its comfortable sofa could easily serve as a third bedroom. A few steps lead up to the sitting room (also with a fireplace), which leads into the dining room and kitchen area. There are two bedrooms, one double and one twin, both with their own bathrooms.

Casa Severino: Two bedrooms, a double and a twin, one bathroom, a large kitchen/dining room, and a small private garden. Minimum stay three nights.

AMENITIES:

English is spoken
Laundry service is available
Parking on the premises
Swimming pool
Your hosts can organize a taxi
    service to pick up guests in Rome,
    Pisa, or Florence
Children under the age of two
    stay free of charge
Pets are welcome

WHERE: The Buonconvento railway station is 8 miles away, while the airport in Florence is 31 miles away.

CATEGORY: **Caffelletto** ✦ RATE: ○○○ ✦ *Member since 1999*

COSONA (SI)

INFO: CAFFÈLLETTO, ITALY

TEL. +39 023311814 OR 1820 · FAX +39 023313009 · E-MAIL: info@caffelletto.it

This large historic estate extends over the hills below Siena, six miles from Pienza, the tiny Renaissance town designed by Pope Pius II Piccolomini in the fifteenth century. The valley of the Orcia River is a part of Tuscany forgotten by the twentieth century, with narrow roads winding through fields of wheat and small sleepy towns. Their churches and museums contain some of the most important works of art of the Trecento.

This is also an important wine growing area. In Montepulciano—a small medieval town with imposing palaces and the famous Pulcinella bell tower—you can taste the Vino Nobile in the wine bars. For one of the most beloved red wines in Italy, you can go to Montalcino and sample the local Brunello. Nearby, the Abbey of Sant'-Antimo—a monastery dating from the twelfth century and one of the most beautiful of its kind in the world—is still occupied by monks, and Gregorian chants can be heard coming from its luminous pale-yellow interior every day at lunchtime. At the center of the estate is this splendid villa, still in family hands, with its old walls covered in Virginia creeper, a tower that dominates the valley, a walled garden, and the family chapel. The interior is in keeping with the magnificent exterior.

ROOMS: Near the villa two ancient poderi (farmhouses) have recently been restored in good taste. The Podere Il Poggiolo has a large living room with fireplace; dining room, three double rooms, two twins, and a single; three bathrooms; and a kitchen. The Podere La Cappella has a large sitting room with a fireplace and kitchenette, three

double rooms with private bathrooms, and a small sitting room en suite with a bedroom. From the gardens there is a fabulous view toward Mount Amiata and the Val d'Orcia. Minimum stay two nights.

AMENITIES:
English, French, and German are spoken
Private parking

WHERE: The railway station is in Buonconvento, 9 miles away, while the nearest airport is in Florence, 50 miles away.

CATEGORY: ✹✹✹✹ · **RATE:** ◯◯ · *Member since 1998*

CETONA (SI)

INFO: CAFFÈLLETTO, ITALY

TEL. +39 023311814 OR 1820 ◆ FAX +39 023313009 ◆ E-MAIL: info@caffelletto.it

This typically Tuscan country house is between Chiusi and Cetona in the middle of one of the most beautiful and unspoiled landscapes of the region. There is nothing ordinary about the interior, however, as both your hosts are antique dealers and have had the courage and flair to juggle styles and centuries to create an exciting and harmonious environment. The garden is a fragrant profusion of lavender, rosemary, and rosebushes. On one side is the swimming pool and on the other, the remains of an Etruscan tomb. This is the heart of ancient Etruria, where the famous tombs and the Archaeological Museum of Chiusi are nearby. In the warmer months breakfast is served under a leafy arbor.

ROOMS: There are three rooms: the Camera dei Fiori (the Flower Room), with a double bed, third bed, and a bathroom (with shower); the Camera delle Nuvole (the Cloud Room), with a double bed that can be separated into twins on request, the option of a third bed, and a bathroom (with shower); lastly, there is the Romantic Suite, with brocade hangings, a sitting room with a third bed, and a bathroom (with shower). All the rooms have private entrances on the ground floor and all open onto the garden. Minimum stay two nights.

AMENITIES:
Open all year except for the month of January
French and some English are spoken
Laundry service is available
Parking on the premises
Swimming pool

WHERE: The nearest railway station is in Chiusi, 2 miles away, while the airport is in Florence, 74 miles away.

CATEGORY: Caffèlletto ◆ **RATE:** ○○○ ◆ *Member since 2001*

PAGANICO (GR)

PODERE SANTO STEFANO ◆ **58048 PAGANICO, GROSSETO**
TEL. AND FAX +39 0564902102 ◆ **E-MAIL: info@poderesantostefano.it**

The Podere Santo Stefano is in one of the most magical corners of Tuscany. Built as a convent in the 1500s, the Podere also served as a resting place for travelers on their way from Siena to the sea. Today it is a country house, only thirty-one miles from Siena, close to the Val d'Orcia and the wine country of Brunello di Montalcino and Montepulciano. The local wine, the Montecucco, has recently been awarded the DOC (a label guaranteeing the quality and origin of a wine). Your hostess, after many years of working in a bank, has realized a lifetime's aspiration to live and work in the country. An accomplished cook, she has created a restaurant under the loggia where breakfasts are served and locals come for dinner and to listen to jazz. Guests are also welcome to use the library.

ROOMS: A total of six rooms that include two doubles, one with a cot, the other with a third bed, both with bathrooms (with shower). There is also a twin room and a single, both with bathrooms (with shower) and a small sitting room with a fireplace. In a separate building, there are two rooms that share a terrace with an independent entrance, one with its own small sitting room and bathroom (with shower), the other with a special bathroom for handicapped guests.

AMENITIES:
English is spoken
Laundry service is available
Private parking
Children under the age of two stay
  free of charge

WHERE: The nearest railway station is in Paganico, 3 miles away, while the airport in Florence is 89 miles away. By car take highway SS 223 Siena–Grosseto and exit at Paganico. Take the Cipressino road toward Monte Amiata. Continue for three miles until you see the sign on the right for Podere Santo Stefano. After less than a mile on a dirt road, you will see the gate to the house.

CATEGORY: ✳✳✳✳ ◆ **RATE**: ○○ ◆ *Member since 2003*

ORBETELLO (GR)

INFO: CAFFÈLLETTO, ITALY

TEL. +39 023311814 OR 1820 ✦ **FAX +39 023313009** ✦ **E-MAIL: info@caffelletto.it**

At the southern tip of the wild Maremma region along the coast of Tuscany is Orbetello, with its famous lagoon and Wild Life Reserve. The Torre Vecchia (Old Tower) is a fascinating old house built in the seventeenth century and surrounded by olive trees and cypresses. There are not one but three gardens on all sides of the house, each more luxurious than the next, with rosebushes, lavender, and fragrant creepers. There is also an inviting pool at the end of a perfectly manicured English lawn.

Orbetello is near the coast and the resorts of Argentario and the beach of Feniglia are nearby. From the jet-set ports of Santo Stefano and Porto Ercole, boats leave for the lovely island of Giglio. This is the heart of ancient Etruscan civilization and the sites of Vulci and Tarquinia are only forty-five minutes away. For thirty years this was a holiday home but your hosts, the husband from an old Genovese family and his French wife, now live here all year-round. Breakfasts are ample and delicious, served outside under an arbor in the warmer months and in the large kitchen in winter.

ROOMS: Two double rooms, both with private bathroom (with bathtub and shower) and one double and one twin-bedded room, that share a bathroom with bathtub. One

of the rooms has a beautiful terrace of its own. In the tower there is a large double room (with the option of a third bed) and a bathroom with shower. Minimum stay two nights.

AMENITIES:
Open from March to November,
*   except for the month of August*
English and French are spoken
Private parking
Swimming pool

WHERE: The nearest railway station is in Orbetello Scalo, 3 miles away, while the airport in Rome is 89 miles away.

CATEGORY: Caffèlletto ✦ **RATE:** ○○ ✦ *Member since 2003*

PIETRASANTA (LU)

RESIDENZA VISDOMINI ◆ **VIA STAGIO STAGI, 83** ◆ **55045 PIETRASANTA, LUCCA**

TEL. +39 058470479 ◆ **FAX +39 0584283277** ◆ **CELL +39 3473863645**

E-MAIL: residenzavisdomini@libero.it

Since the time of Michelangelo, Pietrasanta has been a center of art, artists, and artisans. The streets are lined with workshops with slabs of marble in their yards like packs of cards, while internationally famous sculptors come here to create monuments and masterpieces. In recent years art galleries and trendy restaurants have sprung up in the center of the town.

The Residenza Visdomini is right in the heart of Pietrasanta, and is a bed-and-breakfast that combines the luxury of a first-class hotel with the warmth of a sophisticated home. As is to be expected, the bathrooms are all in marble, as are the original checkerboard floors of the large and quite lovely kitchen, with its fireplace, copper pans, and long wooden table. There is a romantic garden behind the house with a covered veranda where guests may have breakfast in the warmer months, and a swimming pool is in the planning stage.

Your impeccable hosts are two young women, Sabrina and Patrizia, whose professionalism and charm are evident in every feature of this bed-and-breakfast.

ROOMS: On the ground floor there is a double room with a large bathroom and Jacuzzi tub. On the upper floors four large, elegant suites, all with double bedroom and bathroom with shower, sitting room with double sofa bed, and hall with a little kitchen. In the loft is a romantic double room with a kitchen corner and adjacent bathroom. All rooms are furnished with antiques and have air conditioning, and on the ground floor there is a sitting room with fireplace.

AMENITIES:
English and German are spoken
Private parking
Children under the age of two stay free of charge
Pets are welcome

WHERE: The railway station is at 400 yards away, while the Pisa airport is 18 miles away. By car take highway A12 and exit at Versilia. Continue toward Pietrasanta, and the palazzo is in the historic center just near the Piazza del Mercato on Via Stagi.

CATEGORY: Caffelletto ◆ **RATE:** ○○—○○○○ ◆ *Member since 2004*

UMBRIA

Umbria is a landlocked region in central Italy crossed by the Apennines in the east. The towns and villages of this region are found either on hilltops or clinging to hillsides, commanding splendid views of wooded valleys and the snow-topped Sibillini Mountains. A notable exception is Foligno, where the first printed edition of Dante's *Divine Comedy* was produced, nestled alone in the valley.

Umbria is irrigated by the Tiber and the Nera rivers and in the west by Lake Trasimeno, where Castiglione is perched at an enviable position on a rocky promontory. Umbria is surrounded by several culturally rich cities such as Perugia, Orvieto, Todi, Spoleto (home of the Festival of Two Worlds), and Gubbio, with its medieval charm and folklore (the Corsa dei Ceri is held there every year on May 15). Also nearby is Assisi, whose art historical treasures remain intact despite recent earthquakes.

Although less sought-after than Tuscany, it is difficult to say which of the two regions is the more beautiful. Many discerning tourists and prospective house-seekers have shifted their attention to Umbria's natural beauty and artistic heritage. Artisanship is flourishing here, especially in Deruta—since 1487 a world capital of

ceramics. Umbria also has a rich gastronomic tradition. The mysterious black Umbrian truffle found around Spoleto is a prized delicacy and some of the region's best white wines are produced in Orvieto.

THE LOCAL RECIPE

Umbria borders with Tuscany and its food has much in common with its neighboring region. Pork products (salami, ham, etc.) are probably among the best in Italy, and Umbria is also the primary producer of tartufi neri (black truffles)—the ones from Norcia are renowned for their particular flavor. The extremely delicate and tiny lentils from Castelluccio are also very popular. Their color is a brownish-red and their flavor is fresh and slightly sweet.

Castelluccio Lentil Soup

Ingredients (serves 4)

12 oz. lentils
1 carrot
1 shallot
1 small leek
3 parsley sprigs
1 bay leaf

3 cherry tomatoes
2 oz. diced pancetta (bacon)
1 tsp. sugar
4 tbsp. olive oil
cayenne pepper and salt to taste

Wash, trim, and dice all the vegetables. Place them in a pan along with the olive oil, cayenne pepper, and pancetta. Sauté for three to four minutes, then add the parsley, bay leaf, cherry tomatoes, and lentils. Mix and season with salt and sugar. Pour in six cups hot water (or vegetable broth), cover, and simmer on a low flame for about forty minutes, or until the lentils are soft but still hold their shape.

BOVARA DI TREVI–SPOLETO (PG)

CASA GIULIA ◆ **SS. FLAMINIA KM 140** ◆ **06039 BOVARA DI TREVI**
TEL. +39 074278257 ◆ **FAX +39 0742381632**

An ideal starting point from which to visit Spoleto, Perugia, and Assisi, this welcoming and comfortable seventeenth-century house is surrounded by a well-tended

garden of plants and trees and a lovely swimming pool. Your hostess, Alessandrini Petrucci, worked for many years in the fashion industry and her sense of style is evident in the design and decor of her family house. Beautiful old floors and carefully chosen pieces of furniture with matching upholstery create an atmosphere of elegance and sophistication.

ROOMS: Seven double rooms with private bathrooms: one apartment for two and another for three. Minimum stay three nights.

AMENITIES:
English is spoken
Private parking
Swimming pool
Dinner parties and classical
  music concerts may
  be organized
Children under the age of two
  stay free of charge

WHERE: To reach Casa Giulia by car take SS Flaminia Foligno–Spoleto; after 87 miles you will find Bovara di Trevi. From here follow the directions to Casa Giulia. The casa is 7 miles from Spoleto, 13 miles from Assisi, and 24 miles from Todi.

CATEGORY: ✳✳✳✳ ◆ **RATE:** ⦾⦾ ◆ *Member since 1998*

POGGIO D'ASPROLI (PG)

INFO: CAFFÈLLETTO, ITALY

TEL. +39 023311814 OR 1820 • **FAX +39 023313009** • **E-MAIL: info@caffelletto.it**

A short distance from Todi, this romantic little farmhouse is tucked away in a secluded corner of the countryside. The house has been restored by two Neapolitans, a father and daughter, who have taken it upon themselves to build a home in Umbria that would remind them of their own on the Bay of Naples.

The stone walls are brightened by a trellis climbing with blood-orange flowers in summer and autumn, the months when guests will likely be tempted to dine outside. A fragrant garden of rosebushes, lavender, and rosemary surrounds the house. Discreetly hidden by greenery, a swimming pool is available for hotter days. Inside, there is an elegant living/dining room with stone walls, terra-cotta floors, antique furniture, and a centerpiece fireplace where guests may gather on winter evenings. The bedrooms have beamed ceilings and cheerful chintz upholstery, while the most romantic of all has a four-poster bed covered in white piqué. Largely unspoiled, Umbria offers a plethora of different villages and historic cities, including Assisi, Perugia, and Todi, only five miles away.

A winding side road (which can be toured by bicycle) offers panoramic views of the countryside leading to Montefalco, a small town on a hilltop overlooking an expanse of vineyards as far as the eye can see. The excellent wine, Sagrantino of Montefalco, is produced here. In Montefalco household linens are still made from handwoven linen and cotton. Eleven miles away in Deruta is the most famous ceramics factory in Italy, while at Torgiano, seventeen miles away, you can visit an interesting wine museum.

ROOMS: Six double rooms (all the beds can be divided into twin beds on request), each with its own bathroom. In two of the rooms a third bed may be added. Closed from January 6 until March 15.

AMENITIES:
English, French, and German are spoken
Parking on the premises
Swimming pool
Dinner is served on request
Children under the age of two stay free of charge

WHERE: The nearest airport is Rome, 93 miles away and the railway station is Todi-Ponterio at 6 miles away.

CATEGORY: Caffèlletto • **RATE:** ○○ • *Member since 1999*

TENUTA DI CANONICA (PG)

INFO: CAFFÈLLETTO, ITALY

TEL. +39 023311814 OR 1820 ◆ FAX +39 023313009 ◆ E-MAIL: info@caffelletto.it

For the same arbitrary reasons that a restaurant not visibly different from any other restaurant on the street suddenly becomes all the rage, Todi, a delightful medieval town in Umbria, has become a center for expatriates, especially from America. This, however, is not why Daniele and Maria, the owners of Tenuta di Canonica, decided to restore this magnificent manor house, which is part Roman, part medieval, gentrified but untamed.

Your hosts have preserved the core character of the estate, which still possesses its original thick stone walls and loggia, as well as lawns that slope down to the pool, and splendid antiques from the attics of parents and grandparents. All the rooms have a charm of their own, whether it's the view, a romantic four-poster bed, or a welcoming alcove in one of the corners. Maria is not only a delightful hostess; she is a professor of art history and offers guests precious guidance for their cultural itineraries as well as more frivolous advice regarding shopping, especially for handwoven Umbrian textiles. The estate is surrounded by a rolling green countryside ideal for walks, riding, or mountain biking to and around Todi, the valley of the Tiber, and Lake Corbara. At the end of the day, guests can enjoy delicious bread or fresh pasta. Breakfasts include homemade cakes and pastries.

ROOMS: Eight standard rooms, eight doubles, and three junior suites, all with air-conditioning and private bathrooms. Two independent apartments. Minimum stay two nights. Closed from December 16 until January 15.

AMENITIES:
English is spoken
Dinner is served upon request
Swimming pool
Parking on the premises
Children under the age of three stay free of charge

WHERE: The nearest airport is in Rome, 62 miles away, while the railway station is Todi, 3 miles away. By car from Rome take highway A1 (Roma–Milano), and exit at Orte. Take the road for Perugia–Cesena (E 45), exit at Todi–Orvieto; follow signs for Orvieto (2 miles), after about 12 miles turn in the direction of Prodo–Titignagno. After 2 miles at the crossroads for Cordigliano, turn left where you will see the sign for Tenuta di Canonica, and after about a mile you will reach the house. From Milan or Florence, take highway A1 (Milano–Roma), and exit at Orvieto, follow SS 448 Todi–Lago di Corbara for twelve miles, then turn left at the crossroads for Prodo–Titignagno. After two miles at the crossroads for Cordigliano, turn left where you will see the sign for Tenuta di Canonica, and about a mile you will reach the house.

CATEGORY: Caffèlletto ◆ **RATE:** ○○○ ◆ *Member since 1999*

DOGLIO (TR)

INFO: CAFFÈLLETTO, ITALY

TEL. +39 023311814 OR 1820 ◆ **FAX +39 023313009** ◆ **E-MAIL: info@caffelletto.it**

In silver-gray stone, in tune with the gray trunks and the silvery leaves of the olive trees that shade it, this country house stands in a typical Umbrian landscape among rocky hillsides at the end of winding lanes. This farmhouse, dating back to the seventeenth

century, produces excellent olive oil. When your hosts are in residence they live in the main part of the house. Two wings have been prepared to welcome guests, with the bedrooms on one side and the sitting room, library, and playroom on the other, overlooking the translucent blue of the swimming pool. All you might want for breakfast can be found in the individual apartments. Your hosts run various aspects of the tourist business and will have no difficulty assisting guests in planning their itineraries, whether to the nearby Todi or Perugia, or farther afield.

ROOMS: Four apartments: one accommodates four people, which can stretch to sleep six; one for three; and two for two people. The first has two double rooms, one with an overhead loft with room for two; two bathrooms (with shower), a sitting room with a large fireplace and a kitchen corner. The apartment for three has a double room with a third bed, a bathroom (with shower), and a small sitting room with a kitchen corner. The apartments for two overlook the swimming pool and have a double room, a sitting room with kitchenette, and a bathroom (with shower). Minimum stay four nights.

AMENITIES:

Open from March through October
English and French are spoken
Private parking
Swimming pool
Children under the age of two stay free of charge
Small pets are welcome

WHERE: The nearest railway station is in Todi, 6 miles away, while the Perugia airport is 21 miles away.

CATEGORY: ✳✳✳✳ ◆ RATE: ○○ ◆ *Member since 2002*

ORVIETO (TR)

INFO: CAFFÈLLETTO, ITALY

TEL. +39 023311814 OR 1820 ◆ **FAX +39 023313009** ◆ **E-MAIL: info@caffelletto.it**

This is the perfect vacation getaway for those who love horses. Your hosts' daughter, Camilla, is already an expert horsewoman. Guests can ride all day long through woods, sunflower fields or fallow fields with grazing sheep, or in the indoor and out-

door riding ring. Horses are bred and trained here for equestrian events and the owners run a pony club for children, with courses all summer long. The eighteenth-century stone country house is three miles from Bolsena with a view of Lake Bolsena, where those less inclined to ride horses can practice windsurfing or canoeing. Orvieto, with the famous Duomo and majolica pottery shops, is only nine miles away. Even closer is the enchanting ancient hamlet of Civita di Bagnoregio. Breakfast, including homemade cakes and jams, is served in the large dining room, once a stable with the original stone floors and vaulted ceilings.

ROOMS: On the ground floor there is a double room with private bathroom and French windows opening onto the garden. From the garden there is an independent entrance to two more double rooms, both with their own bathrooms. Both rooms are on two levels: the first has two beds and is on the ground floor, and a double bed on the upper level, while the second has two beds on the ground floor and three upstairs; all have wood floors and tiles from the famous workshop of Vietri. Minimum stay two nights.

AMENITIES:

English, French, and Spanish are spoken
Private parking
Swimming pool
Dinner may be served on request
If required, a car service can pick up
*   guests and take them to the airport*
Children under the age of two stay
*   free of charge*
Pets are welcome

WHERE: The nearest railway station is in Orvieto, 10 miles away, while the airport is in Rome, about 68 miles away.

CATEGORY: ✳✳✳✳ ◆ **RATE:** ○○ ◆ *Member since 2000*

SPEDALICCHIO (PG)

CHIESA PAGANO B&B ◆ **STRADA VICINALE ROCCA DI RASINA**
06019 SPEDALICCHIO UMBERTIDE, PERUGIA
TEL. AND FAX +39 0759410730 ◆ **CELL +39 3381404832** ◆ **E-MAIL: chiesapagano@tiscali.it**

Perugia, Assisi, Gubbio, Cortona, and Sansepolcro are all between approximately twenty and forty miles away, although on this hill-top on the border between the provinces of Arezzo and Perugia one has the feeling of being alone with nature. The grandiose view spans out on all sides over woods, fields, and olive groves. Built in stone in the fifteenth century, the old farmhouse was a ruin until your architect host and his English wife restored it to its sumptuous present state. Some of the antiques and artefacts in the stylish interiors are from the far East.

The landscaping of the garden has recently been improved with many cypress trees, olive trees, lavender, and rosemary bushes. A large terrace provides a great view of the valley, sloping down to the lawn and the swimming pool, hewn out of rock with the blue water soothingly spilling over one side. Breakfast features, among other things, fresh fruit and warm croissants served outside in the garden or in a lovely room leading out to it.

ROOMS: Four double rooms on the ground floor, two of which have a small veranda, and each with its own bathroom with shower. On the first floor a double room with bathroom and shower, and two suites. One is a double room with a bathroom and shower and a loft with a third bed. The second has a double room and adjacent single room plus a bathroom with shower. Available from Easter to November 4, and from December 26 to January 7. All rooms have air conditioning, heating, satellite TV, telephone, frigobar, a safe, and a hairdryer. The building is not suited for the accommodation of children.

AMENITIES:
English, French, and German are spoken
Private parking
Swimming pool
Cold meals may be prepared on request

WHERE: The nearest railway station is in Terontola, 20 miles away, while the Perugia airport is 22 miles away. Guests will need a car here. By car, from the North, take highway AI and exit at Val di Chiana. Take the Bettole/Perugia road and exit at Tuoro. Continue toward Umbertide on SS 416 until Spedalicchio. Immediately after the bar turn left and drive up a road that becomes a gravel road for a half mile until you reach Chiesa Pagano. From the South, take highway AI and exit at Orte, take route E 45 and exit at Umbertide, then the SS 416 until Spedalicchio. Then turn right before the bar.

CATEGORY: Caffèlletto ◆ **RATE:** ○○○—○○○○ ◆ *Member since 2004*

NARNI (TR)

INFO: CAFFÈLLETTO, ITALY
TEL. +39 023311814 OR 1820 ♦ **FAX +39 023313009** ♦ **E-MAIL: info@caffelletto.it**

This house reflects the heart and soul of Umbria, its old sand-colored stone blending perfectly into the countryside. A new endeavor, this bed-and-breakfast is full of promise; an irrigation system ensures glossy green lawns leading down to the inviting swimming pool. The house has been carefully restored, preserving its original character and structure. It is furnished with valuable antiques and tapestries from the ancient San Leucio weaving mill, and enhanced by the old terra-cotta floors and the beamed ceilings. Your hostess offers a wine tasting to mark your arrival. The house is conveniently located for day trips to the many historical towns of the area. Each room features all you might need for breakfast, including homemade cakes and biscuits.

ROOMS: Six apartments, each different from the other, four for four people, one for two, and one for five. Large sitting rooms with kitchen corners, double rooms in the overhead lofts, and bathrooms (with showers). In the five-person apartment the double has a single bed in the overhead loft. Minimum stay two nights except during Christmas, Easter time, and in August, when it is four nights.

AMENITIES:
English and some French are spoken
Laundry service is available
Private parking
Swimming pool
Decoration, ceramic, riding, and yoga
  courses can be organized on request
  for a minimum of five people
Pets are not allowed

WHERE: The nearest railway station is in Narni Scalo, 3 miles away, while Rome's airport is 80 miles away.

CATEGORY: Caffèlletto ♦ **RATE:** ○○ ♦ *Member since 2002*

THE MARCHES

The Marches extend inland from the Adriatic coast toward the center of Italy and comprise part of the Apennine range. This is a region of dramatic beauty, and, until recently, was relatively undiscovered and consequently unspoiled. It has a varied landscape with peaks as high as 6,600 feet belonging to the Sibillini Mountains, contrasting with lush valleys around the bed of the Chienti River. One of the major area attractions is the breathtaking Romanesque abbey of Santa Maria Piè di Chienti.

Ancona, the capital city, is on the coast; the other main cities are Ascoli Piceno, Macerata, Pesaro, and Urbino, the birthplace of Raphael. Fabriano was for centuries a thriving center for the manufacture of paper, and a medieval workshop has been preserved at the Museo della Carta e della Filigrana (Museum of Paper and Filigree), where handmade paper is still produced. The most beautiful part of the coast is dominated by Mount Conero, its slopes covered in holm oak groves and Mediterranean maquis, with little bays and rocky coves such as the famous Spiaggia delle Due Sorelle (Beach of the Two Sisters).

The people of the Marches are hardworking and when they relocate to other regions of Italy, it is their farmhouses that stand out from the landscape, characterized by well-tended plots and stucco walls. It is the Marchigiani who get up at dawn to

tend neat rows of tomatoes or pick fruit from trees. But they are not only active agriculturally; industrially they have emerged as an important entity—world leaders in leather manufacture, especially shoes. Diego della Valle, who has shoe boutiques all over the world, for instance, is from the Marches.

THE LOCAL RECIPE

A delicious hors d'oeuvre from this region is stuffed green olives (deep-fried green olives stuffed with meat). Among first courses, a sumptuous dish is vincisgrassi, a mysteriously named pasta pie reminiscent of lasagna from the nearby Emilia–Romagna. Fresh fish abounds in the Marches and is always prepared simply and tastily. Vino cotto, typical of the Marches, is obtained by boiling the must of grapes, though white wine and sherry can be used as a substitute.

Chicken Braised in Vino Cotto (cooked wine)

Ingredients (serves 4)

1 chicken cut into 8 pieces	1 green bell pepper
2 oz. diced bacon	1 bay leaf
1 cup vino cotto	1 sprig of rosemary
3 tbsp. olive oil	1 tsp. tomato paste
1 diced onion	salt and pepper to taste

In a frying pan, sauté the chicken, onion, and bacon, along with the rosemary and bay leaf, in the olive oil. Wash and trim the pepper, cut it into strips, and add it to the pan with the tomato paste. Pour in the vino cotto and let it evaporate for three minutes on a high flame. Season with salt and pepper, cover, and reduce heat to moderate. Cook for about 35 minutes.

CASTELRAIMONDO (MC)

IL GIARDINO DEGLI ULIVI ◦ 62022 CASTELRAIMONDO
TEL. +39 0737642121 ◦ FAX +39 0737640441 OR +39 0737642600

Il Giardino degli Ulivi (The Olive Garden) is situated on the slopes of Mount Gemmo at a height of almost 4,000 feet and commands a spectacular view on all sides of the valley of the Potenza River. A winding road leads up the mountainside lined with

ancient oaks to the tiny hamlet with its romantic old church tower surrounding the house. Il Giardino degli Ulivi has been restored by the owners, a father and daughter. Both are architects, and their expertise and flair as well as a profound love for their house are evident in innumerable details. The old stone paving in front of the house, for instance, has been laid out to resemble a furrowed field. Inside they have tried to respect as much as possible the house's original style. One of the rooms in daily use was once the place where freshly harvested olives were pressed. The dining room with its large fireplace is particularly impressive; here you may want to sample the sophisticated cuisine of your hostess, as do gourmets from all over the area who come to enjoy her regional menus with a highly personal touch. Even the breakfast is in a class all its own with freshly made ricotta cheese and homemade honey from the local acacia bushes.

Il Giardino degli Ulivi is near the village of Castelraimondo and a short distance from many local landmarks, such as Tolentino, home of the splendid church of San Nicola. Also nearby are San Severino and Fabriano, both places infrequently mentioned on the average tourist's route but, like so many small Italian towns, full of cultural and artistic surprises. The abbeys of Santa Maria Piè di Chienti and Treia are also relatively nearby. The landscape lends itself to bicycling or mountain-bike tours.

ROOMS: Six double rooms each with private bath, all in the unique style of the rest of the house, especially the bedrooms with arched windows.

AMENITIES:
English is spoken
Private parking
Dinner is served on request

WHERE: The railway of Castelraimondo is 5 miles away and the Ancona Falconara airport is 37 miles away. From Ancona take the highway to Fabriano, exit at Matelica and follow signs to Castelraimondo.

CATEGORY: ✳✳✳✳ ◦ **RATE:** ◯◯ ◦ *Member since 1998*

MONTEFORTINO (AP)

FRAZIONE PRETATTONI 6 ◆ 63047 MONTEFORTINO, ASCOLI PICENO
TEL. +39 0736859167 ◆ E-MAIL: info@tenutarossibrunori.it

Montefortino, like many tiny townships in The Marches, clings to a hillside surrounded by woodland. The fifty-acre garden of this handsome stone house follows the contours of the hillside. Interspersed with age-old trees, the property is crisscrossed

by paths where guests can take a variety of walks.

The house has been completely restored by your host with the help of his wife, who lives here all year-round. Breakfasts are abundant: homemade cakes and jams, honey from their own beehives, fresh eggs from the barnyard, ricotta cheese, and fruit from their trees. Your hostess is an exceptional cook and is always ready to share some of her regional recipes with guests. Guests are also welcome to participate in the picking of the fruit and harvesting of the grapes and in the preparation of jams, jellies, syrups, and chutneys.

The rooms are palatial, comfortable, and above all panoramic. In Montefortino guests feel pampered and well tended to. Everything, including the surrounding untamed nature, seems in league with making guests feel at home.

ROOMS: The wing reserved for guests has a dining room and a well-equipped kitchen. There is a studio on the ground floor with a sitting room. On the floor above, there is a double room with a bathroom (with bathtub). A second double room has a small adjoining sitting room and a bathroom (with shower). All are furnished with family antiques. Open from April 18 until December 31.

AMENITIES:
English and French are spoken
Parking on the premises
Dinner may be served depending on your hostess's
  commitments
Your hostess is also prepared to organize gastronomic
  and cultural tours of the region

WHERE: The nearest railway station is San Benedetto del Tronto, 37 miles away, while Ancona airport is 74 miles away. Take highway A14 and exit at Fermo–Porto San Giorgio. Take SS 210 to Amandola then follow the directions for Comunanza. At the end of the town turn right after one mile onto a dirt road and follow the signs for Barello–Vena. Drive up; at the first crossroads, turn left, at the second, turn right, then continue for about half a mile until you arrive at the gate.

CATEGORY: Caffèlletto ◆ **RATE:** ○○○ ◆ *Member since 2001*

CUPRA MARITTIMA (AP)

INFO: CAFFÈLLETTO, ITALY

TEL. +39 023311814 OR 1820 ◆ FAX +39 023313009 ◆ E-MAIL: info@caffelletto.it

Cupra Marittima in the Marches is by the sea but its main attraction is undoubtedly this castle of Marano and its surrounding medieval walled hamlet. The gardens with their age-old trees and climbing bushes ramble down toward the sea, while the courtyard is full of flowering tubs and pots lovingly tended to by the caretakers, who take equally good care of guests. The bedroom is covered with frescoes and furnished with family antiques in keeping with the style of the castle. Breakfast is served in the cozy adjacent sitting room complete with a fireplace. Near Cupra Marittima are the famous seaside resorts of Porto San Giorgio, San Benedetto del Tronto, and Grottammare, while there is also much to visit in the hinterland. Next

door to the castle itself is a fourteenth-century church and a palazzo that once belonged to the Sforza family, both of which are open to the public.

ROOMS: A double room with a bathroom (with shower), adjoining sitting room, and private entrance. Closed February and December. Minimum stay two nights.

AMENITIES:
English and French are spoken
Private parking

WHERE: The nearest railway station is San Benedetto del Tronto, 10 miles away, while the airport is in Ancona, 50 miles away.

CATEGORY: **Caffèlletto** ◆ RATES: ○○ ◆ *Member since 2001*

FANO (PU)

VIA DI VILLA GIULIA · LOC. SAN BIAGIO · 61032 FANO, PESARO-URBINO
TEL. AND FAX +39 0721823159 · E-MAIL: INFO@RELAISVILLAGIULIA.COM

Villa Giulia is set in a lush Mediterranean park of pines, cypresses, oaks, beeches, palm trees, oleander, and agaves, with a rare outcrop of bamboo and a variety of flowers. This spacious country residence is the equivalent of an English stately home in the Italian Marches, with its tower, chapel, and terrace looking toward the sea.

Guests have the run of the frescoed salons, terraces, and three gardens, while a path through the olive grove leads to the swimming pool. The bedroom frescoes were expertly painted by your hostess, Countess Passi. Her family has owned this magnificent summer home for generations, and she lives here year round. The villa is furnished with family antiques, and breakfast is served in the garden or dining room.

Fano, Pesaro, and Urbino are all a short drive away, the wide sandy beaches along the Adriatic are less than a mile away, and the surrounding countryside is studded with medieval villages and *trattorie* serving excellent local cuisine.

ROOMS: Two suites and four double rooms. The Blue Suite (double) has a sitting room with sofa bed, and a bathroom with tub/shower. The Coretto Suite (double) has a sitting room, a single room, a bathroom, and a terrace. The Impero Room can be a double or twin. The Yellow Room has a balcony, the Viceré (double) has a bathroom with tub/shower, and the Tower Room (double) in a small tower with bathroom. In the adjacent farmhouse are two romantic studios with double bedrooms, kitchen corner, and bathroom; on the first floor are two double bedrooms with a view of the sea and en suite bathrooms with tub/shower. All the rooms have a hairdryer, shower, and minibar. Minimum stay two nights; in July and August minimum stay five nights.

AMENITIES:
English, French, and German are spoken
Children until the age of two stay free of charge
Private parking
Swimming pool
Candlelight dinners on the terrace over the sea
Pets are welcome

WHERE: The nearest railway station is in Fano, 2 miles away, while the nearby airports are in Ancona, 31 miles away, Rimini, 15 miles away, or Forlì, 37 miles away. By car take the A14 highway and exit at Fano. Drive toward Fano, and from the town center take SS16 (the Adriatica route) toward Pesaro. Continue straight until on the left you will see Via di Villa San Biagio and the signs for Villa Giulia. From here follow the directions on the map that you will find on our Web site.

CATEGORY: **Caffelletto** · **RATE**: ○○—○○○ · *Member since 2005*

SAN BENEDETTO DEL TRONTO–
HISTORIC CENTER (AP)

LOCANDA DI PORTA ANTICA ◆ **PIAZZA DANTE ALIGHIERI 7**
63039 SAN BENEDETTO DEL TRONTO, ASCOLI PICENO
TEL. +39 0735576632 ◆ **FAX +39 0735576631**

San Benedetto del Tronto is in the Marches thirty-seven miles from Ancona on the Riviera delle Palme, so named after the many florid palm trees growing along the sea front. On the terrace of the Locanda di Porta Antica, guests may breakfast overlooking the sea and the ancient twelfth-century Gualtieri Tower. San Benedetto del

Tronto is a famous sea resort and its fish market is well worth a visit, as is the Fishing Museum. Only three miles away is the world's largest collection of shells and coral at Cupra Marittima.

The locanda is a sixteenth-century palazzo, which your hosts have completely renovated. The rooms are decorated with a distinctive verve, and it is your hostess who personally looks after guests. Breakfasts feature fresh pastries every morning.

ROOMS: Two double rooms with a lovely terrace overlooking the square, two twin rooms, and one single; all with private baths (with shower), television set, and safe.

AMENITIES:
English and French are spoken
Laundry service is available
Dinner may be served on request
Small pets are welcome

WHERE: The nearest railway station is San Benedetto del Tronto, a half-mile away, while the airport of Ancona Falconara is 43 miles away. By car take highway A14 Bologna–Bari and exit at Grottamare. Follow the directions for San Benedetto. After about 2 miles, on the left is the Duomo. Drive on past the next traffic light. At the second light, turn right and right again following the signs for Il Vescovado and La Locanda di Porta Antica.

CATEGORY: Caffèlletto ◆ **RATE:** ○○○ ◆ *Member since 2002*

Lazio

Lazio is located in the center of Italy and extends from the Apennines westward to the Tyrrhenian Sea. The region is mostly hilly and mountainous with a narrow coastal plain. Popular resorts, such as Gaeta, Sperlonga, and San Felice Circeo, are strung along the coast, while the delightful island of Ponza and its archipelago are within easy reach.

Apart from the capital city of Rome, the main cities are Rieti, Viterbo, Latina, and Frosinone. On weekends, many Romans take day trips to the Castelli, where the papal nobility built their summer palaces. With hilltop villages and lovely lakes, it is the perfect setting for hearty meals accompanied by the famous Frascati wines.

Lazio is in fact divided into two distinct personalities: topographical and sociological. North of Rome, the countryside was colonized by the Etruscans and it is in towns like Tarquinia that some of the best-preserved ruins of this ancient civilization can be visited, with tombs covered with frescoes dating back to the third and fourth

centuries B.C. South of Rome, the atmosphere becomes more Mediterranean. A 175
slower pace is evident here, dictated by a Bourbon heritage and a balmier climate
where the bougainvillea blooms year-round. Even the bread is different below this
Mason-Dixon line: unsalted above Terracina and salted below.

The Romans and their cousins in the Lazio region are closest to the stereotypi-
cal Italians we know from films: laid-back and affable, especially towards newcomers,
though they do not like to be disturbed in the hot hours of the afternoon—siesta time.

THE LOCAL RECIPE

It is not so easy to find genuine local cuisine in Rome unless you leave the main city
and head for the trattorias in the countryside. You're sure to enjoy the detour: homemade fettuccine, a variety of artichoke dishes made with the popular large and tender
carciofi romani, a special roast lamb, and many other local delicacies.

Spaghetti alla Ciociarìa (an area about fifty miles from Rome)
Ingredients (serves 4)

13 oz. spaghetti	1 clove of garlic
4 oz. pitted green olives	2 tbsp. grated pecorino cheese
2 ripe tomatoes, peeled and diced	4 tbsp. olive oil
1 green pepper	chopped parsley, salt, and pepper to taste

Wash, trim, and dice the green pepper. Pour the olive oil in a frying pan; add the garlic, olives, green pepper, and diced tomatoes. Sprinkle with salt and pepper and sauté
on a medium flame for about 15 minutes. Cook the spaghetti al dente, drain, and add
to the frying pan, stirring for 3 minutes. Serve hot, sprinkled with the pecorino
cheese and parsley.

LUBRIANO (VT)

LE CASETTEVIA MARCONI 19/23 • 01020 LUBRIANO, VITERBO

TEL. AND FAX +39 063215064 • TEL. +39 0761780433 • CELL +39 3389499487

E-MAIL: laghianda@umbriaholidays.it

This medieval hamlet is in northern Lazio on the borders of Tuscany and Umbria and is well situated to take day trips to both. It is difficult to imagine, however, how anyone could tear themselves away from the extraordinary view—the wild landscape of the Valle dei Calanchi, the canyons, or the wonderful city of Civita di Bagnoregio—from the terraces of these studio apartments seemingly suspended in midair. They are furnished with a sort of World of Interiors Greek-island chic of blanched wood and pale fabrics.

The wherewithal for breakfast can be found in the various kitchens. Behind the house is a lawn bordered with roses and climbing plants and another spectacular view. Your hosts live just over a mile away but are on call for any emergency. All apartments have a copy of a guide to the area that they expressly prepared.

ROOMS: On the first floor there are two studio apartments with a beautiful terrace, a double bed, bathroom (with shower), and a small kitchen. On the floor above are two more studio apartments with a living room and sofa bed for two, kitchen corner, and double bed in an overhead loft. The remaining two apartments have access to the garden below. There is also a separate apartment with two twin rooms, a bathroom (with bathtub), kitchen, living room, and terrace.

AMENITIES:

English and French are spoken

Well-behaved pets are welcome

WHERE: The nearest railway station is Orvieto, 10 miles away, while the airport is in Rome, 93 miles away. By car take highway A1 and exit at Orvieto; follow the directions for Orvieto until the roundabout at Orvieto Scalo, follow the signs toward Bagno Regio and then to Lubriano.

CATEGORY: ✳✳✳✳ • RATE: ○ • *Member since 2002*

BAGNAIA (VT)

INFO: CAFFÈLLETTO, ITALY

TEL. +39 023311814 OR 1820 ◆ FAX +39 023313009 ◆ E-MAIL: info@caffelletto.it

La Chiesuola, literally the "itty-bitty" church, takes its name from a hermitage behind the estate where Capuchin monks in earlier times would pause in their wanderings to partake of physical and spiritual nourishment. At about thirty-seven miles from Rome, La Chiesuola is at the foot of the Cimini Hills, surrounded by a large park. The great Roman families of yore used to build country residences here, such as the famous Villa Lante at Bagnaia, whose landscaped gardens and play of fountains makes for a perfect retreat.

A little over a mile away is Viterbo, an Etruscan settlement that came splendidly into its own in medieval times, when the town was the seat of the papacy. Nearby are the magnificent Civita of Bagnoregio, built on a solid base of tufa rock, eroded over centuries, and Bomarzo, a magical park full of grotesque dinosaur-size statues—evidence that Steven Spielberg's *Jurassic Park* had antecedents in the Roman countryside of the Renaissance.

This is an ideal area for nature enthusiasts, as there are endless walking and hiking options. In the fall, the countryside is full of people seeking mushrooms that also feature regularly on local menus. Nearby, there are thermal springs where visitors can relax after a day's exertions.

Hospitality at La Chiesuola has an old-fashioned warmth and formality. Breakfasts include local specialties and homemade baked goods served by the fireplace in a handsome room furnished with period antiques in winter or in the sunny garden by the large swimming pool in summer.

ROOMS: There are two double rooms, each with its own bathroom, as well as a large suite with a memorable view over the surrounding hills. Minimum stay two nights.

AMENITIES:

English and Polish are spoken
Laundry service is available
Parking on the premises
Dinner can be served on request
Swimming pool
Children under the age of two stay
free of charge
Pets are welcome

WHERE: Rome's airport is 62 miles away, while the railway station of Bagnaia is about a mile away. There is also regular bus service.

CATEGORY: ✳✳✳✳ ◆ **RATE:** ○○ ◆ *Member since 1999*

ORTE (VT)

INFO: CAFFÈLLETTO, ITALY

TEL. +39 023311814 OR 1820 · FAX +39 023313009 · E-MAIL: info@caffelletto.it

This old stone house in a verdant garden is in Orte, in the valley of the Tiber River, about thirty-seven miles from Rome and twenty-five miles from Orvieto. Your hostess, a widow with four children, lives in this country house all year-round. Attractive as the imaginatively furnished interiors are, it is the garden with its hammocks, the many places for sitting and relaxing, and the small round wading pool for children that beckon. Although well situated to visit Rome and the rest of Lazio, Orte itself should not be overlooked. A town on a main thoroughfare in ancient times, it dates back thousands of years to the Etruscans and is witness to the many vicissitudes of its history since.

ROOMS: There are two double rooms and a twin room, all with private bathrooms. Closed in July and August.

AMENITIES:

French, English, German, Portuguese, and Dutch are spoken

Private parking

Swimming pool

Children under the age of two stay free of charge

Pets are welcome

WHERE: The nearest railway station is at Orte, 6 miles away, while the Fiumicino airport in Rome is 68 miles away. A direct train between Orte and the airport leaves every hour.

CATEGORY: ✳✳✳✳ · RATE: ○ · *Member since 2001*

VIGNANELLO (VT)

INFO: CAFFÈLLETTO, ITALY

TEL. +39 023311814 OR 1820 ✦ **FAX +39 023313009** ✦ **E-MAIL: info@caffelletto.it**

Vignanello is a real castle with a moat and drawbridge. It is also the comfortably and elegantly furnished residence of the princely Ruspoli family from Rome. Vignanello is most famous for its Italian garden that has remained intact since the seventeenth century. Twelve rectangles of perfectly pruned box trees, each with a different intricate design, surround the central fountain in front of the imposing facade of the castle. The little town of Vignanello is nine miles from Orte, on the way to Viterbo. A night under this castle's roof could prove an unforgettable detour when visiting Rome.

ROOMS: On the second floor of the castle is a magnificent apartment recently renovated with a large living room, fireplace, large kitchen/dining room, and four double or twin bedrooms, all with private bathrooms. The most beautiful of the four is the double room with the fireplace and large bathroom (with bathtub). Terra-cotta floors are covered with antique carpets, and classic château furniture adds an eclectic touch.

AMENITIES:
English and French are spoken
Private parking
Children over the age of twelve
  are welcome

WHERE: The nearest railway station is in Orte, 12 miles away, and the nearest airport is Rome's Fiumicino airport, 50 miles away.

CATEGORY: Caffèlletto ✦ **RATE:** ◡◯◯ ✦ *Member since 2002*

POGGIO NATIVO (RI)

INFO: CAFFÈLLETTO, ITALY

TEL. +39 023311814 OR 1820 • FAX +39 023313009 • E-MAIL: info@caffelletto.it

Your hostess's house is less than half an hour from Rieti, the geographic center of the Italian peninsula. Her name is Marvi and she has traveled all over the world before making her home in this red brick house overlooking one of the lovelier, if less known, corners of Italy—the Sabina region. Marvi has taken many grand tours, from Greece to Turkey to the Balearic Islands, and throughout the Mediterranean basin. Her latest exploit was to Mauritius, where she succeeded in teaching 1,600 women how to embroider linens the Italian way, and she is still in contact with many of her

ex-students. Marvi's house is in perfect harmony with the surrounding landscape; the silver green of the olive trees, the wide valley at its feet, and the mountains in the distance.

The house is less than half an hour away from Rome, the perfect distance for a day trip. After the chaotic choreography of the streets of the Eternal City, nothing could be better than to come home and relax with a glass of wine in

the shade of an olive grove. Around Rieti there are four different Franciscan monasteries dating back to the thirteenth century, each of which is well worth a visit, and no one should leave without seeing the fifteenth-century Farfa Abbey, one of the most impressive monuments of European culture in the Middle Ages. Charlemagne was its patron and, at the height of its fame, the abbey was actually the owner of a large part of central Italy. For skiers, the ski resort of Mount Terminillo is less than an hour away. In addition, every third Sunday of the month from November to February a small antique fair is held in the medieval township of Fara Sabina.

ROOMS: There are two doubles and one twin room. The furnishings are beautiful, down to the smallest details, from the old terra-cotta floors to the antique wrought-

iron and brass headboard in one of the rooms. All rooms have private bathrooms. Minimum stay two nights.

AMENITIES:
English and French are spoken
Laundry service is available
Swimming pool and tennis court less than a mile away
Horseback riding
On occasion, dinners can be arranged
Children under the age of two stay free of charge
Pets are welcome

WHERE: Rome's Fiumicino is 37 miles away, while the nearest railway station is Passo Corese, 15 miles away. Buses run frequently between Rieti and Rome.

CATEGORY: ✳✳✳ • **RATE:** ○ • *Member since 1998*

INFO: CAFFÈLLETTO, ITALY

TEL. +39 023311814 OR 1820 • **FAX +39 023313009** • **E-MAIL: info@caffelletto.it**

Only one hour from Rome by car, Il Casale di Max is an old stone country house surrounded by woodlands, with a charming garden leading down to a pool. Il Casale di Max was named after a beloved German shepherd, Max, and the owners have lived here for nearly thirty years, gradually restoring the building and renovating the delightful interiors of the onetime farmhouse as a refuge from the chaos of Rome.

They frequently drive back and forth in one day, something guests may feel less inclined to do as the combination of lawn, cypresses, and pergola of vines provide such an agreeable alternative. Breakfast is a movable feast, served either in the bedrooms, dining room, or in the warmer months under the arbor beside the pool.

ROOMS: Two doubles, both with everything you need for breakfast. The first one has a small bathroom with a shower and a beautiful terrace. The second one has a four-poster bed, a small sitting room, and a large bathroom with a shower. In a loft above the bed there is a comfortable double mattress for two more guests. Opening onto the swimming pool is a large room with a well-equipped kitchen that can also be rented by guests. Minimum stay two nights.

AMENITIES:
English is spoken
Private parking
Swimming pool
Dinner may be served on request
Pets are not allowed

WHERE: The nearest railway station is in Gavignano, 3 miles away, while Rome's Fiumicino airport is 50 miles away. There is a train that leaves from the Fiumicino airport every 20 minutes and takes you to Gavignano in 1 1/2 hours.

CATEGORY: **Caffèlletto** • **RATE**: OO • *Member since 2002*

ROME–APPIA ANTICA

INFO: CAFFÈLLETTO, ITALY

TEL. +39 023311814 OR 1820 ◆ FAX +39 023313009 ◆ E-MAIL: info@caffelletto.it

We are in Ancient Rome, not the civis romanum but the ancient Roman countryside on the old Appian Way, with bits and pieces of Roman villas and baths cropping up in the surrounding fields. The house itself is a low rose-colored structure covered in creepers in the middle of a lawn edged by flower beds. The room set aside for guests is actually round, as it used to be a well. Your hostess is a widow and lives here with her two teenage children. She is an inexhaustible source of information and is willing to accompany guests on sight-seeing tours. She also organizes private shows for artist friends.

ROOMS: A mini-apartment composed of a large comfortable twin room (which can become a double) with sofa bed, private bathroom, and kitchen corner. Closed in December. Minimum stay three nights.

AMENITIES:
English is spoken
Laundry service is available
Private parking
Dinner may be served on request
Guests can be picked up and accompanied to the airport for an extra charge
Weekly rates available

WHERE: The nearest railway station is in Rome, 19 miles away, while the Fiumicino airport is 37 miles away.

CATEGORY: ✳✳✳✳ ◆ **RATE**: ○ ◆ *Member since 2001*

ROME–AVENTINO

VIALE AVENTINO 110 ◆ 00153 ROMA

TEL. +39 065781035 ◆ FAX +39 06233204519 ◆ E-MAIL: journo@tiscalinet.it

This modern second-floor apartment on the Viale Aventino is within walking distance of the Colosseum and the Roman Forum, right in the heart of the Aventine Hill district and five minutes away by subway from Rome's train station. The apartment is comfortable, airy, and air-conditioned. The kitchen is stocked with everything you need for breakfast. Your host is a professional tourist guide and, thus, of invaluable assistance to guests visiting Rome.

ROOMS: An apartment including a sitting room with sofa bed, a double room with a third bed, bathroom, and a small kitchen. There is no elevator. Minimum stay three nights.

AMENITIES:
English and Japanese are spoken
Children under the age of two stay free of charge

WHERE: The railway station is just over a mile away, while the airport is 19 miles away. From Roma Termini take the Linea B subway line and get out at the Circo Massimo (Circus Maximus).

CATEGORY: ✸✸✸ ◆ **RATE:** ○○ ◆ *Member since 2001*

ROME–COPPEDÈ

INFO: CAFFÈLLETTO, ITALY

TEL. +39 023311814 OR 1820 ◆ FAX +39 023313009 ◆ E-MAIL: info@caffelletto.it

Gino Coppedè was a famous art nouveau architect at the turn of the last century. There are many buildings bearing his unmistakable stamp in Milan and Rome. This whole area of Rome is called Coppedè. The buildings lining this charming residential street all date back to the early 1900s.

The bed-and-breakfast itself is on the ground floor of a yellow Coppedè palazzo with green shutters, with an entrance hall and inner courtyard typical of the eclectic style of the architect. Your hostess lives surrounded by a lifetime's memorabilia and is

delighted to welcome guests to whom she serves breakfast either in the kitchen or the dining room as requested. Frequent buses a short way from the house transport guests to the center of the city.

ROOMS: A room with a double sofa bed and a third bed in an overhead loft with private bathroom (with shower). Minimum stay two nights. Closed during the Christmas season.

AMENITIES:
English and French are spoken

WHERE: The railway station is just over a mile away, while Fiumicino airport is 19 miles away.

CATEGORY: ✳✳✳✳ ◆ RATE: ◯◯ ◆ *Member since 2003*

ROME–FONTANA DI TREVI

INFO: CAFFÈLLETTO, ITALY

TEL. +39 023311814 OR 1820 ◆ **FAX +39 023313009** ◆ **E-MAIL: info@caffelletto.it**

When in Rome, what better place to be than around the corner from the Fontana di Trevi (Trevi Fountain), where every tourist throws a coin into the frolicking waters to ensure that he or she will return? Although this is an area with heavy foot traffic, few

tourists get to see the inside of this seventeenth-century palazzo, with its garden of citrus trees and fountains where goldfish and turtles are long-term residents. Despite being one of the busiest corners in Rome, the only sounds you hear inside are the splashing of water and the twittering of birds. The apartments are furnished in excellent taste and all the elements of breakfast can be found in the stocked kitchens.

ROOMS: Two apartments, one studio, and one two-room apartment. The studio sleeps two to three persons, has a separate entrance, kitchen corner, double bedroom, and bathroom (with shower). (A sitting room with sofa bed is separated from the bedroom by the kitchenette.) The two-room apartment sleeps four and has

two entrances. A double room with bathroom, a sitting room with two sofas, kitchen corner, and another bathroom. Minimum stay four nights.

AMENITIES:
English and French are spoken
Possibility of private parking
Air-conditioning
Pets allowed if permission is requested in advance

WHERE: The nearest railway station is 2 miles away and the airport is 19 miles away.

CATEGORY: ✳✳✳✳ ◆ **RATE:** ○○○ ◆ *Member since 2002*

ROME—MACHIAVELLI

INFO: CAFFÈLLETTO, ITALY

TEL. +39 023311814 OR 1820 • FAX +39 023313009 • E-MAIL: info@caffelletto.it

Via Machiavelli is within easy walking distance of the Colosseum and only one stop on the subway from Rome's railway station. It is in a residential part of Rome, a street lined with imposing nineteenth-century palazzi with tall doorways that open onto inner courtyards painted in pale yellows and faded pinks.

This bed-and-breakfast is on the third floor of just such a palazzo with an awe-inspiring entrance hall leading into a discreet courtyard. The rooms are furnished with eclectic antiques, there is an elevator, and everything you need for breakfast is in each room. Your hostess lives with her family on the top floor. She is a psychoanalyst and an expert on Michelangelo's Rome. She will be delighted to help plan tourist outings within Rome and beyond.

ROOMS: A double room with a communicating single room that shares a bathroom with a shower. One double room and two twin rooms, all with private bathrooms, one with shower, and two with bathtubs. Some rooms have their own small refrigerator and there is a communal kitchen corner available for guests. Minimum stay two nights.

AMENITIES:
English, French, Spanish, and some German are spoken

WHERE: The railway station is less than a mile away, while the airport in Rome is 15 miles away. Take subway Line A, get off at Vittorio Emanuele, and exit to the left onto Via Machiavelli.

CATEGORY: ✳✳✳✳ • **RATE:** ○○ • *Member since 2002*

INFO: CAFFÈLLETTO, ITALY

TEL. +39 023311814 OR 1820 ◆ **FAX +39 023313009** ◆ **E-MAIL: info@caffelletto.it**

While this apartment near Piazza Mazzini is not in the historical center of Rome, it has many other advantages. Large and full of light, it is on the seventh floor with a view over the hills of Monte Mario, Villa Madama, and the Italian Foreign Ministry. Built in 1939, it has the solid and harmonious elegance of that era and the apartment is furnished in a style much favored in those days among the affluent and cultured bourgeoisie.

Antique furniture alternates with well-chosen pieces from the 1930s and 40s. The dining room, where breakfast is served, is particularly arresting, with a large canvas reminiscent of a Picasso and furniture in the style of Frank Lloyd Wright. The apartment reflects the lifetime of your hostess, who moved here with her family as a little girl.

Buses run every ten to fifteen minutes from just outside the apartment building to Piazza di Spagna, Piazza del Popolo, and Piazza San Pietro. The subway is a five-minute walk away.

ROOMS: A large double room furnished with eighteenth-century Venetian antiques, with a panoramic view and a bathroom (with shower). Minimum stay three nights.

AMENITIES:

Open from January 15 to June 15, and from September 15 to December 20

English and French are spoken

Pets are not allowed

WHERE: Roma Termini station is 2 miles away, while Fiumicino airport is 22 miles away. The subway stop is Lepanto.

CATEGORY: ✳✳✳✳ ◆ **RATE:** ○○ ◆ *Member since 2000*

ROME–PALLARO

INFO: CAFFÈLLETTO, ITALY

TEL. +39 023311814 OR 1820 • FAX +39 023313009 • E-MAIL: info@caffelletto.it

This fascinating corner of old Rome takes its name from a game called Pallaro, a centuries-old version of today's lottery. The palace was built on the ruins of Pompey's Theater (where Julius Caesar was assassinated) and the third floor apartment looks down on a courtyard—too small to merit being called a square. From the living room windows, the splendid cupola of the baroque church of Sant'Andrea della Valle seems almost close enough to touch. Just around the corner from Piazza Navona, the apartment is at the vortex of ancient and modern Rome. The style of furnishing is rather more modern than ancient, eclectic, and personal in the choice of prints and paintings—a Roman hideaway for intellectuals who don't mind walking up three flights without an elevator.

ROOMS: A large living room with a modern kitchen corner, sofa bed, and double room with bathroom (with shower). Minimum stay two nights.

OPTIONS:
English and Spanish are spoken
Air-conditioning
The kitchen is fully equipped and contains
*   everything you will need for breakfast*
Pets are not allowed

WHERE: Roma Termini station is just over a mile away, while Fiumicino airport is 15 miles away.

CATEGORY: ✳✳✳✳ • **RATE:** ○○ • *Member since 2000*

ROME–PANTHEON

INFO: CAFFÈLLETTO, ITALY

TEL. +39 023311814 OR 1820 ◆ **FAX +39 023313009** ◆ **E-MAIL: info@caffelletto.it**

In the very heart of old Rome, just around the corner from the Pantheon, this apartment occupies the first floor of a seventeenth-century palazzo that opens onto the Via dei Pastini. The street was named after the artisans who made extraordinary sculptures out of dough to adorn the allegorical floats used in festive processions in the sixteenth century.

The apartment is in a part of Rome where the temptation to stroll down the narrow streets and discover unexpected squares and curiosities is irresistible. The Via dei Pastini is included on one of the most recommended walking tours of Rome, from the Trevi Fountain, past the Pantheon, Piazza Navona, Via dei Coronari (a fascinating street lined with artisans' workshops), to Castel Sant 'Angelo. Your hosts live in the same palazzo and can suggest unusual guided tours of Rome, with visits to noble palaces and concerts in the nearby churches and cloisters.

ROOMS: A separate apartment with two double rooms, a sitting room with sofa bed, a bathroom, and a kitchen. Minimum stay three nights.

AMENITIES:
English and French are spoken
Laundry service is available
Children under the age of two stay
  free of charge
Pets are not allowed

WHERE: Fiumicino airport is 20 miles away, while Roma Termini station is about 2 miles away. The nearest bus stop is the number 64 in Piazza Argentina, with buses also going to the Termini.

CATEGORY: ✳✳✳ ◆ **RATE:** ○ ◆ *Member since 1999*

ROME–PARIOLI

INFO: CAFFÈLLETTO, ITALY

TEL. +39 023311814 OR 1820 · FAX +39 023313009 · E-MAIL: info@caffelletto.it

The Parioli district of Rome is the most residential, affluent, and green in the city, whose quiet streets and houses with verandas and rooftop terraces, manicured lawns, and cars parked in garages make for a peaceful atmosphere compared to the bustling city center. This is a comfortable apartment on the ground floor of a modern palazzo, full of sunshine and with a small terrace. Your host, an architect who lives in the same palazzo with his family, will greet guests personally upon arrival. Although guests can choose to be completely independent, your host is always available to solve practical problems or give helpful advice.

Near the apartment is the entrance to the large and stately Villa Borghese Park, where the famous Borghese Museum is located. The city center is not far and can be reached by subway from the nearby Piazzale Flaminio.

ROOMS: The apartment has wood floors and is made up of a hall, sitting room with French windows opening onto a terrace, two bedrooms, one double and one twin, and a bathroom. The kitchen is very well equipped with a washing machine, and guests will find all they need for breakfast. A child's cot can be added on request. Minimum stay three nights.

AMENITIES:

English is spoken

Children under the age of two stay free of charge

Pets are not allowed

WHERE: Rome's Fiumicino airport is 19 miles away, while Roma Termini station is about 2 miles away The subway is a ten-minute walk from the apartment.

CATEGORY: ✳✳✳ · **RATE**: ○○ · *Member since 2000*

ROME–QUIRINALE

INFO: CAFFÈLLETTO, ITALY

TEL. +39 023311814 OR 1820 ◆ FAX +39 023313009 ◆ E-MAIL: info@caffelletto.it

From the bedrooms of this eighteenth-century palace in the center of the city, Rome is a visionary sight. From the morning sun at dawn to the late afternoon sunset, when the sky and the baroque cupolas of Santa Susanna, Santa Maria della Vittoria, and San Bernardo turn a whole gamut of pinks, puce, and blushing apricots. The sun sets in Rome in a glorious chorus of light. All this is seen from your hostess's home, just

around the corner from the Quirinale. At ground level, shops, boutiques, restaurants, and trattorias compete for space on the bustling streets, where visitors are encouraged to pause at the Bar delle Terme, famous for its cappuccino and warm brioche. In the middle of the nearby San Bernardo Square is the Fountain of Moses, next to an ancient pillar from the Baths of Diocletian. Nearby, too, are the well-known local landmarks, the Taverna Flavia restaurant, and the Punturi delicatessen, where residents line up for the famous mozzarella or a quick snack in the middle of the day. The rooms are on the fifth floor of the palazzo, accessible by elevator. They include a sitting room beautifully furnished with antiques and a Chinese screen that befits a Roman palazzo.

ROOMS: There is a double bed that can be divided into two single beds, an Empire-style sofa that can also serve as a third bed, and a private bathroom. Minimum stay three nights.

AMENITIES:
English and French are spoken
A small kitchen stocked with breakfast foods
A washing machine is available

WHERE: Roma Termini station is less than a mile away from the apartment, while Fiumicino airport is about 19 miles away. The house is near a bus stop and a subway station, as well as a taxi hub.

CATEGORY: ✳✳✳✳ ◆ **RATE:** ○○ ◆ *Member since 1999*

ROME—SAN TEODORO

INFO: CAFFÈLLETTO, ITALY

TEL. +39 023311814 OR 1820 · FAX +39 023313009 · E-MAIL: info@caffelletto.it

Step out of the front door, find yourself in the very heart of ancient Rome, and pinch yourself to see that it isn't a dream. At the foot of the Capitol Hill, this charming little apartment is tucked away between the Forum and the Circus Maximus. Dating back to the beginning of the eighteenth century, this typical little Roman palazzo, with its rust colored walls covered with Virginia creeper, is just next to the church of San Teodoro. Behind it the delightful little streets, Via dei Foraggi and Via dei Fienili, the Fodder and Haystack streets, are a reminder of the days before Rome was a capital city, and was more of a sprawling country town. All the goods for a fantastic breakfast can be found in the little kitchen.

ROOMS: An enchanting little apartment on the ground floor was recently renovated, and has a sitting room with sofa bed, an overhead gallery with two single beds, a kitchenette, and a and bathroom with shower. Minimum stay two nights.

AMENITIES:
English is spoken
Children under the age of two are free of charge

WHERE: Roma Termini, the main railway station, is a half-mile away, while the Roma Ostiense railway station is 500 yards away, with trains running to and from the airport. The Rome Fiumicino airport is 15 miles away, and Piazza Venezia is within short walking distance.

CATEGORY: ✳✳✳✳ · RATE: ○○ · *Member since 2004*

INFO: CAFFÈLLETTO, ITALY

TEL. +39 023311814 OR 1820 · FAX +39 023313009 · E-MAIL: info@caffelletto.it

Trastevere (literally, "across the Tiber") is the Roman equivalent of Paris's Left Bank, the abode of struggling artists, Rome's radical, chic, and so-called Trasteverini.

The vicolo della Penitenza is a pretty and elegant narrow street, flanked on one side by gardens and trees and on the other by centuries-old palazzos. The apartment is on the first floor of a palazzo dating back to the late nineteenth century, with win-

dows looking out onto the green foliage of the next-door neighbor's garden. Completely restored, the apartment maintains its original charm, from the old red and black hexagonal-tiled floors and old-fashioned white door and window frames, to the original bathroom tiles. The furniture is modern and cheerful and in excellent taste, with white sofas, framed posters of art exhibitions, and well-chosen artifacts.

Your charming hostess has prepared detailed suggestions and maps for guests who wish to visit Rome. It is just next to the Botanical Gardens, parallel to the Tiber, and around the corner from the Villa Farnesina (where frescoes of Raphael can be seen) and Palazzo Corsini, an elegant palace and art gallery.

Across the river, in the area known as Trastevere, is the heart of old Rome, ten minutes by foot from Campo dei Fiori. The main square of Trastevere itself is bordered by lively trattorias spilling out onto the street, and the loud and infectious confusion that sums up the charm of Rome is audible throughout the day.

ROOMS: A light and airy two-bedroom apartment with a sitting room, well-equipped kitchen corner, sofa bed, and two bathrooms (with shower). Minimum stay four nights.

AMENITIES:
English and French are spoken

WHERE: The nearest railway station is Roma–Trastevere less than a mile away, while Roma Termini is 2 miles away. Fiumicino airport is 19 miles away.

CATEGORY: ✳✳✳✳ · RATE: ○○ · *Member since 2001*

ROME–TRASTEVERE MONTEFIORE

INFO: CAFFÈLLETTO, ITALY

TEL. +39 023311814 OR 1820 · **FAX +39 023313009** · **E-MAIL: info@caffelletto.it**

Located in the heart of Trastevere on a narrow side street, this pale yellow house built in the late eighteenth century has recently been renovated. The ground-floor apartment is available for guests and is on two levels, with an overhead loft and a small

balcony perched above a cobblestone street. The apartment is comfortably furnished with taste and charm. Air-conditioning has been installed, although not much sun passes through the windows, which can be an advantage during Rome's torrid summers. Your hostess lives nearby and is always on hand to welcome guests. The apartment is ideally situated near the river and a ten-minute walk from the old ghetto. Apart from the more obvious sights, the church of San Giovanni dei Genovesi is well worth a visit for its beautiful cloisters, while in Piazza Apollonia the Sachertorte (Viennese chocolate layer cake with apricot jam filling) is simply unforgettable. Near the Church of Santa Cecilia, on the street with the same name, there is a small shop that makes ties to order.

ROOMS: An independent apartment with a living room, a kitchen corner, a double room, and a bathroom with a shower. Minimum stay two nights; three nights in May, September, and October.

AMENITIES:
Some English and French are spoken
Children under the age of two stay
  free of charge

WHERE: The railway station is a mile away, while Fiumicino airport is 19 miles away.

CATEGORY: ✳✳✳✳ · **RATE**: ◯◯ · *Member since 2003*

ROME—TRIONFALE

INFO: CAFFÈLLETTO, ITALY

TEL. +39 023311814 OR 1820 · **FAX +39 023313009** · **E-MAIL: info@caffelletto.it**

The Prati—Trionfale neighborhood is a central part of Rome, very close to the Vatican. This large apartment is in an imposing palazzo, five minutes from the Vatican Museums and from the Ottaviano—San Pietro subway stop. Alternately, all the different areas of town are easy to reach by bus. Breakfast is served in the beautiful dining room and the whole apartment is comfortably furnished and full of curious memorabilia.

ROOMS: A large double room furnished with antiques and a private bathroom (with bathtub). Minimum stay three nights.

AMENITIES:
English and French are spoken
Laundry service is available
A garage two minutes from the house is available at a daily rate

WHERE: Roma Termini station is 3 miles away (5 minutes by subway), while Fiumicino airport is 19 miles away.

CATEGORY: ✳✳✳✳ · RATE: ○○ · *Member since 2002*

ROME—BORGHI VATICANI

INFO: CAFFÈLLETTO, ITALY

TEL. +39 023311814 OR 1820 • **FAX +39 023313009** • **E-MAIL: info@caffelletto.it**

This little gem of a bed-and-breakfast is right in the heart of the elegant neighborhood adjacent to the Vatican, only four hundred metres from both St. Peter's Cathedral and Castel Sant'Angelo along the Tiber River.

The apartment is on the top floor of an art nouveau palazzo, with elevator, dating back to 1923 and has been completely restored. Guests are housed in a very comfortable attic room furnished with period pieces belonging to the family with fireplace, Turkish bath, a little kitchen, and terrace. The terrace, thirty square yards in size, commands an enviable view over the roofs of Rome, and there are chairs and tables under a sunshade where guests can breakfast in the warmer months. At any other time, an exquisitely prepared breakfast tray is served in the room. Your hosts, who also live in the same building, could not be more charming and helpful.

ROOMS: An elegant, romantic attic with independent entrance is available, in addition to a large bedroom/sitting room with double bed and the option of a third bed, a fireplace, bathroom with shower and Jacuzzi massage, Turkish bath, kitchen, and terrace. Air conditioning and satellite TV are included. Minimum stay two nights.

AMENITIES:
English and French are spoken
Children under the age of two stay free of charge

WHERE: The nearest railway station is 2 miles away, while the Fiumicino airport is 18 miles away. From the airport there is a train to the main railway station, and from here the subway's A line (direction Battistini) will bring you to the Ottaviano-San Pietro stop, 600 yards from the house. The nearest bus stop is 200 yards away.

CATEGORY: Caffèlletto • **RATE:** ○○○ • *Member since 2005*

TREVIGNANO ROMANO (Rome)

CASA PLAZZI ◆ **VIA OLIVETELLO 23** ◆ **00069 TREVIGNANO ROMANO, ROME**
TEL. +39 069997597 ◆ **FAX +39 0699910196** ◆ **CELL +39 3356756290**
E-MAIL: welcome@casaplazzi.com

This modern villa in a garden with a swimming pool has a spectacular view of Lake Bracciano, nineteen miles from Rome. One of the cleanest in Europe, it is on this lake that the city depends for the bulk of its water supply. Five minutes from the villa, the lake offers every kind of water sport, as well as archery and an eighteen-hole golf course.

Your host used to work in show business and now lives here all year-round. He is an excellent chef and is delighted to cook for guests, drawing much of his inspiration from his vegetable garden, where everything is organically grown. Breakfasts feature homemade jams.

ROOMS: The master bedroom is a double with its own terrace and bathroom with a Jacuzzi, as well as a television set, stereo, fireplace, ceiling fan, and the option of adding a baby bed. Matteo's room has two beds that can be joined into a double and a bathroom with a shower. Maddalena's room is small with a queen-size bed and bathroom with a shower. Margherita's room has a double bed with French windows leading onto the garden and a bathroom with a shower. Mimma's room has a double bed and one single with a bathroom with a shower. Marco's room is a double with an independent entrance from the garden and a bathroom with a shower. Marta's apartment has an entrance from the garden, a double room, a living room with sofa bed, a bathroom with a shower, and a small, well-equipped kitchen. Use of the kitchen is available for those who do not rent with the bed-and-breakfast package.

AMENITIES:
English is spoken
Laundry service is available
Swimming pool
Private parking
Lunch and dinner may be served on request

WHERE: The nearest railway station is Bracciano, 6 miles away, while Fiumicino airport is 37 miles away. By car take highway A1 and exit at Orte. Take the Orte–Viterbo highway and exit at Viterbo Nord in the direction of Rome, on the Via Cassia. Drive through Vetralla, Capranica, and Sutri. After 30 miles, turn right following the directions for Trevignano. Drive 7 miles and then turn left at the crossroads. After about 2,000 feet, immediately after the IP gas station, turn left onto Via Olivetello. The house is number 19 on the left.

CATEGORY: ✳✳✳✳ ◆ **RATE:** ○○ ◆ *Member since 2002*

BRACCIANO (Rome)

INFO: CAFFÈLLETTO, ITALY

TEL. +39 023311814 OR 1820 · **FAX +39 023313009** · **E-MAIL: info@caffelletto.it**

Lake Bracciano is only a half hour from the center of Rome by subway and is set in an idyllic landscape of wooded hills. A favorite Roman resort during weekends, Lake Bracciano is also sufficiently romantic for prominent foreign visitors to decide to hold their weddings in the imposing castle belonging to Prince Odescalchi.

From the house, Bracciano and the lake can be glimpsed between the tall trees and lush green of the hedges and bushes surrounding it. The house is comfortable and welcoming, full of books, prints, paintings, and music, which reflect the personality of your host, a journalist, excellent cook, and conversationalist. Here guests are ideally situated for visiting Rome while avoiding the madding crowd of the Eternal City, especially during the holidays. That said, Bracciano and its lake are well worth the detour, with the Odescalchi Castle and many little trattorias serving fish fresh from the lake. In summer the lake is a perfect place for surfing, canoeing, and other water sports.

ROOMS: One double room with a terrace and private bathroom; two double rooms with shared bathroom. Minimum stay two nights.

AMENITIES:

English is spoken
Laundry service is available
Private parking
Dinner may be served on request
Children over the age of ten
are welcome

WHERE: The nearest railway station is in Cesano, 3 miles away; trains to Saint Peter's leave every 15 minutes. Buses between Rome–Lepanto and Bracciano leave every hour. Fiumicino airport is 31 miles away.

CATEGORY: ✳✳✳✳ · **RATE:** ○○ · *Member since 2000*

SANTA MARIA DI GALERIA (Rome)

INFO: CAFFÈLLETTO, ITALY

TEL. +39 023311814 OR 1820 ⬩ FAX +39 023313009 ⬩ E-MAIL: info@caffelletto.it

Only twelve miles from the heart of Rome, in the middle of five acres of parkland, lies this beautiful country house near the medieval village of Santa Maria di Galeria. In some ways, the green hills studded with spreading oak trees are reminiscent of the

English countryside—until you see scattered, unmistakably Roman ruins, that is. The house is surrounded by a large garden with a swimming pool, orchards, and pines. Much effort has been put into the interiors, with cheerful wallpaper on the bedroom walls, chintzes, and bright bedspreads on the wrought-iron beds.

This is an ideal base for day trips to Rome or to simply enjoy the countryside around the capital. Lake Bracciano is just six miles away; it draws surfers, all sorts of sailors, and canoe enthusiasts, while those less athletically inclined can enjoy long lunches in the typical rustic trattorias in the area.

The Etruscan cities Veio and Tarquinia, with their painted tombs and museums, are rich in a culture that preceded the Romans and which, according to D.H. Lawrence, "is closer to today's Italy than the classical era which followed."

ROOMS: On the first floor of the main building there is an independent apartment called "Tarquinia." It has three bedrooms, one double and one twin, a living room that opens onto a loggia with a view of the park, two bathrooms, and a well-equipped kitchen. There is also a charming independent cottage called "Ceri" with a beamed ceiling, a double bedroom, a twin room, a living/dining room, a kitchen, and a bathroom. In all the kitchens guests will find what they need for breakfast. Each apartment has its own television. Minimum stay two nights.

AMENITIES:
English, French, and Spanish are spoken
Laundry service is available
Parking on the grounds
Private swimming pool
Children under the age of two stay free of charge
Pets are not allowed

WHERE: Regular buses run between Santa Maria di Galeria and Rome; the bus stop is 2 miles from the house, while the subway is 4 miles away. Rome's Fiumicino airport is 25 miles away.

CATEGORY: ✳✳✳ ⬩ **RATE:** ○ ⬩ *Member since 1999*

ACQUAFONDATA (FR)

INFO: CAFFÈLLETTO, ITALY

TEL. +39 023311814 OR 1820 · FAX +39 023313009 · E-MAIL: info@caffelletto.it

Acquafondata has a special quiet and peaceful charm, most likely due to the fact that for many years the village was rather isolated. Built in the eighteenth century on the ruins of a fifteenth-century fortress, the house stands poised on the edge of the mountainside with a wooded valley at its feet and a view over distant peaks—the closest Italy comes to a monastery in Nepal. The nearest landmark is indeed a monastery, the famous Abbey of Monte Cassino, bombed by the Allies during the Second World War. The Monks have slowly restored it to its former magnificence, employing, among others, fifty Florentine artisans who took ten years to restore the extraordinary wooden choir stalls, of which no two are alike.

Acquafondata has always been in the hands of the same family, the leading family in the area, the eldest son of each generation traditionally becoming a doctor. Today your hostess is the daughter of the last of these doctors and it was she who rescued the house from a long period of neglect and restored it to its former glory, living here in the summertime with her husband and two children.

Acquafondata is at the crossroads between three Italian regions—Lazio, Campania, and Molise—which comprise a little hamlet 3,300 feet above sea level, with a delightful square, church, and bell tower. For a place that prides itself on its monastic calm, there is a lot going on at Acquafondata. During the month of August the piazza turns into an outdoor theater where festivities and much merrymaking take place. In July on the feast of the Madonna of Mount Carmel there is a procession with lighted torches, while in May an international bagpipe festival is held with participants arriving all the way from Scotland. In the village there are two excellent trattorias. Twelve miles away is the splendid national park in Abruzzo where you can walk, mountain bike, or hike. The stunning Reggia di Caserta is twenty-five miles away.

ROOMS: One whole floor has been put at the disposal of guests with its long glass-enclosed veranda overlooking the valley and the bell tower. There is also a large double room with Art Nouveau–style furniture and a living room with two sofa beds, stereo, and two large bathrooms. Minimum stay two nights.

AMENITIES:
Open from May to October
English and French are spoken
Laundry service is available
Private parking
Afternoon tea is served on the veranda at five o'clock
Children under the age of two stay free of charge

WHERE: The nearest railway station is Cassino, 15 miles away. The airports are either in Rome, 100 miles away, or closer still in Naples, 50 miles away.

CATEGORY: ✳✳✳✳ · RATE: ○ · *Member since 2000*

ABRUZZO

Abruzzo is the Italian equivalent of France's Massif Central, with three mountainous backbones running parallel from north to south including the peaks of Laga, the Gran Sasso d'Italia, Maiella, Velino, Sirente, Marsica, and Meta, as well as Simbruini and Ernici in the west. Unlike nearly all other parts of Italy, this region was colonized neither by the Greeks nor by the Etruscans. The fiercely independent people of Abruzzo spent most of their time rebutting the advances of the many succeeding civilizations that tried to dominate them. In more recent history, they made a valiant stand against the Fascists. The famous statue of the Warrior of Capestrano in Chieti's National Museum of Archaeology dates back to the sixth century and is one of the rare works of art from that era free from classical influence.

Abruzzo is a region of contrasts. L'Aquila, the capital city, is a cultural center, hosting musical events of international importance, and is home to one of Italy's most audaciously innovative theaters. Pescara, which in the last decades has been the fastest-expanding city in Italy, holds frequent significant art exhibitions and film festivals. Only a short way up the mountainside one can find villages that still live in a world of the past, with archaic customs and religious festivals that are more pagan than Christian and impenetrable dialects that originated in pre-Christian times.

Abruzzo boasts one of the country's most important natural reserves, the Gran Sasso d'Italia, protecting endangered species such as bears and wolves.

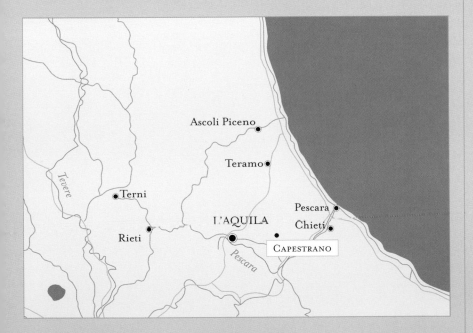

THE LOCAL RECIPE

Abruzzo boasts a long coastline as well as the Gran Sasso, making the local cuisine extremely varied, ranging from seafood originating in the coastal areas to dishes subtly flavored with saffron threads collected in the foothills. The threads are actually the pistils of the crocus nativus, a delicate flower that grows in the region. The harvesting of the precious pistils is still done by hand only in the cool hours of the early morning and late afternoon, when the flower's bouquet is at its best. Along the coast, saffron is used to flavor brodetto pescarese, a type of tasty fish soup. Another delicious soup from the central region is the scrippelle 'mbusse, cheese-filled crepes drenched in a hot chicken broth. From the small city of Sulmona comes the sugarcoated confetti, white as snow, exported all over the world.

Fettuccine all'Abruzzese
Ingredients (serves 4)

12 oz. fresh fettuccine

1/3 cup unsmoked pancetta (bacon)

1/3 cup grated pecorino cheese

1 medium onion

1 tbsp. chopped parsley

2 tbsp. chopped basil

3 tbsp. olive oil

salt and pepper to taste

Chop the onion and bacon, or pancetta, and sauté in a large skillet with the olive oil. Season with salt and pepper and then add the basil and parsley. Cook for about 30 minutes, moistening with broth if necessary. Cook the fettuccine al dente, drain, and stir into the skillet. Sprinkle with the pecorino and serve piping hot.

CAPESTRANO (AQ)

INFO: CAFFÈLLETTO, ITALY

TEL. +39 023311814 OR 1820 · FAX +39 023313009 · E-MAIL: info@caffelletto.it

This small medieval village founded on a rocky hilltop with a sweeping view over the valley of the Tirino River seems so far away from everything that it might be the very reason to visit. Halfway between Pescara and L'Aquila, Capestrano is ninety-nine miles from Rome and thirty-seven miles from the Adriatic coast.

Located in a palazzo that dates back to 1400, this bed-and-breakfast has been expertly restored to preserve its magical atmosphere, with original floors and walls in warm apricots, yellows, and reds. From the garden, three large terraces brimming with flowers, creepers, and vegetables, you can see the ruins of the medieval Piccolomini Castle in the center of Capestrano. Breakfasts, abundant with homemade jams and cakes, have a British colonial flair as your hosts spent many years in Kenya and South Africa. Capestrano takes the notion of "getting away

from it all" to a new level while offering a wealth of opportunities for trekking, climbing, or discovering medieval abbeys and villages.

ROOMS: Two double rooms, each with its own bathroom, the Red Room (with bathtub) and the Blue Room (with shower). In a separate wing of the building with a private entrance and small garden, there is an apartment with a double room, living room with two sofa beds, a kitchen corner, and a bathroom (with shower). Minimum stay two nights.

AMENITIES:
English and French are spoken
Children under the age of two stay free of charge

WHERE: The nearest railway station is Bussi, 6 miles away, while Pescara's airport is 24 miles away.

CATEGORY: **Caffèlletto** · RATE: ○○ · *Member since 2002*

MOLISE

Molise, after Valle d'Aosta, is Italy's smallest region, comprising only 1.5 percent of Italy's entire territory. Of this, 55 percent is mountainous and 40 percent grassland, which leaves only 5 percent of land composed of valleys sloping down to the Adriatic Sea. There is little industry and tourism to employ the local population, many of whom have emigrated north or sailed to the Americas to seek their fortune. In recent years, however, Molise has seen remarkable development, particularly in the area of Isernia, where textile industries have sprung up.

Yet Molise has remained a place of beauty unspoiled by factory chimneys or hordes of tourists. Each village is represented by a patron saint whose name day is feted with a procession of papier-mâché floats and relics reverently carried on shepherds' shoulders. The main city, Campobasso, is renowned for its wrought-iron work, while nearby Agnone produces church bells that hang in cathedrals all over the world. At Isernia the elderly women are adept at lace-making, a tradition their great-great-great-grandmothers learned from Spanish nuns in the seventeenth century.

Molise is the youngest region in Italy. It obtained its "independence" from Abruzzo in 1965. Agnone has a Renaissance center and some beautiful eighteenth- and nineteenth-century buildings, while more recent architecture too often seems to concentrate on massive municipal buildings to house the wielders of rubber stamps.

THE LOCAL RECIPE

If so many great chefs are from Molise there must be a good reason! Cooking here is still very traditional. Meat, especially lamb, is often baked in a wood oven. Each home has its own bunch of red chili pepper called diavolino ("little devil"), the hottest in Italy, which can transform a bland tomato sauce into something. . .fierce! There are even liquors made with Diavolino. Pasta alla Chitarra (guitar-shaped macaroni) is a local specialty. A traditional festive meal in Molise known as panarda may well consist of thirty different dishes!

Molise Ham and Cheese Pie
Ingredients (serves 4)

FOR THE PASTRY:
1 1/2 cups flour
3 oz. butter
1 whole egg
salt to taste

FOR THE FILLING:
6 oz. sliced Parma ham
1/2 pound sliced mozzarella
1/3 cup milk
3 egg yolks
nutmeg, salt, and black pepper to taste

In a mixing bowl, combine the flour and salt, then mix in the softened butter and egg until the dough is smooth (add a few drops of water if the dough is too hard). Let it rest for 20 minutes. Dust the dough with flour and roll it into a quarter-inch-thick round. Fit the round into a buttered pie plate. Arrange the sliced ham and mozzarella on the surface. Beat the egg yolks with the milk, flavor with nutmeg, and season with salt and pepper. Pour the mixture over the ham and mozzarella. Bake in a 350° F oven for about 35 minutes or until custard is set.

VENAFRO (IS)

DIMORA DEL PRETE DI BELMONTE · VIA CRISTO 49 · 86079 VENAFRO, ISERNIA
TEL. AND FAX +39 0865900159 · E-MAIL: dorvolpe@tin.it

Venafro is a delightful town located in a valley at the foot of Mount Santa Croce, one hour's drive from Naples. One of Italy's natural treasures, the national park of Abruzzo, is only six miles away. The Palazzo del Prete was built in the sixteenth century on Roman foundations, although its current neoclassical style dates back to the last century, when it underwent major restorations. Right in the center of the old town, the Palazzo looks out on the Piazza del Cristo next to a church with the same name. In the courtyard there is an enchanting inner garden with palm trees.

The owners returned to Venafro twenty years ago to bring the family home back to life and to take charge of the estates. In Roman times, Horace, Martial, and Pliny the Elder all praised Venafro for its moderate climate and excellent olive oil. The upper floors of Palazzo del Prete have been transformed into guest rooms. An elegant dining room frescoed with views of the town and the Del Prete country estates serves as a breakfast room. Venafro has an interesting Romanesque cathedral with a portal flanked by two marble lions and three apses built with materials from Roman tombs. The Lombard Castle, built in the thirteenth century and remodeled in the mid-fifteenth century, has recently been restored, bringing to light a life-size relief of horses, unique in its genre, commissioned by the castle's owner, a famous horse breeder at the start of the sixteenth century.

Venafro is also eighteen miles from the famous Abbey of Montecassino—bombed by the Allies during the Second World War and completely restored to its original splendor—and thirty-six miles from Caserta and its Royal Palace, often called Italy's Versailles. The ancient Teatro Sannitico di Pietrabbondante is well worth a visit. Your hosts are happy to offer gastronomic specialties of the Molise region, as well as the excellent oil and wine from the estate.

ROOMS: Four double rooms furnished with antiques, all with private bathrooms. A suite with air-conditioning.

AMENITIES:
English and French are spoken
Laundry service is available
Dinner is served on request
Children under the age of two stay free of charge

WHERE: The nearest airport is in Naples, 50 miles away, while there is a railway station at Venafro. By car from the north, take highway A1 and exit at San Vittore, or at Caianello if coming from the south. Follow signs to Isernia.

CATEGORY: Caffelletto · **RATE:** ○○ · *Member since 1999*

CAMPANIA

The region of Campania in Southern Italy extends from the Apennines west to the Tyrrhenian Sea, and from the Garigliano River south to the Gulf of Policastro. Naples, the capital of Campania, was once part of the kingdom of the Two Sicilies and, like Sicily, has been swept by the waves of many different civilizations. Originally a Greek colony, Campania is home to magnificent ruins of Greek temples in Paestum to the south. The presence of the Romans, surprised in their sleep by the eruption of Vesuvius, is documented at Pompeii and Herculaneum and at the Museo Archeologico Nazionale in Naples. Today's Naples is a mixture of ancient culture and modern chaos, with its honking horns, colorful residents, and cacophony of sounds, smells, and sensations.

From the Bay of Naples, boats and hydrofoils leave regularly for the islands of Capri, Ischia, and Procida. Amalfi's coastal road, teetering around hairpin bends at the edge of a precipice with a deep blue sea lapping against the rocks below, is perhaps the most spectacular in Europe. It winds from Sorrento, past Positano and Ravello, to Amalfi, a casbah of whitewashed streets with echoes of a Saracen past.

There are three things that taste better in Naples and its surroundings than anywhere in the world: tomatoes, pizza, and mozzarella di bufala—made from the milk of black buffalo that roam the northern plain. Caserta is considered the heartland of mozzarella, although it is better known for its beautiful royal palace built by Vanvitelli for the Bourbon kings. The Neapolitans and their cousins in Campania are remarkably warm and friendly to visitors and with their constant query: "Ma le piace Napoli?" (How do you like Naples?)—there is no question that they are talking about the most beautiful city in the world.

THE LOCAL RECIPE

Say "Naples" and immediately pizza comes to mind. But there's also another kind of cuisine that you can find in Naples. Many foreign overlords have influenced Neapolitan cuisine—the French in particular—which is why the city boasts Italy's best brioches, not to speak of the wonderful timballi, fragrant pastry crusts concealing different kinds of pasta in wonderfully rich sauces. Seafood is equally important.

Cauliflower Salad with Pickles

This tasty salad is a traditional Christmas dish in Naples; it can be made to last until the New Year with the addition of a few ingredients each day.
Ingredients (serves 4)

1 cauliflower	1 tbsp. capers
1/4 cup pitted green olives	4 anchovies
1/4 cup pitted black olives	1 tbsp. vinegar
1/4 cup pickles	olive oil and salt to taste
1 marinated bell pepper	

Wash and trim the cauliflower heads and boil until al dente, 15 to 20 minutes. Drain and separate the florets into a salad bowl. Add the olives, capers, diced pepper, pickles, and anchovies. Toss with plenty of good olive oil, mild vinegar, and salt.

BOSCARELLO (BN)

INFO: CAFFÈLLETTO, ITALY

TEL. +39 023311814 OR 1820 ◆ FAX +39 023313009 ◆ E-MAIL: info@caffelletto.it

In the heart of Campania's countryside, about half an hour from the Royal Palace of Caserta, is this unusually attractive guesthouse which has been completely restored and remarkably landscaped by its owners. Naples is forty-five minutes by car, while nearby, at the Terme di Telese, is a spa with turn-of-the-last-century charm. Guests may stay in the delightful dependance (cottage), which is beautifully furnished and full of sunshine. The living room has an open fireplace and French windows that face the garden.

ROOMS: The dependance is divided into a sunny living room with a double sofa bed and a double bedroom with a bathroom. In the main building there is a large double bedroom with a private bathroom attached to a smaller room with twin beds.

AMENITIES:

Open from January 4 to December 20
English and French are spoken
Laundry service is available
Private parking
Swimming pool
Dinner may be served on request in the
  dining room of the main house
Children under the age of two stay free of charge
Well-behaved pets are allowed

WHERE: The nearest airport is at Capodichino in Naples, 25 miles away, while the Telese railway station is 6 miles away.

CATEGORY: ✳✳✳✳ ◆ **RATE:** ◯◯ ◆ *Member since 1998*

ISOLA DI PROCIDA–TORTUGA (NA)

INFO: CAFFÈLLETTO, ITALY

TEL. +39 023311814 OR 1820 · **FAX +39 023313009** · **E-MAIL: info@caffelletto.it**

What could be more magical than to bob at anchor in a little old world fishing port called Chiaiolella, on the island of Procida, before a backdrop of pink and yellow fishermen's cottages with geraniums flowering in the window boxes while ducks swim around the hull and seagulls circle overhead? The island of Procida is less well known than its bigger sisters Capri and Ischia, preserving its authentic quality, and the fishing boats come in every morning with the night's haul, some of which ends up on the tables of one of the best restaurants in Procida on the port, called Crescenzo.

This particular fishing boat has a mahogany hull and all the quaint fixtures of old-fashioned boats as well as fully modern equipment. It is thirty-three feet long, nine feet wide, and has spacious decks with reclining beds both in the prow and stern. Your host is a genial and charming sea dog whose favorite pastime is magic, as he is a professional magician. He will prepare a delicious breakfast on deck for guests, and usually takes everyone for a boat trip around the island on the first day. He is also willing to organize excursions to Capri, Ischia, Positano, Amalfi, Sorrento, and Naples.

ROOMS: A small cabin with a double bed and another with bunk beds share the small bathroom with a washbasin and W.C. The maximum number of guests the tiny boat will house is four. The boat is equipped with a little kitchen corner with a fridge and small sofa bed. The shower is outside, for the time being hot water is yet to be installed, and there is a TV and stereo aboard.

AMENITIES:

English is spoken
Children under the age of two stay free of charge
All safety devices are installed, but children under the age of eighteen are the responsibility of their parents
The boat is available from April until October

WHERE: the nearest railway station and airport are in Naples. There are hydrofoil boats leaving from Mergellina and ferries from the Beverello pier leaving every half hour. From the main port of Procida to Chiaiolella there is a bus service until ten o'clock at night, as well as taxi service available.

CATEGORY: ✳✳✳ · **RATE:** ○○ · *Member since 2005*

CALITRI (AV)

INFO: CAFFÈLLETTO, ITALY

TEL. +39 023311814 OR 1820 • **FAX +39 023313009** • **E-MAIL: info@caffelletto.it**

This white house stands amidst fields in southern Italy that vary from season to season, turning yellow with sunflowers and green with young wheat—all organically grown. From Il Tufiello, guests can choose a compass point and venture east to Apulia, west toward Naples, or south to Basilicata. Your hosts, three generations of a Neapolitan family, embody the warmth and generous hospitality you would expect from the south. You might be tempted to participate in the life of a family farmstead, helping the children gather zucchini, watching as they lay the tomatoes out to dry or gather the chestnuts in autumn. Antonietta and Cietta transform the produce into delicious sauces for pasta and fresh salads. Breakfasts are accompanied by honey made from the bees of Il Tufiello's hives, and pecorino cheese.

Pleasant drives in the area lead to castles of Norman, Gothic, or Roman origin, some of which were chosen as residences by Federico II of Swabia, the dominant figure of southern Italy's history. Don't miss the Castel del Monte, built in 1240 for Federico II as his shooting lodge and later converted into a prison by the Angevins. It stands high on a hillock near the  village of Andria. The nearest historic center is Calitri, an ancient town overlooking the Ofanto River valley, known for its ceramics, terra-cotta, and wine, made from southern grapes such as the Aglianico del Vulture, the Greco di Tufo, and the Taurasi. Guests can sample wines with vintners while visiting nearby wine cellars carved from tufaceous rock. In May wine afficionados from all over travel here to attend the popular open house during which the locals hold wine tastings.

The family has restored two cottages, the Masseria and the Casa del Nonno, while the Stalla, or stable, has is now a library and living room with a fireplace—an ideal meeting point.

ROOMS: Four double rooms with private bathrooms, and two apartments with a double bedroom, bathroom, living room, and kitchenette.

AMENITIES:
Open from Easter until the end of October
English and French are spoken
Swimming pool
Parking on the premises
Bicycles are available
Children under the age of two stay free of charge

WHERE: The nearest airport is in Naples, 74 miles away. The Calitri Scalo railway station is 6 miles away.

CATEGORY: ✹✹✹ • **RATE:** ○ • *Member since 1999*

NAPLES–CUMA

INFO: CAFFÈLLETTO, ITALY

TEL. +39 023311814 OR 1820 ◆ FAX +39 023313009 ◆ E-MAIL: info@caffelletto.it

Twelve miles from Naples and eighteen miles from Pompeii, Pozzuoli is the birthplace of Sofia Loren and best known for the archaeological site of the Campi Flegrei (Phlegraean Fields). The Villa Giulia is an attractive old house, characteristically Mediterranean in appearance, with a flat roof, thick white walls, and green shutters to keep out the sun. Your hostess spent many years in England and it shows, particularly in her large garden with its perfectly manicured English lawn, accented by rosebushes and fruit trees. She also breeds Siberian huskies and has five champions among her brood. Eucalyptus trees shade the swimming pool and there are beaches a short distance away. The famous Agnano thermal baths are nearby and boats leave regularly for Procida, Ischia, and other islands from the port of Pozzuoli.

ROOMS: The elegantly furnished Iris room has a double bed with a fireplace and bathroom (with shower and bathtub). Demetra, a double that shares a bathroom (with bathtub) with Giacinto, a single room. The three rooms are in a separate building and may be rented as an apartment by the week. There is also a living room and kitchen. On the grounds are two romantic annexes: Priscilla, with a double room, kitchen, living room, dining room with a fireplace, and bathroom (with bathtub); and Arancia, a studio apartment with two beds, fireplace, kitchen corner, and bathroom (with bathtub). Minimum stay two nights.

AMENITIES:
English and French are spoken
Private parking
Swimming pool
Dinner may be served on request
Children under the age of two stay free
  of charge

WHERE: The railway station in Pozzuoli is a mile away. Both the Naples Mergellina station and the airport in Naples are 12 miles away.

CATEGORY: **Caffèlletto** ◆ RATE: ○○○ ◆ *Member since 2003*

DONNA REGINA B&B ⬧ **VIA L. SETTEMBRINI 80** ⬧ **80139 NAPLES**
TEL. +39 081446799 ⬧ **FAX +39 081446799** ⬧ **E-MAIL: m.mazzella@libero.it**

In the heart of old Naples, this bed-and-breakfast was once part of a nunnery, commissioned in the fourteenth century by Queen Mary of Hungary, hence the name Donna Regina, "the Lady Queen." The building is the last example of Gothic architecture left in Naples and is similar to Sainte-Chapelle in Paris, due to the fact that many French artists and artisans were brought to the city by the Angevins.

The bed-and-breakfast is on the fourth floor and was once the private apartment of the Mother Superior. There are vestiges of her private chapel in what is now an enormous and quite splendid kitchen with hand-painted tiles from the sixteenth century and an antique refectory table where breakfast is served. A beautiful terrace looks down on the sixteenth-century cloisters of the convent, frescoed beneath the arches; one fresco is attributed to the fourteenth-century Renaissance master Giotto. Here guests may sit in the sun or shade and admire the amazing architectural complex, of which the bed-and-breakfast is only a small part, and which includes the domes of Donna Regina and the cathedral of Naples.

Recently restored by a family of artists, the result is a unique palimpsest of Naples' fascinating past and the equally engrossing artistic milieu of today. Your hosts are charming, serve sumptuous breakfasts enhanced by Neapolitan pastries, and are well-informed about the city and its surroundings. The street where Donna Regina is situated is a pedestrian zone and thankfully very quiet in what can be a somewhat noisy city.

Around the corner is Spaccanapoli, so named because it cuts through the city, with the church of Gesù Nuovo, the monastery of Santa Chiara, and San Gregorio Armeno, where all the workshops on the street are devoted to making figures for the famous Neapolitan crèche scenes.

ROOMS: Two doubles, both with an overhead loft with two single beds for couples with children, and a single room with a double bed. The bathrooms are modern, recently installed with showers. Minimum stay two nights.

AMENITIES:
Closed from August 1 to 20
English is spoken
Dinner may be served on request for four or more people
Elevator
Children under the age of two stay free of charge
Pets are not allowed

WHERE: The nearest railway station is Napoli–Centrale, 6 miles away. The Capodichino airport is 3 miles away.

CATEGORY: ✳✳✳✳ ⬧ RATE: ○○ ⬧ *Member since 2003*

NAPOLI–TOLENTINO

INFO: CAFFÈLLETTO, ITALY

TEL. +39 023311814 OR 1820 • FAX +39 023313009 • E-MAIL: info@caffelletto.it

Funiculì, funiculà...the best way to find your way around Naples is by the funicular, a series of cabins that link all the landmarks of the city within minutes. This bed-and-breakfast is on a street parallel to the Corso Vittorio Emanuele, and is close to the Funicolare Centrale, which brings the whole historic centre of Naples together: the Piazza Plebiscito, the Teatro San Carlo, the Maschio Angioino, and other famous sights. The apartment is charming, on the third floor without a lift but with a lovely view over the Gulf of Naples, Capri, and the Sorrento coastline. Small and cozy, the rooms are sunny and furnished with taste. Your hostess will meet guests on arrival and provide the basics for a good breakfast.

ROOMS: There is one sitting room with double sofa bed, a bedroom with single sofa bed and small balcony, an overhead balcony with small double bed, and a kitchen and bathroom with shower.

AMENITIES:
French is spoken
Children under the age of two stay free of charge
A garage for parking by the hour is a short way away

WHERE: Napoli Mergellina, the nearest railway station, is a couple of miles away, while the airport is 5 miles away.

CATEGORY: ✳✳✳ • **RATE:** ○○ • *Member since 2005*

NAPLES—MONTE DI DIO

INFO: CAFFÈLLETTO, ITALY

TEL. +39 023311814 OR 1820 ◆ FAX +39 023313009 ◆ E-MAIL: info@caffelletto.it

This apartment is on the third floor (accessible by elevator) of an eighteenth-century palazzo on a Neapolitan street that couldn't be more characteristically warm, colorful, and chaotic. That said, the windows look out over silent and sunlit gardens fragrant with orange blossoms. The apartment has been furnished with the impeccable taste and inimitable style and humor of your host, a multifaceted personality combining a successful career as a doctor with a passion for collecting fine paintings. The apart-

ment is near the main historic monuments of Naples and the elegant shopping streets—from Piazza dei Martiri to Via dei Mille and the Riviera di Chiaia. On this wide seaside promenade resides Italy's most famous tie-maker, Maurizio Marinella. In his tiny store you can choose from among myriad different silks and, like many famous men the world over, have a tie custom made. A variety of seaside restaurants

are clustered around the Castel dell'Ovo, the stout Anjou fortress jutting into the sea, and in the recently spruced-up Borgo Marinaro at its feet, where Neapolitans break for a coffee or a generous plate of maccheroni and fish fresh from the gulf.

ROOMS: The apartment is composed of a double room, living room with a sofa bed, bathroom, and kitchen. Minimum stay two nights.

AMENITIES:
English and French are spoken
Laundry service is available
Dinner can be served on request
Children over the age of ten are
  welcome
Pets are not allowed

WHERE. The Naples airport is 7 miles away. The Mergellina railway station is about a mile away, while the main railway station is 2 1/2 miles away.

CATEGORY: ✳✳✳ ◆ **RATE:** ○○ ◆ *Member since 1999*

NAPLES–MONTESANTO

INFO: CAFFÈLLETTO, ITALY

TEL. +39 023311814 OR 1820 ⬧ **FAX +39 023313009** ⬧ **E-MAIL: info@caffelletto.it**

This is a very large apartment in an eighteenth-century palazzo at the heart of historic and histrionic Naples, with all the colorful hustle and bustle that this implies.

Your hosts have recently restored their home. They are both doctors and live here all year-round with their three children. The apartment exudes a happy family atmosphere with a large kitchen in the center and a living room full of books and music.

The apartment has been designed on two levels in order for guests to be completely independent and assured of their privacy. Privacy being a very English concept somewhat alien to the Neapolitans, your hosts will only be too glad to share their space and time with guests who choose to chat or listen to music in the living room. On warm summer evenings guests may dine on the terrace with the city of Naples in full view. The apartment is located at the center of the city's cultural hub. Within easy reach is the extraordinary Museo Archeologico Nazionale; the Monastery of Santa Chiara, whose eighteenth-century majolica-tiled cloister is not to be missed; the Church of San Lorenzo, a palimpsest of different eras and styles; and the Cloister of San Gregorio Armeno, where all year-round, but especially in the months before Christmas, artisans in tiny workshops create the scenery and protagonists for the legendary Neapolitan crèche. Everyone is welcome in Neapolitan Bethlehem. In addition your hosts can provide invaluable information about restaurants serving Neapolitan specialties and, in particular, where to find the best pizza in town.

ROOMS: Two doubles each with private bathroom. Minimum stay two nights.

AMENITIES:
English is spoken
Laundry service is available
Dinner can be served on request
Children under the age of two stay free of charge
Pets are not allowed

WHERE: The Mergellina and Napoli–Centrale railway stations are about 2 1/2 miles away. The Naples airport is 7 miles away.

CATEGORY: ✳✳✳✳ ⬧ **RATE:** ⵔ ⬧ *Member since 1999*

NAPLES–SANTA LUCIA

BORGO MARINARO · 80121 NAPLES
TEL. +39 08124052 · FAX +39 0817645619 · CELL +39 3477748238
E-MAIL: info@jordanandjordan.it

This boat, a brand-new Jeanneau 45.2 over forty-six feet long, is moored in the Bay of Naples at the Borgo Marinaro. Naples's famous seafront promenade displays a pompous nineteenth-century facade of luxury hotels and myriad little shops and restaurants in the pedestrian area below. From the portholes there is a magnificent view of Vesuvius, while at night the Castel dell'Ovo alternates in color from red to yellow to azure blue. Guests may watch the variegated colors of the Neapolitan scenario pass by from the deck of the boat. Breakfast is served in the warm cherry-wood interior with walls of marine blue and white. A strong cup of Neapolitan coffee will be offered but your hosts are also pleased to honor a lighter alternative; they are young and enthusiastic, determined to make this unusual new venture a success. The boat is moored within a short walking distance of the main Piazza del Plebiscito and the San Carlo Opera House.

ROOMS: The boat has four double cabins. There are two bathrooms with showers, central heating, and television. The boat is under surveillance during the day, while at night the gates to the port are locked. Minimum stay two nights.

AMENITIES:
Open from October 15 to March 25
English and French are spoken
There is a covered parking lot for a fee
* not far from Borgo Marinaro*
Short cruises in the bay can be arranged
* for a fee*
Children under the age of two stay free
* of charge*

WHERE: The Napoli–Mergellina railway station is about 2 miles away, while the city airport is about 18 miles away. By car take highway Roma–Napoli, exit at Napoli Porto Via Marina, and follow the road toward the Tunnel della Vittoria. Before entering the tunnel turn left and follow the signs for Santa Lucia until you come to Borgo Marinaro.

CATEGORY: ✳✳✳✳ · **RATE**: ○○○ · *Member since 2002*

SANT'ANTIMO (NA)

INFO: CAFFÈLLETTO, ITALY

TEL. +39 023311814 OR 1820 • **FAX +39 023313009** • **E-MAIL: info@caffelletto.it**

This aristocratic palazzo, in the heart of the historic town of Sant' Antimo, is six miles from Naples. Surrounded by churches and convents, the house itself is steeped in history. Erected between 1600 and 1800, it is built around a large courtyard (4,300 square feet) paved in volcanic stone from Vesuvius with two gateways large enough to accommodate heavily loaded horse-drawn carts. In the middle, a magnificent palm tree reminds us that we are in southern Italy, within thirty minutes, not only from Naples, but also from Caserta and its royal palace, San Leucio, and its silk looms—as well as the Neapolitan coastline. Your hostess, an artist who works in an atelier on the ground floor, has lovingly restored the palazzo to its former glory. The delicate eggshell-blue walls of the interiors set off the polished sheen of the antique furnishings and the old-master paintings on the walls. Breakfasts are served in the dining room and feature delectable specialties of the region from bread baked in age-old ovens to the justifiably renowned Neapolitan sfogliatella, a flaky shell-shaped pastry.

ROOMS: One double room with a private bathroom.

AMENITIES:
English is spoken
Private parking
Guests may be picked up from the airport in Naples for a fee

WHERE: The nearest railway station is in Naples, 9 miles away, while the airport is 6 miles away.

CATEGORY: Caffèlletto • **RATE:** ○ • *Member since 2003*

CICCIANO (NA)

INFO: CAFFÈLLETTO, ITALY

TEL. +39 023311814 OR 1820 · **FAX +39 023313009** · **E-MAIL: info@caffelletto.it**

The town of Cicciano is an ideal starting point for day trips to Naples, Caserta, Sorrento, or the Amalfi Coast. The highway can be picked up at nearby Nola, while Cicciano is linked to Naples by the convenient Circumvesuviana railway line. Trains leave every twenty-five minutes and arrive in the historic center of Naples in about forty minutes.

Casa Palazziata is an eighteenth-century palace whose inner courtyard smells of fragrant jasmine and whose walls are covered with bright bougainvillea. The garden is shaded by stout palm trees and is redolent with the scents of magnolia and citrus. You

will be welcomed by Sistke, the charming Dutch owner responsible for the beautiful garden. An expert in flowers and plants, she will also be glad to suggest itineraries to help you discover the local flora. The apartment available for guests looks out over the courtyard and is furnished with antiques belonging to the family.

ROOMS: There are two apartments, both with separate entrances. In one apartment there is a double bedroom, a single room, and a bathroom; in the other, a hall, a double bedroom, and a bathroom. Minimum stay two nights.

AMENITIES:

English, German, French, and Dutch are spoken
Dinner can be served on request in the dining room of
*   the main villa*
Laundry service is available
Private parking
Swimming pool and tennis courts are nearby
Children under the age of two stay free of charge
Pets are welcome

WHERE: While the railway station is in Nola, 3 miles away, the nearest airport is the Capodichino airport in Naples, 18 miles away. A five-minute walk from the villa, there is regular bus service to Nola and other interesting spots in the area to be discovered.

CATEGORY: ✳✳✳✳ · **RATE:** ○ · *Member since 1998*

PIANO DI SORRENTO (NA)

INFO: CAFFÈLLETTO, ITALY

TEL. +39 023311814 OR 1820 · FAX +39 023313009 · E-MAIL: info@caffelletto.it

This house, not far from Sorrento and Positano, is in the main square of the historic village of Mòrtara. The square itself is com-posed of a Mediterranean scenario with the facade of the church along one side and a small booth selling coffee and lemon granita (a refreshing crushed-ice drink) on the other. The house has a garden on three sides with fruit trees, bougainvillea, palm trees, and hydrangea bushes.

Built at the beginning of the eighteenth century, the villa surrounds a fascinating courtyard with a beautiful kitchen on the ground floor. A stairway leads up from the courtyard to the main floor and its suite of salons, bedrooms, and the family chapel. The house was a wedding present to a favorite niece and has changed little over the years, ancestral charm prevailing over modern plumbing. It is one of the five villas along the coast of Sorrento that are considered landmarks. Although he lives in Rome, your host finds every excuse to take refuge in his villa where, in the warmer months, breakfast is served on the terrace.

ROOMS: A suite made up of a double room with living room and a bathroom (with shower) to which another bedroom can be added with a small functional bathroom (without shower). In both cases the bathrooms are in the corridor. Recently two delightful apartments have been restored. The first one is on the ground floor and features a living/dining room with a double sofa bed and kitchen corner, and one double bedroom with a bathroom (with shower); the second is an air-conditioned loft with an elegant double bedroom, a small kitchen, and a bathroom (with shower). Minimum stay two nights.

AMENITIES:
Open from January 15 to July 30 and from
September 1 to December 20
English, French, and Spanish are spoken
Dinner may be served on request
Children under the age of two stay
free of charge
Pets are welcome

WHERE: The nearest railway station is Piano di Sorrento, less than a mile away, while the airport is in Naples, 31 miles away.

CATEGORY: **Caffèlletto** · RATE: ○○ · *Member since 2001*

ASTAPIANA (NA)

VIA CAMALDOLI 25 · 80070 VICO EQUENSE, NAPLES
TEL. +39 0818024392 · FAX +39 081403797 · E-MAIL: giuliael@tin.it

Once a monastery, Astapiana was built near Vico Equense at the beginning of the seventeenth century by order of Matteo da Capua, prince of Conca and lord of Vico Equense. The monks were forced to leave under Napoleonic rule, while the monastery became the refuge of Gioacchino Murat in 1815 after the debacle of Waterloo. Since 1976, the Italian Beni Culturali (National Trust), due to its historic and architectural value, has protected Astapiana. With a view of the sea and Mount Faito, the house is in an ideal position to enjoy the lure of the sun and the ocean, as well as the welcome shade and cool breeze of the hillsides, where there are plenty of walking trails.

Astapiana is roughly two miles from Sorrento, Positano, Praiano, and Amalfi, all well known for their beaches, restaurants, boutiques, and cultural events. Ravello, an enchanting town a little further down the coast, holds a concert festival each summer: Theatrical performances, popular feast days, and picturesque religious pageants especially during Easter week and on the various saints' days, are celebrated and held.

The present owner of Astapiana is a determined young woman who decided to

restore the property to its former splendor. The living room is furnished with period pieces typical of Southern Italy in the last century with silk upholstery in mellow golden tints and floors made from the local volcanic stone. Guests may either breakfast in the majestic kitchen of the old guest house with the original ceramic tiles and large fireplace or, in warmer weather, on the terrace overlooking orange trees, grape arbors, and the sea.

ROOMS: Four rooms, one double and three with twin beds, with two bathrooms. The rooms are large, airy, and pleasantly furnished with care and good taste. Minimum stay two nights.

AMENITIES:
English and French are spoken
Parking on the premises
Dinner can be served on request
Children under the age of two stay free of charge
Pets are not allowed

WHERE: The airport in Naples is about 28 miles away. The Circumvesuviana line is 4 miles from the house. By car from the north take highway A1 Milano–Napoli, and then merge onto Napoli–Salerno. Exit at Castellammare. Follow the directions to Sorrento and Positano. At Seiano make a left toward Monte Faito, continue on the Via Raffaele Bosco, after 3 miles turn right toward Camaldoli.

CATEGORY: ✳✳✳✳ · RATE: ○○ · *Member since 1999*

NAPOLI–VIA PETRARCA

INFO: CAFFÈLLETTO, ITALY

TEL. +39 023311814 OR 1820 · FAX +39 023313009 · E-MAIL: info@caffelletto.it

Via Petrarca is in the affluent quarter of Naples, and is a quiet residential street with grandiose views sweeping over the Gulf of Mergellina. Some of the most elegant cafés of Naples are here, with wide terraces where the unhurried locals sit and sip their aperitifs in the early evening watching the sun begin its descent into the bay.

The apartment is on a side street off Via Petrarca, with a secluded terrace looking out over a slice of sea. Here, surrounded by flowers and greenery, guests are served breakfast on sunny mornings. This is a well-maintained and dignified palazzo with a doorman and elevator (although there is an additional short flight of steps up to the front door). The décor is cool and congenial, in various shades of blue, with majolica floors, comfortable chairs, flower vases, and personal touches like family photographs. Dinner can be served in the elegant dining room, where the oval table is always laid with family silver, and there is a veranda above green trees and lush foliage where guests can sit for afternoon tea. The hostess, always accompanied by Cherie, her inseparable Dachshund, prepares everything herself, using only organic products and baking her own cakes and focaccia.

In Naples it is a joy to stroll in the streets, and Via Petraca leads all the way to the Parco Virgiliano, where a rather dubious legend sustains that Virgil is buried. From here the hillside plunges down to the sea, and the view spans out over Vesuvius and Sorrento as far as Pozzuoli and the Campi Flegrei.

ROOMS: Two double rooms share a bathroom with shower. Sheets embroidered by hand decorate the light, charming rooms fragrant with potpourri. Both rooms have views towards the sea on one side and trees on the other.

AMENITIES:

Basic English and French are spoken
Internet connection available for a small fee
Children under the age of two stay free of
 charge
Lunch and dinner may be served on request
Use of washing machine
Garage space available upon advance
 request at time of reservation

WHERE: The nearest railway station is Napoli Mergellina about 2 miles away, while the airport is 6 miles away. From Mergellina hydrofoil service leaves regularly for Capri, Ischia, Procida, and the Aeolian islands. There is a bus stop at the end of the park.

CATEGORY: ✳✳✳✳ · **RATE:** ○○ · *Member since 2005*

SCALA (SA)

INFO: CAFFÈLLETTO, ITALY

TEL. +39 023311814 OR 1820 ◆ **FAX +39 023313009** ◆ **E-MAIL: info@caffelletto.it**

The coastline of Amalfi needs little introduction, but here we are further inland on Mount Amalfi itself, with a splendid view from the terrace toward Ravello and, of course, the sea. A path leads down through the fields to the nearest beach at Atrani. Similar to the other houses built on the hillside, this was once a peasant cottage with terraced steppes for orange and lemon trees, olive groves, and bougainvillea. The house itself, the summer home of two architects who teach at the University of Naples, is cheerful and colorful, with a garden bordered by lavender bushes and a stepped path, typical of the Amalfi coast, leads to the house. Breakfast features homemade jams and baked goods.

ROOMS: A double room with a bathroom (with shower). A second room is available

with a terrace (with shared bathroom). Guests will want to spend most of their time on the panoramic terrace above and there is also an indoor sitting room. Minimum stay two nights.

AMENITIES:

Closed during August
English and French are spoken
Children over the age of twelve are welcome
Pets are not allowed

WHERE: The nearest railway station is in Salerno, 21 miles away, while the airport in Napoli–Capodichino is 37 miles away. Buses run regularly from Salerno and Naples.

CATEGORY: ✳✳✳✳ ◆ **RATE:** ○ ◆ *Member since 2001*

GIUNGANO (SA)

DOMUS LAETA B&B ◆ **VIA FLAVIO GIOIA 1** ◆ **84050 GIUNGANO, SALERNO**
TEL. +39 0828880177 ◆ **CELL +39 3398687983** ◆ **E-MAIL: domuslaeta@libero.it**

The national park of Cilento is protected under the World Heritage Fund. It comprises more than four million acres of land, with 3,500 vegetable species and signs of human habitation dating 600,000 years back. Eighty villages are surrounded by a spectacular landscape. Giungano is a village in the park at the foot of the Alburni Mountains and was founded a millennium ago by peoples from the coast seeking refuge from Saracen pirates.

The Domus Laeta (the Latin name of this bed-and-breakfast) was originally a fortress—the ancient turrets and slit windows are still visible today. The Domus Laeta has always been self-sufficient, with spring water in the terraced garden, lush vines and fruit trees, its own stables, stone oil press, winery, and wood oven on one level, and with a fresco-covered loggia, library, and reception rooms above. The ancient pool that once collected rainwater has been converted into a splendid swimming pool with a Jacuzzi. The house is impeccably furnished with family antiques.

The area is famous not only for its closeness to the Greek temples of Paestum and Vella, but also for its castles, sanctuaries (Santuario della Madonna del Granato, Getsemani, and Certosa di Padula, which alone is worth the detour), and grottoes (Castelcivita and Pertosa). For those who like simply to lie in the sun, the coast is rich with coves and sandy beaches. In the plain, herds of black buffalo provide the rich milk used to make mozzarella di bufala, unlike anything you will taste elsewhere.

ROOMS: One suite with a double bedroom and a room with twin beds with private bathroom (with shower) and a small bathroom, and two double bedrooms, each with private bathrooms (with showers). Minimum stay two nights.

AMENITIES:
English and French are spoken
Laundry service is available
Dinner may be served on request
Children over the age of eight are welcome
Pets are welcome

WHERE: The railway station at Paestum is 7 miles away, while the Naples airport is 68 miles away. By car take highway Salerno–Reggio Calabria and exit at Battipaglia. Follow the signs for Paestum. One mile after Paestum you will find the sign for Giungano on the left.

CATEGORY: Caffelletto ◆ **RATE:** ○○ ◆ *Member since 2000*

CASTELLABATE (SA)

LA MOLA ◆ VIA A. CILENTO 2 ◆ 84014 CASTELLABATE, SALERNO
TEL. +39 0974967053 ◆ FAX +39 0974967714 ◆ CELL +39 3351292800
E-MAIL: lamola@lamola-it.com

This ancient palazzo with a medieval tower sits above the town of Castellabate and boasts breathtaking views of the Gulf of Cilento. On clear days, one can see as far as the island of Capri. From the splendid terrace with its flourishing bougainvillea and lemon and olive trees, a path lined with rosemary bushes and pomegranate trees leads down to a terraced garden. Your hosts have renovated the tower and furnished it with valuable family antiques, including a seventeenth-century Neapolitan crèche. White walls and fluttering white curtains with pale patterns contribute to the delightfully cool interiors. Breakfasts feature homemade pastries and can be served either in the dining room or on the terrace overlooking the sea. Beaches are not far, and small boats can be rented to visit the Punta Licosa and the grottoes of Palinuro.

ROOMS: All rooms have a refrigerator and television set and all but one looks out over the sea. Tarassacum is a double with the option of a third bed, with a bathroom (with shower). Arnica is a large and comfortable double room with a sofa bed, and a bathroom (with shower) next to the bedroom. Angelica is a lovely room with a wrought-iron double bed and a bathroom (with bathtub and shower). There is also a small apartment with a private entrance, with two rooms, one with a double bed and one with two single beds, and a small terrace. All double beds can be converted into twin beds on request. Minimum stay two nights.

AMENITIES:
English and French are spoken
Laundry service is available
Dinner may be served on request
Children under the age of two stay free of charge
Pets are welcome

WHERE: The nearest railway station is Agropoli, 11 miles away, while the Naples airport is 62 miles away. By car take highway A30 Salerno–Reggio Calabria and exit at Battipaglia. Follow directions for Agropoli, toward Santa Maria di Castellabate. Once you reach the sign for Santa Maria, continue for another quarter mile and turn left toward the center (centro storico) of Castellabate and La Mola.

CATEGORY: Caffèlletto ◆ RATE: ○○○ ◆ *Member since 1999*

SAN MARCO DI CASTELLABATE (SA)

INFO: CAFFÈLLETTO, ITALY

TEL. +39 023311814 OR 1820 · FAX +39 023313009 · E-MAIL: info@caffelletto.it

Villa Giacaranda is a charming nineteenth-century villa surrounded by a fragrant Mediterranean garden. The villa is a short distance from the Greek temples of Paestum. Your hosts, an aunt and her two nieces, like to call the Villa Giacaranda "the domain of cats and other details," which is similar to Laurence Durrell's "my family and other animals," in that the cats are the unchallenged masters of the home.

Fortunately it is your hostesses, rather than the cats, who have supervised the furnishing of the rooms with hand-embroidered linens, antique cupboards and chests of drawers, and stereo equipment in every room so that guests may listen to a choice of classical or modern music. Breakfast is served either in your room or in the garden with marmalade and peach or apricot jams all prepared exclusively for the guests. Your

charming hostesses are justifiably proud of their Mediterranean, or more precisely Cilento, cuisine. With a glass of white wine at cocktail hour comes sage fried in olive oil, ricotta cheese with mint, and celery-flavored pickled olives. But this is just an overture to the stuffed rice timbales, ravioli with rosemary, fish fritto misto, cherry tarts, and almond cake.

But Villa Giacaranda is not just a food lover's paradise. The house organizes seminars from April to October and excursions to places of cultural interest are constantly on the agenda. In the vicinity are the temples of Paestum, more beautiful than any in Greece, the castle of Agropoli, and the town of Laureana Cilento with its historic palazzos and classical music festival held each summer. Also nearby at Palinuro and Camerota are beaches and the clear, translucent sea.

ROOMS: Seven double bedrooms, each with its own bathroom.

AMENITIES

English, French, German, and Greek are spoken
Laundry service is available
Parking on the premises
Dinner may be served on request
Tennis court
Baby-sitting service if required
Children under the age of two stay free of charge

WHERE: The nearest airport is in Naples, 74 miles away. The railway station is in Agropoli, 7 miles away. By car from Rome take the Salerno–Reggio Calabria highway and exit at Battipaglia. Follow the directions for Agropoli and exit at Agropoli Sud. Drive to San Marco di Castellabate; once you are there, call your hosts, and they will come and pick you up.

CATEGORY: ✳✳✳✳ · RATE: ○○ · *Member since 1999*

Apulia

Apulia is the heel of the Italian boot, surrounded on three sides by water—the Adriatic Sea to the east, and the Strait of Otranto and Gulf of Taranto in the southwest. The main cities are Bari, Brindisi, Taranto, Foggia, and Lecce. Visitors are most likely to want to explore Lecce for its splendid baroque facades. This lovely city has nothing to envy in Florence, the famous Renaissance center further north. Although Apulia could not be further south geographically, people are more "northern" in spirit than their neighbors. Bari, for instance, has a flourishing economy and, with its elegant boutiques and tree-lined boulevards, it could just as easily be likened to Milan or Turin.

In Apulia, it is the small centers that are particularly rewarding. Travelers flock to Alberobello, where the famous limestone trulli (conical dwellings dating back to the Middle Ages) are nestled together on steep slopes. Other worthwhile destinations are Otranto, from where the crusaders left to fight the infidels; Gallipoli and Monopoli, whose names hark back to the Greeks who colonized this part of Italy; Trani, whose splendid eleventh-century Duomo is silhouetted against the sea, many coastal resorts; and the Tremiti Islands. This region is far enough south for the sea;

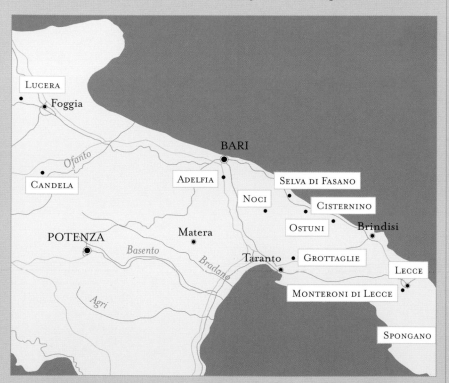

228 to be free of pollution and crystal clear. The countryside is flat and fertile with a rich red soil and olive trees with old twisted trunks, making this region famous for its olive oil cultivation.

THE LOCAL RECIPE

Apulia's long coastline faces Greece. Most of the land is fertile and its food reflects a mingling of seaside fare and agricultural products. The culinary tradition of Apulia often mixes vegetables with fish, a fortunate combination emphasized by the inventiveness of this creative cuisine.

Squid and Potato Casserole

Ingredients (serves 4)

24 oz. potatoes
4 medium-sized squid
1 tbsp. minced parsley
1 tbsp. grated pecorino cheese

1 tbsp. breadcrumbs
2 cloves of garlic
olive oil, salt, and pepper to taste

Pour a half cup of hot salted water in a casserole dish. Wash and peel the potatoes, then slice and spread them evenly on the bottom of the casserole dish. Wash and trim the squid, cut them into strips, and distribute them over the potatoes. Make a second layer of sliced potatoes. Put the garlic on top and sprinkle with the pecorino cheese, parsley, and breadcrumbs. Season with salt and pepper and drizzle with abundant olive oil. Bake for about 45 minutes at 325° F.

CANDELA (FG)

MASSERIA CANESTRELLO · 71024 CANDELA, FOGGIA
TEL. AND FAX +39 0885660792 · E-MAIL: giorgio@masseriacanestrello.it

This sprawling, attractive farmhouse seems to stand alone, stark white against a blue sky, in a landscape that stretches straight into the horizon. It was once a resting place for shepherds and their herds descending from the mountains of Abruzzo, where they had spent the summer on their way to winter pastures in Apulia. It is here that the wheat for which Apulia is famous is grown. The bed-and-breakfast is on the banks of the Ofanto River,

which marks the boundary with the region of Basilicata and is surrounded by orchards. Cherries, figs, apricots, and pears grow among the olive trees and giant cactus plants. The interiors are spacious, vaulted, and whitewashed with beamed ceilings, cobalt blue doors and shutters. Your hosts are gentlemen farmers who started restoring the house ten years ago. Breakfasts include jams made from the apricots or cherries growing in the garden. Because of its position on the cusp of both regions, this is an excellent starting point when touring both Apulia and Basilicata.

ROOMS: All six rooms—each with their own private entrance—are on the ground floor and can be heated in fall and winter. The largest room has a small sitting room with satellite television and a double bed with a bathroom (with bathtub). There is another double room with a bathroom (with shower), and a sitting room with a fireplace and television. Another room has three twin beds and a bathroom (with bathtub); another has two twin beds and one double bed, a bathroom (with bathtub), a kitchenette, and a washing machine. The fifth room has a double and a twin bed, a bathroom (with shower), kitchenette, and a washing machine. The last one is a double with a bathroom (with shower) and kitchenette that looks out over the swimming pool.

AMENITIES:
Open April 15 to October 15 and in winter on request
English, French, and Spanish are spoken
Private parking
Large swimming pool
Dinner, when requested, is simple and guests are invited
  to participate and suggest their own recipes
Children under the age of two stay free of charge
Pets are welcome

WHERE: The nearest railway station is Candela, 7 miles away, while the airport in Foggia is 28 miles away. There is a comfortable coach service from Naples, which takes 1 1/2 hours. By car take highway Napoli–Bari and exit at Candela. Turn left and then turn immediately right, following the directions to Rocchetta (Strada Provinciale 98). At the Rocchetta intersection go straight on Strada Provinciale 97. Six miles from the Candela exit, turn right at the crossroads at an abandoned house. After about 2 miles there is a sign, "Apo Foggia Cooperativa La Croce Farascusa." Turn right again and at the end of the road, past the Cooperativa and a short dirt road, you'll reach the Masseria Canestrello.

CATEGORY: ✳✳✳✳ · RATE: ○○ · *Member since 2002*

230 ADELFIA (BA)

INFO: CAFFÈLLETTO, ITALY

TEL. +39 023311814 OR 1820 · FAX +39 023313009 · E-MAIL: info@caffelletto.it

This is a grand palazzo with a suitably grand name: Palazzo De Bianchi Dottula di Montrone at Adelfia, a little town nine miles from Bari. It is one of the few noble mansions still intact in the area. The palazzo dates back to the fourteenth century, when it was built by the feudal lord Nicolo Dottula. Since then many owners have come and gone, each leaving behind a different architectural legacy until, at the end

of the eighteenth century, the Marquis Luigi De Bianchi di Montrone married Francesca Dottula, the last descendant of the original owner. The palazzo still belongs to their descendants today. However, the role of host has been more than adequately taken over by the aptly named Angelo. He tends to the flowers in the central courtyard, where he also serves breakfasts in the warmer months. His love for the palazzo is evident in every corner of every room and it is his smiling face that greets guests upon arrival. He is also a collector of ancient tools, which he keeps in the old

cellar. Adelfia is ideally situated for touring Apulia and visiting its Romanesque abbeys and Swabian castles. The sea is only seven miles away.

ROOMS: On the palace's first floor is a suite with frescoed ceilings and two large independent double rooms, a kitchen, and a third room with a queen-size sofa bed. Each room has a private bathroom. On the same floor is a room with two sofa beds, a terrace, and a bathroom (with shower). Minimum stay two nights.

AMENITIES:
Open May through November, and other times if due notice is given
English and German spoken
Private parking
Pets are welcome

WHERE: The nearest train station is Adelfia, 2 miles away, which offers daily service to Bari, whose airport is 12 miles away.

CATEGORY: **Caffèlletto** · RATE: ○○○ · *Member since 2001*

INFO: CAFFÈLLETTO, ITALY

TEL. +39 023311814 OR 1820 ◦ **FAX +39 023313009** ◦ **E-MAIL: info@caffelletto.it**

In Apulia, a "masseria" is a rather grand term for a farmhouse, in that when a farmer became a gentleman farmer he went to great lengths to make his house reflect his new status. The Albanese family, who built this farmhouse in the eighteenth century, went to such lengths that local architectural journals often print learned essays on the "Masseria Albanese." The grandfather of your hosts purchased the masseria from the last of the Albanese family, whose fortunes went into a dramatic downward spiral as a result of their republican leanings during the reign of the Bourbon kings. Your hosts, mother and daughter, are both excellent cooks, a talent guests are made well aware of from breakfast onward. It is what journals call a "cubic masseria," a handsome neoclassical square building.

The masseria is five miles from Alberobello, the famous village in Apulia where all the cottages ("trulli") are conical, with tall, white thatched chimneys built around a central fireplace. The splendid seacoast of Apulia is half an hour away. The surrounding countryside is among the loveliest in southern Italy, with cherry and almond trees and the ancient trunks of olive trees firmly planted in the brick-red soil, swathed in a veil of delicate white flowers.

ROOMS: A double and twin-bedded room, both with their own bathroom, in the masseria. In the guest wing, a double room with bath, sitting room, and small kitchen. This apartment also has a patio and separate entrance.

AMENITIES:
Open from March 15 until January 15
English, French, and Spanish are spoken
Parking on premises
Laundry service is available
Dinner may be served on request
Children under the age of two stay free
of charge

WHERE: The nearest railway station is in Noci, less than 5 miles away, while the airport in Bari is less than 40 miles away.

CATEGORY: **Caffèlletto** ◦ RATE: ○○ ◦ *Member since 2000*

SELVA DI FASANO VILLA ELENA (BR)

INFO: CAFFÈLLETTO, ITALY

TEL. +39 023311814 OR 1820 • **FAX +39 023313009** • **E-MAIL: info@caffelletto.it**

Selva is one of the most popular places to take pre-teen children because of its Safari Zoo, which boasts 1,000 animals roaming wild around (and all over) your car. Selva is in a landscape of remarkable natural beauty at 1,000 feet above the sea. This house, built a century ago, commands a spectacular view of the area from the garden, whose pines, cypresses, olives, and oaks are at least as old as the house itself. The Mediterranean vegetation jostles for space with rosemary, jasmine, and viburnum bushes. Breakfast can be enjoyed in various unexpected corners of the garden, under the shade of a pergola or gazebo, on the terrace overlooking the valley, or in the dining room or kitchen of this fascinating old house. Your hostess has lived here since she was a child and it has been in her family for generations. She is rightfully proud of her Apulian roots and delighted to share many lesser-known aspects of the countryside, culture, and cuisine.

ROOMS: A double room with a bathroom (with both bathtub and shower), and a

twin room with a bathroom (with shower), which can be rented in conjunction with another room, preferably for one person, to become an independent suite. Minimum stay three nights.

AMENITIES:
French is spoken
Laundry service is available
Lunch or dinner may be served on request

WHERE: The nearest railway station is in Fasano, 4 miles away, while the Brindisi airport is 25 miles away.

CATEGORY: Caffèlletto • **RATE:** ○○ • *Member since 2002*

CISTERNINO (BR)

INFO: CAFFÈLLETTO, ITALY

TEL. +39 023311814 OR 1820 ⋅ FAX +39 023313009 ⋅ E-MAIL: info@caffelletto.it

Anyone who has been to Apulia will have been fascinated by the trulli, white limestone dwellings with conical roofs surrounded by olive trees almost as old as they are. This place close to Cisternino is just such a village, bought by a family from Brindisi who took the ancient structures apart stone by stone and put them together again, transforming them internally into comfortable cottages. Almost every trullo has a kitchen corner, although breakfast may also be served on the patio of the main trullo, where your hosts live themselves. The whole family—Marilena, Luca, Erika, and Francesca—

is involved in the running of this bed-and-breakfast and will organize sight-seeing tours to many beautiful spots in Apulia. They also organize courses in Italian, cooking, and acting (with an actor friend), and in the warmer months there are concerts nearly every evening in Cisternino's main square and in the beautiful towns of Ostuni and Martina Franca.

ROOMS: Two communicating trulli for four people with kitchen corner, fireplace, bathroom (with shower), and two overhead lofts with two queen-size futons. Two larger trulli, with three rooms each—one for five people, the other for six. All rooms

have a bathroom and kitchen corner. Three single trulli, two of which have queen-size beds and the other a bunk bed.

AMENITIES:

English and some German are spoken
Dinner may be served on request,
featuring local fresh produce such as
cheeses, tomatoes, cold cuts, and
vegetable preserves as well as delicious
pasta and bread
There is a riding school less than a mile
away with a restaurant
Pets are welcome

WHERE: The nearest stations are Cisternino for local trains, 3 miles away, and Ostuni for all others, 9 miles away. The airport is in Brindisi, 31 miles away.

CATEGORY: ✳✳✳✳ ⋅ **RATE:** ○○ ⋅ *Member since 2001*

OSTUNI (BR)

234

IL FRANTOIO ✦ **STATALE 16 KM 874** ✦ **CAS. POST. 25** ✦ **72017 OSTUNI**
TEL. AND FAX +39 0831330276 ✦ **E-MAIL: armando@trecolline.it**

Il Frantoio is Italian for the place where olives are pressed into olive oil and this magnificent fortified structure dating back to the seventeenth century is surrounded by 4,200 olive trees and has been built on the foundations of an ancient olive oil press. Its white walls are almost blinding in the Mediterranean sun. Although completely restored, the Frantoio has preserved its authentic character as a Masseria Pugliese (large Apulian farmhouse). Neither villa nor castle nor manor house, this handsome complex of buildings at one time housed the entire rural hierarchy, from the lord of the manor down to the day-old chick freshly hatched from the egg. The Frantoio is near the old hilltop town of Ostuni, four miles from the Adriatic coast and the sea.

Nearly all the windows look out onto a courtyard blooming with fragrant flowering plants. As soon as the evenings are warm enough, dinner is served in the courtyard under a starry sky, with menus inspired by the produce from the farm.

ROOMS: There are eight rooms with two to five beds in each, all with a bathroom. Each room is furnished in a different style, with the inimitable flair of your hostess.

AMENITIES:
Open all year-round
A library with more than 1,500 old books
Table tennis, mountain biking, horseback riding
Two private sandy beaches, five minutes away by car
Deck chairs and umbrellas available for guests
For guests who are interested, organically grown farm products are for sale

WHERE: The nearest airport is in Brindisi, 22 miles away, while the railway station is in Ostuni, 3 miles away. If you are traveling by car, take superstrada 379 from Bari to Pezze di Greco where you will find road signs for Ostuni. Follow them on State Road 16 until you reach the Frantoio.

CATEGORY: Caffelletto ✦ **RATE:** ○○○○ ✦ *Member since 1998*

INFO: CAFFÈLLETTO, ITALY

TEL. +39 023311814 OR 1820 F FAX +39 023313009 F E-MAIL: INFO@CAFFELLETTO.IT

Grottaglie is a hilltop town in Apulia known for its artisans working in ceramic. With as many as a thousand potters tucked away behind their wheels along the narrow side streets, the city offers a trove of handmade objects. Your host is a writer and winner of a literary prize for his first novel, while his wife is the author of a successful cookbook of local recipes; she also organizes cooking courses.

The Palazzo Pignatelli belongs to the Pignatelli family and has an ineffable storybook charm. Its sixteenth century facade, baroque balcony, and art nouveau frescoes convey a whimscal and playful atmosphere. From under the pergola (where breakfast is served during the warmer months) with its splendid majolica tiles, the garden slopes down the hillside under a series of baroque arches. Travelers should visit the Hellenic Museum of Taranto where a unique collection of ancient Greek goldsmith's objects is on view.

ROOMS: A suite with a spacious double bedroom, frescoed ceiling, and a double room with a bathroom. Minimum stay 2 nights.

AMENITIES:
English, French, Spanish, and Portuguese are spoken.

WHERE: The railway station is less than a mile away, while the Brindisi airport is 30 miles away. The Grottaglie airport will soon be opened and will be 2 miles away.

CATEGORY: **Caffèlletto** · RATE: ⭕⭕ ·
Member since 2001

ANDRIA (BA)

BIOMASSERIA LAMA DI LUNA ◆ **LOC. MONTEGROSSO** ◆ **70031 ANDRIA, BARI**
TEL. AND FAX +39 0883569505 ◆ **CELL +39 3280117375** ◆ **E-MAIL: info@lamadiluna.com**

This *masseria* is grouped around a beautiful courtyard with forty chimneys pointing into the intense blue sky. Lama di Luna is heated by fireplaces as it was centuries ago, while forty solar panels do the rest. It is a total *feng-shui* experience where energy flows uninterrupted; north-facing beds are made of pine and olive wood, linens are unbleached cotton, and olive oil soap is used.

The estate covers 444 acres of olive groves, vinyards, almond and cherry orchards, sheep pastures, and various crops. Some of these products become break-fast, and everything is cooked on a wooden stove at the heart of the complex. Your host is a highly cultured agronomist who tends the estate year-round. Lama di Luna is near the seaside towns Barletta and Trani, and seminars are held here by Professor Lorenzo Ostuni, who is known worldwide for his research in philosophy.

ROOMS: Seven double rooms with vaulted ceilings and terracotta floors, all deco-rated with a sophisticated simplicity. One room has three beds, another has four, and all have their own bathroom with shower, fireplace, and French windows with a court-yard view. For those staying a full week, the seventh night is free.

AMENITIES:
English, French, and Spanish are spoken
Children under the age of two stay free
of charge
Private parking
Dinner may be served on request
Pets are welcome
Laundry service is available

WHERE: the nearest railway sta-tion is 12 miles away in Barletta, while the Bari airport is 44 miles away. By car take highway A14 and exit at Canosa di Puglia. Turn right as you exit towards Canosa, then drive on toward Andria on the SS 98, and after 37 miles take the turn for Montegrosso. From here drive towards Castel del Monte, and after 2 and 3/4 miles two pillars of tufaceous rock on your left mark the entrance to the avenue leading up to the *masseria*.

CATEGORY: **Caffelletto** ◆ **RATE**: ○○○ ◆ *Member since 2005*

CISTERNINO–2 (BR)

INFO: CAFFÈLLETTO, ITALY

TEL. +39 023311814 OR 1820 ♦ FAX +39 023313009 ♦ E-MAIL: info@caffelletto.it

Cisternino Trulli Country House is four miles from Alberobello, famous for its *trulli*, the conical whitewashed stone architecture typical of Apulia.

Here, too, there are *trulli* dating back to 1700 in an L-shaped *masseria* blazing white against the blue sky. The ancient trunks of olive trees are rooted in red clods of earth that look good enough to eat, surrounded by lacy white flowers like icing, twisted and contorted like children's illustrations by Arthur Rackham.

Your hostess is from Verona, has fallen in love with the area, and has restored this group of *trulli* respecting the original style and character with personal touches of her own. The result is full of charm, producing a harmonious combination of earthy colors and low-slung sofas and futon beds against whitewashed walls. Because she is a professional photographer, she always takes a portrait of guests before they leave and sends it to their home address.

Breakfasts are served on the patio under the mulberry tree. Cisternino is six miles from the sand beach of Ostuni and eight miles from the lovely sand and rock beach of Torre Canne. The medieval village of Cisternino comes alive in summer, when tables are set out in the narrow streets and on Sundays classical music accompanies the traditional aperitif. A magnificent golf club, the Golf Club San Domenico, is five miles away and has greens overlooking the sea.

ROOMS: Two double rooms with the option of a third bed and private bathroom, one with shower and one with shower and bathtub, as well as a romantic *trullo* with its own bathroom, though not en suite. Minimum stay two nights; in August minimum stay one week. Open from Easter to October. Out of season, groups of six and over are also welcome.

AMENITIES:
English and German are spoken
Private parking
Children under the age of five stay free of charge
Small pets are welcome
Massage and beauty treatments available for guests

WHERE: The nearest railway station is in Cisternino, six miles away, while the Bari airport is 37 miles away.

CATEGORY: ✱✱✱✱ ♦ **RATE:** ○ ♦
Member since 2004

LECCE–VITTORIO EMANUELE

INFO: CAFFÈLLETTO, ITALY

TEL. +39 023311814 OR 1820 ◆ **FAX +39 023313009** ◆ **E-MAIL: info@caffelletto.it**

This apartment is at the heart of the historic center of this beautiful Baroque city. Just around the corner from the Duomo, the bell tower can be seen from the garden and the guests' windows. The apartment is in the garden of the Carrelli Palombi family's palazzo. Built between the seventeenth and eighteenth centuries, it is perfectly typical of the Lecce Baroque style.

Your hosts do not live here all year-round, but their personality is palpable throughout the house: in the vivid choice of colors and furnishings, all in excellent taste, and the joyous atmosphere. Breakfast supplies can be found in the kitchen while just outside the palazzo gates is a bar, which serves some of the best croissants in Christendom!

ROOMS: An independent apartment on two levels: on the second level a sitting room with two sofa beds, one double and one single, and a bathroom (with shower). On the ground floor, a large sitting room with a single sofa bed, a bathroom (with

shower), and a fully-equipped kitchen with French windows opening onto the garden.

AMENITIES:
English and French are spoken
Children under the age of two stay free of charge

WHERE: The nearest railway station is in Lecce, a mile away, while the airport in Brindisi is 19 miles away.

CATEGORY: Caffèlletto ◆ **RATE:** ○○○ ◆ *Member since 2001*

MONTERONI DI LECCE (LE)

INFO: CAFFÈLLETTO, ITALY

TEL. +39 023311814 OR 1820 ♦ **FAX +39 023313009** ♦ **E-MAIL: info@caffelletto.it**

Stark against a blue sky, Panariello is a typical Mediterranean country villa not far from Lecce. Almost Moorish in style on the outside, the interior is ablaze with yellows and contrasts with the cool stone of the granite floors. The fireplace is highly decorative and is studded with ancient tiles. The rooms either open out onto gardens with Mediterranean palms, orange trees, pomegranate bushes, and weeping willows, or onto the pool behind the house. The upper floor has terraces on both sides of the villa, which look out over the countryside of Lecce.

The owners bought this house, built at the beginning of the twentieth century, in the early 1990s and your host not only supervised the restoration in every detail but also personally laid the oak floors in the bedrooms. He owes his mastery of woodwork to his experience in boat building. He constructed his twenty-six-foot sailing boat with his own hands. Your hostess is a German journalist. Two large dogs, chickens, geese, and a horse complete the family circle.

ROOMS: In the villa itself one double room with large windows overlooking the garden, wrought-iron bed, and a bathroom shared by the delightful single room in an alcove under a vaulted ceiling with a floor like the deck of a ship. In the guest wing downstairs there is an independent apartment with a small kitchen, double room, and bathroom that opens out onto the garden and a patio with stone benches where guests may breakfast nearly all year-round. Minimum stay two nights.

AMENITIES:

English and German are spoken
Parking on the premises
Swimming pool
Dinner is served on request
Your host will also organize outings on his
  sailboat from Otranto and Gallipoli
Children under the age of two stay free of charge
Pets are welcome

WHERE: The nearest railway station is in Lecce, 3 miles away, while the Brindisi airport is 28 miles away.

CATEGORY: **Caffèlletto** ♦ RATE: ○○ ♦ *Member since 2000*

SPONGANO (LE)

INFO: CAFFÈLLETTO, ITALY

TEL. +39 023311814 OR 1820 ✦ **FAX +39 023313009** ✦ **E-MAIL: info@caffelletto.it**

Only three miles from the sea at Castro Marina, with the whole Salento coast within easy reach, Spongano is an ideal starting point from which to tour southern Apulia, Lecce, Gallipoli, and Otranto. Spongano is a baronial palace still in family hands after five centuries. In the second half of the sixteenth century it was a castle. At the beginning of the seventeenth century it was transformed into a palace, incorporating the original medieval fortifications. Another floor was built in the second half of the nineteenth century by Baron Filippo to accommodate his fourteen children. The family still lives in the palazzo in the summer months.

ROOMS: There are four elegantly furnished double bedrooms with modern, en suite bathrooms and a fully-equipped kitchen overlooking a spacious terrace. A long imposing oak-beamed loft runs the whole length of this wing. There are also two large double bedrooms and one triple room with modern bathrooms (with both shower and bathtub). The immense drawing room with open fireplace at one end opens onto a series of terraces overlooking the main courtyard and the palace gardens below. On the ground floor there is an elegant suite and a small apartment with four beds, a bathroom, and a small kitchen (reservations for a minimum of six people). There are also three small cottages at the end of a Mediterranean garden with citrus groves; each of them has two double bedrooms with private bathrooms and a kitchen. In all the kitchens, guests will find the wherewithal for breakfast. Minimum stay seven nights.

AMENITIES:

English is spoken
Private parking
Swimming pool
Children under the age of two stay free of charge
Pets are not allowed

WHERE: The nearest railway station is Spongano, while the Brindisi airport is 59 miles away.

CATEGORY: Caffèlletto ✦ **RATE:** ○○○ ✦ *Member since 1998*

BASILICATA

Looking at the boot of Italy on a map, Basilicata corresponds to the area above the ankle to the instep, from the Gulf of Policastro in the west to the Ionian Sea. It is a beautiful mountainous region. In ancient Roman times, the region was known as Lucania, after the Lucani who occupied Basilicata from the seventh to the fifth century B.C. Ever since, the ancestors of the Lucani have lived in isolated communities in the hills, raising their sheep as the modern world passed them by. Sociologically and economically, the Lucani have presented a stumbling block for Italian governments since the beginning of the twentieth century, when the then—prime minister traveled the length of Basilicata in a cart drawn by oxen—the only means of transportation—to ascertain for himself the root of the problem. Every government pledges to redeem Basilicata and the rest of the Italian south, but little is achieved. Until recently, Italian railways bypassed the two main cities of Matera and Potenza on their way south, despite the fact that the famous sassi (stones) of Matera, rock-hewn dwellings carved into the face of a steep ravine, are sufficiently awe-inspiring to be designated a UNESCO World Heritage Site. Between 1950 and 1970 a third of the population left to find work in other regions of Italy or abroad. They remain staunchly attached to their homeland, however, and it is largely their savings that sus-

tain their relatives today. Tourism is bringing new life to the economy; ironically, the very things that prompted latter-day Lucani to leave for new worlds are what increasingly lure visitors to this unexplored region.

THE LOCAL RECIPE

Basilicata is rich in pastureland, allowing for a large production of cheeses: caciocavallo, scamorza, different kinds of pecorino, goat cheese, and ricotta, which can be fresh and creamy, suitable for desserts, or aged and sharp for grating on the lamb or mutton ragouts that often accompany pasta dishes. Pork salami and sausages are also very popular, including one bearing the ancient name of its region, lucanica, flavored with wild fennel. The queen of Basilicata, however, is pasta. From fusilli to cavatelli (a sort of dumpling), strascinati (similar to orecchiette) to lasagna, the different shapes and sizes are seemingly endless. In the sixth century B.C., Greeks brought a grapevine called aglianico, which even today produces the famous Aglianico del Vulture wine.

Lasagna with Fresh Beans
Ingredients (serves 4)

1 1/2 cup freshly shelled beans
2 garlic of cloves
lard
cayenne pepper to taste

FOR THE LASAGNA:
2 cups hard wheat flour
salt and water

Cook the fresh beans in a large quantity of salted water for about an hour. Mix the flour with the salt and water and knead the dough until it is smooth and elastic. Roll the dough very thin, fold, and cut into wide flat noodles. Sauté the pepper and garlic in the lard. Cook the lasagna al dente, drain, and transfer to a large bowl. Drain and add the beans and the lard, toss well, and serve very hot.

MARATEA (PZ)

INFO: CAFFÈLLETTO, ITALY

TEL. +39 023311814 OR 1820 ⋅ FAX +39 023313009 ⋅ E-MAIL: info@caffelletto.it

Maratea is a delightful seaside town along a rocky coastline not unlike that of Amalfi further north, but is less tourist-trodden. The sea itself is among the most translucent in the Mediterranean, with inviting little bays tucked into the coastline.

The house, typically Mediterranean in style, is found in a private complex of villas with lush gardens, and built around an inner courtyard with a splendid view over the bay. It is furnished with an elegant simplicity that befits a seaside residence. Squirrels scamper among the terraced gardens, unheeded by the two shar-peis, Eolo and Olivia, and by the dedicated and friendly gardener. Guests may use the swimming pool and tennis court, and a private beach is a fifteen-minute walk away. Breakfasts are wholesome and vary according to season.

ROOMS: A double room with a bathroom (with shower and bathtub) and another double room with the option of a third bed, a bathroom (with shower), and a private entrance from the inner courtyard. On the ground floor there is a large living room with a refrigerator, where guests can gather after a day on the beach. Minimum stay two nights.

AMENITIES:

*Open in August, September, and, weather
  permitting, October*
English is spoken
Laundry service is available
Private parking
Private beach access
Swimming pool and tennis court
Dinner may be served on request

WHERE: The nearest railway station is in Maratea, 2 miles away, while the airport in Naples is 186 miles away.

CATEGORY: Caffèlletto ⋅ RATE: ○○○ ⋅ *Member since 2002*

METAPONTO

INFO: CAFFÈLLETTO, ITALY
TEL. +39 023311814 OR 1820 · FAX +39 023313009 · E-MAIL: info@caffelletto.it

You don't have to play golf to stay at this golf club, but after a visit to this wedding-cake-white bed-and-breakfast set in the middle of emerald-green lawns surrounded by orange trees, you might be tempted to try.

The Metaponto is not strictly a bed-and-breakfast, but the large, luminous bedrooms with terraces overlooking the greens are furnished with the patrician decadence typical of gracious country-house living in the South. The large sitting room with its fireplace has the cozy comfort of clubhouses everywhere while substantial breakfasts are served in the elegant dining room. The area around the Metaponto Club House is of great artistic and archaeological interest, and includes the sassi (stones) of Matera, a UNESCO World Heritage Site. Also nearby are a museum, ancient ruins of Metaponto, the trulli of Alberobello, and Grottaglie, one of the most famous centers in Italy for hand-painted ceramics. The splendid white beaches of the Ionian Sea are only five miles away.

ROOMS: Four luxury double rooms and one suite all with Jacuzzi tubs, air-conditioning, television, telephone, safe, and minibar.

AMENITIES:
English, French, and German are spoken
Private parking
Restaurant and bar
TV lounge
Pro-shop
Sauna
18-hole championship golf course
Guests are welcome to use the facilities at the nearby Riva dei Tessali Hotel & Golf Resort

WHERE: The nearest railway station is in Metaponto, 2 miles away, while the Bari or Brindisi airports are an hour away.

CATEGORY: **Caffèlletto** · RATE: OOO · *Member since 2004*

SAN TEODORO NUOVO (MT)

TENUTA DI SAN TEODORO NUOVO ◆ 75020 MARCONIA

TEL. +39 0835470042 ◆ FAX +39 0835470223 ◆ E-MAIL: info@santeodoronuovo.com

In the heart of what was once the Magna Graecia, only sixteen miles from the white beaches of the Ionian Sea, San Teodoro Nuovo has been in the hands of a prominent aristocratic family for generations, and is surrounded by 370 acres of olive groves and vineyards. Inner courtyards are swathed in bougainvillea, while rose and orange blossoms perfume the air. Mediterranean bushes fringe the swimming pool. Your gracious hosts, mother and daughter, also run an organic agricultural enterprise. Breakfast is served in the farmhouse next to the villa and features ricotta cheese from flocks of sheep grazing nearby, as well as freshly squeezed orange juice. The farmhouse also doubles as a restaurant exclusively for villa guests. Beaches and two golf courses in the area are a short drive away.

ROOMS: In the villa itself, two large twin-bedded rooms each with their own bathroom, one with a sitting room and fireplace. On the grounds, four apartments with vaulted ceilings each house up to four people. In the farmhouse, there are also four twin-bedded rooms, each with their own living room and private bathroom.

AMENITIES:

English, French, and German are spoken
Private parking
Swimming pool
Dinner may be served on request
Children under the age of two stay free of charge
Pets are welcome

WHERE: The nearest railway station is in Metaponto, 4 miles away, while the airport in Bari is 37 miles away. By car take highway A14 Bologna–Taranto, exit at Palagiano, and take SS 106 toward Metaponto. After 275 miles, drive toward San Teodoro Nuovo Az. Visconti. From highway A3 Salerno–Reggio di Calabria exit at Sicignano and drive toward Potenza. Follow the Basentana road until you reach highway SS 106. Drive toward Reggio di Calabria. After 275 miles drive toward San Teodoro Nuovo Az. Visconti.

CATEGORY: Caffèlletto (rooms in the villa); ✳✳✳✳ (rooms in the farmhouse) ◆
RATE: ○○ ◆ *Member since 2004*

CALABRIA

A peninsula projecting between the Ionian, and the Tyrrhenian Sea, separated from Sicily by the narrow Strait of Messina, Calabria is at the toe of the Italian boot. Two narrow coastal strips are separated by Scilla, a mountainous area of spectacular beauty, wooded with conifers, where, despite its southern location, snow often falls in winter.

Catanzaro is the capital city and other main cities are Cosenza and Reggio di Calabria. Historically one of the most depressed areas in Italy, a victim of earthquakes and emigration, farming remains the chief occupation of this region, where citrus orchards alternate with olive groves and goats graze along the mountainsides. Colonized by the Greeks, Calabria was an integral part of ancient lore: it was through the Strait of Messina (ancient Scylla and Charybdis) that Ulysses sailed on his way back to Ithaca at the end of the *Odyssey*.

The low-lying areas are littered with fragments of ruins belonging to Corinthian

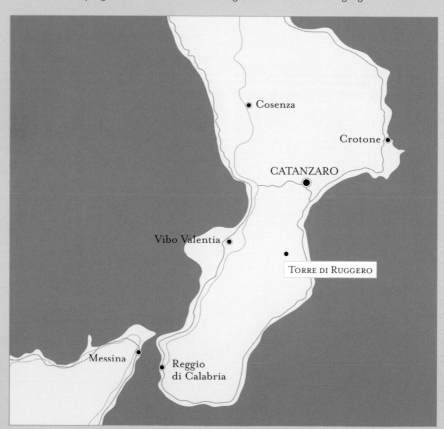

columns, Greek temples, and arenas. There is a haphazard quality to Calabrian architecture, a temporariness that makes the buildings along the coast contrast with their
Greek ancestors. At the extreme tip of the Calabrian toe, however, the beaches are
wreathed in fragrant jasmine bushes and bergamot orange trees. The people of Calabria are among the most hospitable of Italians, making it a point of honor to divide
the last loaf and fish with their guests.

THE LOCAL RECIPE
Although Calabria is flanked by two different seas—the Ionian and the Tyrrhenian—it
is also a mountainous country, and its pastureland yields particularly good lamb and
goat meat.

Fried Eggplant with Tomatoes
Ingredients (serves 4)

3 eggplants
3 large ripe tomatoes
3 whole eggs
1 tbsp. grated pecorino cheese
olive oil, salt, and pepper to taste

Wash the eggplants, dice them, and deep-fry in olive oil. Drain well, salt them, then
set aside. Dice the tomatoes. Discard three-quarters of the oil from the pan and stir
in the tomatoes. After a few minutes, add the eggplant. Beat the eggs with the grated
pecorino, salt, and pepper, and add to the pan. Combine well and cook until the eggs
are just set. Serve hot or lukewarm.

TORRE DI RUGGERO (CZ)

AZIENDA AGRITURISTICA I BASILIANI DI MARINA MARTELLI

88060 TORRE DI RUGGERO, CATANZARO

TEL. +39 0967938000 OR +39 03683395338 · **E-MAIL: info@ibasiliani.it**

Two thousand feet above Catanzaro, I Basiliani is a mountain retreat surrounded by glorious woodland, where the last carbonai (miners) still practice one of the oldest trades in the world. All over Italy they used to spend months in makeshift cabins in the woods, cutting down trees and burning the wood into charcoal. I Basiliani is almost equidistant from the coast of the Ionian Sea, fifteen miles away, and the Tyrrhenian Sea, twenty-one miles to the other side. From here you can leave for the Aeolian Islands (also known as the Lipari Islands), an hour away by hydrofoil. I Basiliani itself is built on the ruins of the Greek Orthodox monastery of Saint Basil, of which it is still possible to see remnants of the arches. The house is surrounded by a large garden with shady lime and cherry trees, which form a backdrop for the solarium and the swimming pool that takes its shape from an old reservoir.

Your host's cuisine is fresh and spontaneous, made with fresh ingredients, including produce grown in the vegetable garden.

This is a trekker's paradise. I Basiliani is marked on the Sentiero Italiano (Italian Way), the official hiking map of Italy. Mountain bikes can be rented and guides will take you on horseback along the woodland paths. Not far from I Basiliani is Serra San Bruno, known for its beautiful churches; the medieval township of Badolato; and the cascades of Marmarico. Local artisans are famous for their basketwork, while people come here from all over Italy for the briar pipes made in Brognaturo.

ROOMS: Your host's grandfather, a well-known humorist and illustrator of satiric journals, is responsible for the frescoes in the bedrooms, which have come to assign a name to each room, such as the Harvest Room or Butterfly Room; even some of the bathrooms have had the same treatment. There are six bedrooms, all with private bathrooms, and in three of them it is possible to add an extra bed. Minimum stay two nights.

AMENITIES:

Open from May to October; closed December 20 to January 7, and Easter
English and French are spoken
Laundry service is available
Horseback riding lessons
Dinner is served on request
It is possible to follow a meal plan during your stay
Baby-sitting service is available
Children under the age of two stay free of charge

WHERE: The airport and the railway station are both in Lamezia Terme, 28 miles away. By car exit from the Autostrada del Sole at Pizzo Calabro, then take highway SS 110 until the turn for Monte Cucco Pecoraro. From here, take SS 182 toward Soverato until the 40-mile (65-kilometer) milestone.

CATEGORY: ✳✳✳✳ · **RATE:** ○ · *Member since 1998*

SICILY

Sicily is the largest of the Mediterranean islands, and is covered almost entirely by hills and mountains. At the tail end of the Apennine chain, Sicily's highest peak is Mount Etna, an active volcano over 10,000 feet high. The region also includes the Egadi Islands, the Aeolian Islands, Lampedusa, Pantelleria, and Ustica, floating in the bluest, most translucent sea in Italy. The main cities are Palermo, Agrigento, Caltanissetta, Catania, Enna, Messina, Ragusa, Siracusa, and Trapani.

Over the centuries, Sicily has been ruled and occupied by the Phoenicians, Greeks, Carthaginians, Romans, Byzantines, Arabs, Normans, Angevins, Aragons, and Bourbons, until 1860 when it was conquered by Garibaldi and became part of the Kingdom of Italy. All these civilizations have left their mark on the culture and architecture of Sicily, which remains, however—as Giuseppe Tomasi di Lampedusa so eloquently wrote in *The Leopard*—a prisoner of her own history. The Sicilians themselves are physically a mixture of blue-eyed Norman, Spanish elegance, and uncompromisingly Arab profiles.

There are important Greek and Roman ruins in Agrigento, Siracusa, Segesta, and Selinunte. There are also splendid examples of Byzantine, Arab, and Norman influence in palaces and churches all over the island. Antonello da Messina is perhaps Sicily's most famous artist, but most of his canvases have left the island. Similarly, many native

islanders have left Sicily, as it is one of the poorest parts of Italy, a victim of the corruption and hegemony in recent decades of the Mafia.

The exceptionally mild climate and long summers favor the cultivation of grapes, olives, citrus trees, and almonds (used to make the delicious pasta alle mandorle), as well as the succulent palms and exotic plants in Sicily's numerous botanical gardens. The work of local artisans is an explosion of color and gaiety, from the painted donkey-drawn carts, life-size performing puppets, local costumes, and the ceramics of Caltagirone. The people of Sicily have a sense of hospitality, which is said to be Arabic in its intensity, Bourbon in its formality, and Italian in its degree of warmth.

THE LOCAL RECIPE

Sicily is a land of mystery and exotic flavor, where everything reminds you of the nearness of the North African coast. Spices, sweet and sour preparations, and the frequent use of almonds, honey, and orange-flower essence are the legacy of the Arabs.

Swordfish Roulades
Ingredients (serves 4)

12 oz. swordfish, thinly sliced	1 whole egg
2 oz. grated Parmesan cheese	4 oz. breadcrumbs
1 tbsp. pine nuts	1 tsp. chopped basil
1 tbsp. raisins	1 tsp. chopped parsley
1 tbsp. capers	olive oil, salt, pepper, and fresh mint leaves to taste

Mix together the breadcrumbs, capers, Parmesan cheese, raisins, pine nuts, parsley, basil, and whole egg. Season with salt and pepper. Wrap each fish slice around two teaspoons of the stuffing mixture to obtain a roulade. Seal securely with toothpicks. Grill and serve drizzled with olive oil and sprinkled with fresh mint leaves.

SALINA (ME)

INFO: CAFFÈLLETTO, ITALY

TEL. +39 023311814 OR 1820 · FAX +39 023313009 · E-MAIL: info@caffelletto.it

The seven islands that make up the Aeolian archipelago look like pebbles kicked into the sea by the toe of the Italian boot, but they were once, eons ago, active volcanoes spewing lava into the Mediterranean. The Pollara beach on the island of Salina still has black volcanic sand and a sea that ripples in the center of a collapsed volcanic crater. This is one of the most remote and fascinating parts of Italy where, even in November the temperature is subtropical. The island of Salina, the most fertile of the Aeolians, takes its name from a small salt lake where the locals fetch salt to preserve capers, which they export all over the world. Salina is also famous for its dessert wine, the amber-colored and ambrosia-flavored Malvasia.

This bed-and-breakfast belongs to the Pittorino family, one of the most prominent Sicilian families living on the island. There is even a statue of your host's grandfather, the first doctor on the island, in the main square. He was said to have made house calls for his patients in remote villages, reaching their mountainside homes astride a mule.

The house is surrounded by a garden overrun by tropical plants, banana trees, hibiscus, poinsettias, green pepper plants, and "bread marmour" of Madagascar, which contains medicinal properties discovered by the family's illustrious grandfather, who also invented a digestive tonic called the "Eupeptico Pittorino."

At 495 feet above sea level, the house is high enough for a sea breeze to make evenings on the terrace comfortably cool, and for the lights and hubbub of the fisherman's port of Rinella to seem sufficiently far away. It is in fact less than a mile on foot from the house to the harbor and guests can take boats from here to the neighboring islands—Lipari, Vulcano, and furthest away, Stromboli, an hour's boat ride—or go deep-sea fishing. The beach of Malfa with its round stepping-stones is also a short distance away, with some of the clearest waters in the Mediterranean.

Your hosts are rightly proud of their family tradition and of their island. They offer a trove of information for guests, who will also be frequently urged, with the insistence typical of "southern hospitality," to partake of brimming baskets of fruit from the garden—lotus, pomegranates, oranges, tangerines, apricots, plums, figs, grapes, mulberries, and cactus fruit, depending on the season. The same fruit will be transformed into marmalades and jams for breakfast on the terrace.

ROOMS: Dependent upon the season. A large double room with a balcony over-looking the sea with a small sitting room with television set and a private bathroom in the corridor; a double room on two levels with en suite bathroom; an independent

one-room apartment with two sofa beds, kitchen corner, bathroom, and an overhead loft with a double bed. Breakfast is not provided for guests who stay in the apartment. All rooms are furnished with family antiques. Minimum stay three nights.

AMENITIES:
English and French are spoken
Laundry service is available
Parking on the premises
Car, moped, and boat rentals
available at the port of Rinella

WHERE: The nearest airport is either Palermo or Reggio di Calabria, 40 nautical miles away, while hydrofoils and ferries leave from Naples, Palermo, and Milazzo.

CATEGORY: ✳✳✳✳ ◆ **RATE:** ○ ◆ *Member since 2000*

PETTINEO (ME)

INFO: CAFFÈLLETTO, ITALY

TEL. +39 023311814 OR 1820 ◦ FAX +39 023313009 ◦ E-MAIL: info@caffelletto.it

Not all Italian gardens have regimented borders and box hedges neatly clipped to portray geometrical shapes. The gardens of Casa Migliaca are a wanton profusion of narcissi, roses, and geraniums clustering around the trunks of the olive trees and tumbling down the stepped terraces toward the sea and Cefalù. To create such careful chaos has taken many generations. The same flawless taste and respect for natural harmony can be observed in the house itself, with its soft yellow walls made out of volcanic rock and swathed in creepers. In the eighteenth century the building housed an olive press, but it was turned into a country house over a century ago. The floors and ceilings have been restored to their original state and dinner is served on the old grindstone, which once turned the mill. In summer, guests can eat outside under the arbor with a view of the citrus-tree groves and stout-trunked olive trees that surround the house. In the nearby villages, local shepherds will sell you their products and you can visit the seamstresses of Mistretta, who are famous for their embroidery—in Castel di Lucio they still weave linen in the traditional way. Two miles away is Cefalù, one of Sicily's most fascinating landmarks, where a Norman cathedral, cloisters, and beautiful mosaics, as well as the temple of Diana, are noteworthy stops.

ROOMS: There are eight rooms with bathrooms, all furnished with antiques; some have balconies and others a terrace.

AMENITIES:
English and French are spoken
Laundry service is available
Dinner is served on request at Contrada
 Migliaca, where you can sample the excellent regional cooking
Children under the age of two stay free of charge

WHERE: The nearest airport is in Palermo about 62 miles away, while the railway station in Tusa is 4 miles away.

CATEGORY: ✳✳✳✳ ◦ **RATE:** ○○ ◦ *Member since 1998*

SALEMI (TP)

INFO: CAFFÈLLETTO, ITALY

TEL. +39 023311814 OR 1820 · **FAX +39 023313009** · **E-MAIL: info@caffelletto.it**

Here on a hilltop, not far from the town of Salemi in the northwest corner of Sicily, is a microcosm of the island. The melting pot of culture that makes up the heart and soul of Sicily is nowhere more apparent than here. From the farmhouses covered with vines, the odd giant date tree swaying in the wind, the Greek ruins half an hour away

at Selinunte and Segesta, to the medieval Marsala and the Arab-Norman castle of Salemi, Sicily's rich past is here brought to life.

The house itself is warm and welcoming and represents a style departing from the more recent local history. Built in the middle of the nineteenth century by your hostess's uncle, photographic portraits of their ancestors—esteemed physicians after whom squares and

streets of Salemi have been named—line the walls. Last but not least comes the proverbial hospitality of Sicilians: your hosts, experts on the local art, lore, and cuisine of Sicily, are more than happy to accompany guests on their discovery of the island and to tempt them with local delicacies. Breakfasts are served on the lawn outside the house with a view of the surrounding countryside, or in the dining room if desired.

ROOMS: Three double rooms and two singles with two bathrooms (with bathtubs). Minimum stay two nights.

AMENITIES:
English, French, and German are spoken
Laundry service is available
Private parking
Dinner may be served on request
Children under the age of two stay free of charge

WHERE: The nearest railway station is Salemi, 5 miles away, while the Marsala Birgi airport is 22 miles away.

CATEGORY: ✳✳✳✳ · **RATE:** ○ · *Member since 2002*

PALERMO—MONDELLO

INFO: CAFFÈLLETTO, ITALY

TEL. +39 023311814 OR 1820 ◦ FAX +39 023313009 ◦ E-MAIL: info@caffelletto.it

For lovers of flowers and beautiful gardens, this subtropical paradise in a residential area of Palermo is a must on any European tour. Twenty years ago your hostess trans-

formed an abandoned orange tree orchard into a lush garden, which is English in its apparent wanton profusion and Mediterranean in its abundance of heady fragrances and exotic plants. It has been featured in all the important gardening magazines and your hostess also makes excellent flower arrangements. An enchanted oasis only fifteen minutes from the bustling center of Palermo, the silence is only broken by the sweet songs of birds throughout the day and by the chirping of crickets in the evening. It is only four minutes from the beach in Mondello. At breakfast, fruits from the garden are served together with homemade jams and, for those who wish, fresh eggs are available from your hostess's own chicken coop. The large house stands in a spacious courtyard behind high gates and has a patrician Arabic air, with tall windows, turrets, and wrought-iron balconies, while the interior exudes an English charm and is decorated with chintz prints and crammed bookshelves lining the walls.

ROOMS: On the first floor a double room with bath and a suite consisting of a double and a single room sharing a bathroom. Minimum stay two nights.

AMENITIES:
English, French, and some German are spoken
Laundry service
Parking on the premises
Dinner is served on request
Children over the age of twelve are welcome
Pets are not allowed

WHERE: The railway station in Palermo is 9 miles away, while the Punta Raisi airport is 12 miles away.

CATEGORY: Caffèlletto ◦ RATE: ○○○ ◦ *Member since 2001*

PALERMO–TEATRO MASSIMO

INFO: CAFFÈLLETTO, ITALY
TEL. +39 023311814 OR 1820 ◦ FAX +39 023313009 ◦ E-MAIL: info@caffelletto.it

At the historic center of Palermo, this apartment is on the third floor of a palazzo built at the beginning of the eighteenth century. Your hosts are a young and charming couple: he is from Palermo and she is from Tuscany. She is an interior decorator

who has completely restored the apartment, trying as much as possible to preserve its unique style. The cool floors are in the original gray and white marble, while the bedroom is paved with antique majolica tiles. A frescoed ceiling enhances the sitting room, while the apartment as a whole is furnished in excellent taste ranging from the old to the antique. Guests will find the wherewithal for breakfast in the sitting room with a view of the terrace.

You are within minutes of the Via Macheba, where you can explore the inexhaustible plethora of churches, palazzi, typical Sicilian gardens, and squares, whose colorful weekly markets make up the fascinating kaleidoscope that is Palermo. In the street below the apartment you can find restaurants serving the best couscous in the city while typical local restaurants with vaulted ceilings offer delicious daily variations of Sicilian cuisine. The Teatro Massimo is also only two minutes away.

ROOMS: One double room and one single, each with its own bathroom (one with bathtub, the other with shower). Each share a small sitting room with a sofa bed which opens out onto the terrace. Minimum stay two nights.

AMENITIES:
English, French, and some German are spoken
Laundry service is available
Private parking
Dinner may be served on request
Children over the age of twelve are welcome
Guests should be aware that there is no elevator

WHERE: The nearest railway station is a mile away, while the airport in Palermo is II miles away.

CATEGORY: ✳✳✳✳ ◦ **RATE:** ⭕⭕ ◦ *Member since 2001*

CAMPOREALE (PA)

MASSERIA PERNICE 90043 ◆ **AGRO DI MONREALE, PALERMO**
TEL. AND FAX +39 092436797 ◆ **E-MAIL: f.delatour@tiscalinet.it**

This is a masseria (a large farm) where you can spend unforgettable hours in an atmosphere full of aromas, colors, flavors, and local traditions. The owners offer their guests the opportunity to choose among four apartments. They are furnished in the style of the most famous Provençal *maison d'hôtel*: family furniture, Sicilian ceramics, and period prints. An outdoor baglio (overhang) is covered with bougainvillea, jasmine, roses, and geraniums.

Behind the masseria, surrounded by a marvelous garden with pine and eucalyptus trees, there is a large swimming pool where you can have a pleasant swim on a hot summer day. Next to the swimming pool there is an open courtyard where breakfast is served in the summer. In winter, guests enjoy breakfast (which is based on genuine and healthful products from the countryside) in a spacious living room accented by a large fireplace.

Sallier de La Tour is a firm that belongs to the owners' family. Their 333 acres of land, divided into vineyards, olive groves, orchards, and pastures, provide the perfect setting for unforgettable walks, and horse and bike rides at anytime of the year. Furthermore, you can taste Sallier de La Tour oil and wines, visit their nineteenth-century winery La Monaca, as well as take part in the grape and olive harvest.

The owners often organize concerts in summer and winter. In addition to the beauty of the location and its peaceful atmosphere, you can also experience the ancient and aristocratic tastes of Sicily.

ROOMS: Casina delle Piume: a double room with a large bathroom (with bathtub); Casina delle Papere: double room, small living room with two comfortable beds, one bathroom (with bathtub). Casina dei Fiori: one double room, one room with two beds, one bathroom (with bathtub), one living room with a fireplace, and a small kitchen. Casina della Caccia: one double room, one small living room with a cooking area, one bathroom (with shower).

AMENITIES:
English and French are spoken
Private parking
Swimming pool
Laundry service is available

WHERE: The nearest railway station is in Palermo, 25 miles away, while the Palermo Falcone–Borsellino airport is 28 miles away. By car, take SS Palermo–Sciacca, exit at Camporeale–Zabbia and follow the signs for Case Pernice.

CATEGORY: Caffelletto ◆ **RATE:** ○○○○ ◆ *Member since 2002*

CAMPO FELICE (PA)

STRADA PROVINCIALE 129 KM 3 ⬧ **90016 COLLESANO**
TEL. +39 0916167839 ⬧ **CELL +39 3494634300** ⬧ **E-MAIL: abaziafloris@hotmail.com**

This bed-and-breakfast is located thirty-one miles from Palermo in open countryside that is a delightful hybrid between country life and the seashore. From the house there is an enticing view of the sea and Cefalù, nine miles away. The property is right on the edge of the Natural Reserve of Madonie, for those who favor walks and communing with nature. The house and gardens are also hybrids: a peasant cottage furnished like a palazzo with family antiques and patrician taste, with gardens of well-tended flower beds, olive groves, and farmland. Your hostess has completely renovated the house where she lives almost all year-round. She is very active in the organic production of olive oil and the old oil press and Ali Baba–like jars used over the centuries can still be seen on the ground floor. Breakfasts are served in the large kitchen, which has been equipped with all the modern appliances without altering the timeless charm of the antique tiles and worn surfaces of peasant kitchens. During the warmer months guests can breakfast under the mulberry tree, and when the chickens are in form there are fresh eggs, as well as ricotta cheese and delectable homemade bitter-orange marmalade.

ROOMS: A double room in an alcove with private bathroom (with shower). An attractive apartment with a double room (the beds can be transformed into twins),

bathroom (with shower), small sitting room with a fireplace, and kitchen. Minimum stay two nights.

AMENITIES:
English and French are spoken
Parking on the premises
Dinner may be served on request
Children over the age of eight are
   welcome
Pets are welcome

WHERE: The nearest railway station is Campo Felice di Roccella, 3 miles away, while the Palermo airport is 50 miles away.

CATEGORY: Caffèlletto ⬧ **RATE:** ◯ (rooms); ◯◯ (apartment)
⬧ *Member since 2001*

CATANIA–LUNGOMARE

INFO: CAFFÈLLETTO, ITALY

TEL. +39 023311814 OR 1820 ✦ FAX +39 023313009 ✦ E-MAIL: info@caffelletto.it

On the residential seafront of Catania, this ninth-floor apartment has a large terrace swathed in orange begonia, jasmine, and oleander bushes, with a sweeping view of the sea. Here guests may enjoy excellent homemade breakfasts in the shade of nineteenth-century gazebos. In winter, breakfasts are served in the sunny and elegant dining room charmingly furnished by your hostess with unusual china and ceramics. She is extremely hospitable and, as she works in tourism, is brimming with information about the surrounding sights. A twenty-minute walk away is the baroque center of Catania, while Taormina, Siracusa, and Noto are all easy day trips. Guests may swim at the beach below the apartment or go to the famous Plaja beach nearby.

ROOMS: An elegant double room with a four-poster bed, antique furniture, and large hand-painted bathroom (with bathtub); two singles, one with a shower in the corridor, the other with a small basic bathroom en suite. Guests may also use the small sitting room and library with television set. Minimum stay two nights.

AMENITIES:
English and French are spoken
Dinner may be served on request
Children over the age of ten are welcome

WHERE: The nearest railway station is at a short distance away, while the Catania Fontanarossa airport is a mile away.

CATEGORY: ✳✳✳✳ ✦ **RATE:** ⭕⭕⭕ ✦ *Member since 2003*

LINGUAGLOSSA (CT)

INFO: CAFFÈLLETTO, ITALY

TEL. +39 023311814 OR 1820 • FAX +39 023313009 • E-MAIL: info@caffelletto.it

It is not often that we have the chance to be guests at the foot of an active volcano. Below Mount Etna—at nine miles from Taormina and eleven from the ski resort of Piano Provenzana—this house is in the center of a farm with olive groves, apricot trees, chestnut woods, and an army of prickly pears. As your hosts themselves say, it is the perfect compromise of life in the mountains and by the sea. At the heart of the complex there is a low building made of lava stone where grapes used to be pressed; here, guests may meet, relax, and make use of the kitchen corner. The rooms have chestnut-wood beams with details and Sicilian terra-cotta floors that are warm and welcoming, with a rustic elegance all their own.

ROOMS: A double room with queen-size bed, a double room with a small sitting room with another two beds, a double room with an overhead loft with another two beds, a triple room, and another double for handicapped guests. All rooms have their

own private bathroom with shower.

AMENITIES:
English is spoken
Private parking
Air-conditioning
Mountain bikes can be rented
Barbecues are frequently organized
*Dinner may be served, on request, at
    the farm, one mile away*
*Children under the age of two stay
    free of charge*
Pets are welcome

WHERE: The nearest railway station is in Taormina, 9 miles away, while the airport is in Catania, 22 miles away. By car take highway A18 Messina–Catania and exit at Fiumefreddo. Take the SS 120 until you reach Linguaglossa. Follow the signs for Zafferana. After just under a mile you will see a sign for the Azienda Agrituristica Contrada Arrigo.

CATEGORY: ✳✳✳✳ • **RATE:** ○ • *Member since 2001*

INFO: CAFFÈLLETTO, ITALY

TEL. +39 023311814 OR 1820 · FAX +39 023313009 · E-MAIL: info@caffelletto.it

The Villa Agavi is everything a visitor would want to find in Sicily: hillsides covered in olive groves, lemon trees that slope down to an impossibly blue sea, palm trees with their fronds swaying in the breeze, and wisteria smothering the walls of a patrician villa. The scene is dominated by Mount Etna, whose nightly red glow is verdant in summer and glistening with snow in winter.

The villa has belonged to the same family since time immemorial, although they have often lived far from the island. Your host and hostess now live here all year-round, while their children study in Milan. The rooms are typical of the cool elegance of aristocratic Sicilian interiors with stone floors, polished antique furniture, and old-master paintings on the walls. Breakfasts are also very Sicilian as is the warm hospitality extended by your hosts. Lemon sorbet and warm brioche are served in the shade of the loggia. There are plenty of cool corners in the gardens while the pool, surrounded with plants, merges into the horizon.

Your hosts can organize yachting trips including deep-sea fishing, fishing by night, or excursions to the tip of the crater on Mount Etna in a land rover. There is an eighteen-hole golf course nineteen miles away and the thermal baths of Acireale are two miles away. Taormina is thirteen miles away.

ROOMS: The Yellow Room is a double suite (the beds can be separated into single beds) with a bathroom, adjoining sitting room with sofa bed, fireplace, and terrace overlooking the sea. The Blue Room is also a double with a bathroom, and there are two Green Rooms, one of which has a terrace covered in creepers overlooking Mount Etna; they share a bathroom (with shower). Minimum stay three nights.

AMENITIES:
*Open all year except for the month of August
    and between December 20 and 26*
English and French are spoken
Laundry service is available
Parking on the premises
Dinner may be served on request
Children under the age of two stay free of charge

WHERE: The railway station is in Acireale, 4 miles away, while the airport of Catania is 15 miles away.

CATEGORY: **Caffèlletto** · RATE: ○○ · *Member since 2001*

AGRIGENTO

INFO: CAFFÈLLETTO, ITALY

TEL. +39 023311814 OR 1820 · FAX +39 023313009 · E-MAIL: info@caffelletto.it

This charming farmhouse with a biblical name is only two miles from the famous Valley of the Temples in Agrigento and about one mile from the sea. The ancestors of today's owners bought the farm from a religious order, which no doubt explains why Fattoria Mosè is named after a pillar of the Old Testament, rather than an ancient Greek figure. The estate covers 117 acres, producing oranges, almonds, pistachio nuts, fruit, and vegetables in season, as well as olive oil from the gnarled old trees of a century-old olive grove. Everything is organically grown. Your hostess is an architect and has spent much of the preceding years initiating organic farming on the estate and restoring part of the old house and stables.

The Fattoria Mosè is made up of a complex of old buildings grouped around three large courtyards. The main house overlooks one of these, while the other two act as a stage set with little cottages made out of the old stables all opening onto courtyards. The main house goes back to the first half of the nineteenth century, with a tower and a large archway, which are certainly from a much earlier date.

There is much to see in the area, from the Port of Sciacca, which has been famous since Roman times for its natural springs, to many examples of medieval architecture, such as the twelfth-century Duomo and the Luna Castle, built in the late 1300s. Along the coast is the archaeological site of Eraclea Minoa, the ancient City of Gold, while twenty miles away is the natural oasis of Torre Salsa.

ROOMS: In the villa there are two floors, on the first: two communicating rooms, one double, and one single with a bathroom and two large double rooms in the old tower each with its own bathroom. On the second floor: another two communicating rooms, one double and one single with a bathroom. There are six cottages (the old stables); the largest has six beds and two bathrooms, one of which is suitable for handicapped guests. The others each have a shower, bathroom, and a two- to four-bed capacity. All have a kitchen corner and a personal share of the courtyard, where guests can dine or relax outside. Minimum stay three nights.

AMENITIES:

English, French, and Spanish are spoken

Laundry service is available

Parking on the estate

The farmhouse sells produce made on the estate

The central courtyard has a covered terrace overlooking the countryside with a barbecue, ideal for alfresco dinners on summer evenings

Dinner may be served on request

Children under the age of two stay free of charge

Pets are not allowed

WHERE: The airports of Palermo and Catania are about 117 miles away, while the nearest railway station is in Agrigento, 2 miles away.

CATEGORY: ✳✳✳✳ ◆ **RATE:** ○○ ◆ *Member since 1999*

SIRACUSA–HISTORIC CENTER

INFO: CAFFÈLLETTO, ITALY

TEL. +39 023311814 OR 1820 ◆ **FAX +39 023313009** ◆ **E-MAIL: info@caffelletto.it**

In the heart of Siracusa, the Ortigia, this little pink-and-white two-story building, dating back to 1887, has been restored and transformed by your hosts into a very comfortable and pleasant bed-and-breakfast. The communal sitting room is outdoors, Sicilian-style, in the little square with tables and chairs under wide umbrellas. Breakfast, served on the rooftop, is made memorable by the almond-flavored cakes and tarts typical of the region. Ideally situated to visit Siracusa and its surroundings with their world-famous archaeological sites. The sea is only 600 feet from the house.

ROOMS: Six double rooms and one twin room named after flowers or plants, all with bathrooms with showers, air-conditioning, and televisions. Two of the rooms have a balcony and the option of a third bed. There is also a bathroom for handicapped guests. Minimum stay two nights.

AMENITIES:
English is spoken
Laundry service is available
Children under the age of two stay
  free of charge
Pets are welcome

WHERE: The nearest railway station is Siracusa, less than a mile away, while the Catania airport is 25 miles away.

CATEGORY: ✳✳✳✳ ◆ **RATE:** ○○ ◆ *Member since 2003*

SIRACUSA–ORTIGIA

INFO: CAFFÈLLETTO, ITALY

TEL. +39 023311814 OR 1820 • **FAX +39 023313009** • **E-MAIL: info@caffelletto.it**

Few bed-and-breakfasts can boast such proximity to a temple to Apollo. But here we are in Ortigia, the historic heart of Siracusa, where consorting with the ancients is part of everyday life. This bed-and-breakfast is a delightful palazzo dating back to the eighteenth century and recently ably restored by your hostess. The atmosphere is undoubtedly Mediterranean, with pink walls outside, blues and whites characterizing the tastefully decorated interior, and fresh flowers in all the vases. For the time being, breakfast is a voucher for a frothy cappuccino and Sicilian pastries in the bar of the spectacular Piazza Duomo. In the future, the wherewithal for breakfast will be provided in all of the rooms. In the meantime, guests may make tea in their rooms sweetened with the famous Sortino honey. Your hostess works for the regional department of agriculture and is the official taster of olive oil, cheese, and honey. She is also a mine of information about the area. The sea is nearby, as is the Archaeological Museum. The Ciane Natural Reserve should not be missed.

ROOMS: One double and one twin room share a bathroom (with shower). Two apartments open onto inner courtyards, both with a double room with a bathroom (with shower) and a sitting room with a kitchen corner and two lounge chairs. Minimum stay two nights for the rooms and three nights for the apartments.

AMENITIES:
English is spoken
Children under the age of two stay free of charge

WHERE: The nearest airport in Catania is less than an hour away, while frequent buses run between Catania and Siracusa.

CATEGORY: ✳✳✳ • **RATE:** ○ • *Member since 2003*

INFO: CAFFÈLLETTO, ITALY

TEL. +39 023311814 OR 1820 ◆ **FAX +39 023313009** ◆ **E-MAIL: info@caffelletto.it**

This is a true hidden treasure. In the small town of San Pietro Clarenza on the outskirts of Catania, when you least expect it, the wide gates of the Villa Lionti open onto a fascinating little enclave, a Sicilian "Secret Garden." A lawn, studded with eighteenth-century stone seats and fragrant jasmine, pale blue plumbago, and climbing bougainvillaea surround an extraordinary ancient well, oil press, variously arrayed stone columns, and a wide swimming pool. The eighteenth-century house, built out of lava stone, was purchased in near ruins by your charming hostess and her daughter, who have put much love and good taste into its restoration. The daughter is heavily involved in sailing and is delighted to organize varied excursions in sailing or fishing boats. The rooms are all furnished with antiques in excellent taste and overlook the enclosed garden, while guests may browse in the library where they can also check their e-mails. Breakfast is served in the garden with marmalades made from the local, and rightly famous, Sicilian oranges and lemons. Guests are not far from the historic centre of Catania, while Taormina is half an hour away and Mount Etna is only ten minutes away and provides an unforgettable experience: slopes layered with both extinct and recent lava in a silent and eerie world.

ROOMS: One double room with alcove, adjoining sitting room, and bathroom with shower, while the Etna Room is a loft with an overhead gallery bathroom with tub, double bed, and roomy kitchen. The Ulisse Room is a large double and sitting room with sofa bed and bathroom with tub, while the Polifemo Room is a double room with bathroom adapted for handicapped guests. The Ionio Room is a small single room with adjoining dressing room and bathroom with shower. Minimum stay three nights.

AMENITIES:

French, Spanish, and a little English
are spoken
Private parking
Dinner may be served on request
Laundry service is available
Oven and barbecue equipment in the
garden

WHERE: The nearest railway station and airport are in Catania, 9 miles away.

CATEGORY: Caffèlletto ◆ **RATE:** ○○○—○○○○ ◆ *Member since 2004*

INFO: CAFFÈLLETTO, ITALY
TEL. +39 023311814 OR 1820 ◦ FAX +39 023313009 ◦ E-MAIL: info@caffelletto.it

Modica is just inland from Sicily's southern coast and is famous for its chocolate, pronounced by the famous Sicilian writer Leonardo Sciascia as "unparalleled in flavor, such that tasting it is like reaching the archetype, the absolute." It is also less than one hour from the archaeological sites at Pantallica, the haven of the ancients, and Cava d'Ispica, and the Roman amphitheater at Siracusa, while the sea is only thirty minutes away. Modica is ideally situated to visit one of the loveliest and less well-known parts of Sicily. Opening onto typically Sicilian courtyards lined with terra-cotta vases full of lush green plants, the two comfortable apartments have been constructed on two levels beneath exquisite stucco and painted ceilings. Your hosts, a pediatrician and his wife, live on the ground floor. Kitchens are equipped with all you need for breakfast and there is an excellent restaurant on the same street. Modica is also famous for its cuisine.

ROOMS: Two entirely independent apartments. The first is a duplex with sitting room and kitchen corner and sofa bed as well as a bathroom (with shower) on the first floor, and double bedroom above. The second is the same only larger. Both have terraces with plants and creepers. Four double bedrooms each one in a different color: la chambre verte (the green room), la chambre rouge (the red room), la petite chambre (the little room), and la chambre

jaune (the yellow room) with an extra bed—all offer private bathrooms, air-conditioning, minibar, and television set.

AMENITIES:
English, French, and Spanish are spoken
Garage for parking at extra cost
Air-conditioning
Children under the age of two stay
   free of charge

WHERE: The railway station in Modica is less than a mile away, while the nearest airport is in Catania, 74 miles away.

CATEGORY: ✳✳✳✳ ◦ **RATE:** ○○ ◦ *Member since 2001*

INDEX

NOTES

NOTES

NOTES